PENS
POCKE

CW00519332

1996

NTC PUBLICATIONS LIMITED

IN ASSOCIATION WITH

BACON & WOODROW

PENSIONS POCKET BOOK
1996 Edition

ISBN 1 899314 24 5

Produced and published by NTC Publications Ltd, Farm Road, Henley-on-Thames, Oxfordshire RG9 IEJ, United Kingdom.
Telephone: (01491) 574671. Fax: (01491) 571188.

Comments and suggestions for future editions of this pocket book are welcomed. Please contact: Editor, Pensions Pocket Book, NTC Publications Ltd at above address.

Whilst every effort has been made in the preparation of this book to ensure accuracy of the statistical and other contents, the publishers and data suppliers cannot accept any liability in respect of errors or omissions or for any losses or consequential losses arising from such errors or omissions. Readers will appreciate that the data contents are only as up-to-date as their availability and compilation, and printing schedules, will allow and are subject to change during the natural course of events.

Printed and bound in Great Britain by Biddles Ltd, Guildford and King's Lynn.

NOTES

(i) Symbols used:
  – *or* n/a = data not available or not available on a comparable basis.

(ii) Constituent figures in the tables may not add up to the totals, due to rounding.

(iii) For full definitions readers are referred to the sources given at the foot of the tables.

(iv) Some topics are mentioned in more than one table but the information is not necessarily from the same source. Any differences are likely to be due to difference in definition, method of calculation or periods covered.

ACKNOWLEDGEMENTS

The publishers would like to thank all those who have contributed to this compilation of pensions data, in particular Bacon & Woodrow – coproducers of the book – whose contribution and support have been invaluable.

Other contributors, including Government departments whose help is gratefully acknowledged, include:

Allied Information Technologies Ltd
A.P. Information Services
Central Statistical Office (CSO)
Combined Actuarial Performance Services Ltd
Employment Gazette
Government Actuary's Department
Institute of Actuaries
The National Association of Pension Funds Ltd
National Readership Survey (NRS Ltd)
Office of Population Censuses and Surveys (OPCS)
The Pensions Management Institute
Pensions Research Accountants Group
Securities and Investments Board

Bacon & Woodrow was established over 70 years ago and is the largest independent actuarial consulting partnership in Europe. It is the UK member firm of Woodrow Milliman, an international network represented in principal cities worldwide.

We advise organisations of all types and all sizes, multinational or local, on all aspects of pay, pensions and employee benefits. Our work is remunerated by fees only.

Our overriding aim is to excel at what matters most to our clients, recognising that each has different needs, priorities and expectations.

Bacon & Woodrow is regulated in the conduct of UK investment business by the Institute of Actuaries.

NTC Publications Ltd, part of the Allied Information Technologies Group, is a specialist provider of professional publishing, market research, industry forecasting, database management and marketing services. Its business – often in collaboration with leading trade associations, government bodies, research companies, advertising agencies, service organisations and industry – is to provide information to business and management professionals; researched, packaged and disseminated according to the user's needs.

FOREWORD

The foreword of our first **Pensions Pocket Book** in 1989 referred to *"the continually changing world of pensions"*. Here we are with the eighth edition, and this legend is as valid as ever.

The new Pensions Act is now with us and we have revised this year's contents to reflect the new legislative requirements and all they imply for trustees, pension fund managers, their actuarial advisers, consultants and investment managers. Further, as I write this foreword, the first effects of the Greenbury Code are being felt by quoted companies. Extra care is being taken to ensure that Annual Reports comply with the pension aspects of disclosure of directors' total remuneration, and questions will undoubtedly be asked of remuneration committee chairmen at AGMs. This is proof, if proof were needed, that the subject of occupational pensions is higher on the agenda in the boardrooms of corporate Britain than ever before.

I hope that you will find this latest edition of the **Pensions Pocket Book** as convenient, authoritative and indispensable as ever.

Duncan Ferguson
Senior Partner
Bacon & Woodrow

CONTENTS

Section 4: UK SOCIAL SECURITY BENEFITS

**Section 5: SOCIAL SECURITY AND OTHER RETIREMENT BENEFITS
           OVERSEAS**

Section 6: INVESTMENT DATA

ECONOMICS

THE INTERNAL AND EXTERNAL VALUE OF THE POUND: 1966–95

	General Index of UK Retail Prices (1990 = 100)		Exchange Rates[1] (Foreign Currency per £ Sterling)			
	Index	Yr-on-Yr % Change	Trade-Weighted Sterling Index (1990 = 100)	US$	DM	Yen	ECU
1966	12.2	3.9	. .	2.793	11.168	1012.0	–
1967	12.5	2.5	. .	2.750	10.955	995.9	–
1968	13.1	4.7	. .	2.394	9.555	863.2	–
1969	13.8	5.4	. .	2.390	9.379	856.5	–
1970	14.7	6.4	. .	2.396	8.736	857.8	–
1971	16.1	9.4	. .	2.444	8.530	844.6	–
1972	17.2	7.1	. .	2.502	7.975	752.3	–
1973	18.8	9.2	. .	2.453	6.540	664.6	–
1974	21.8	16.1	. .	2.340	6.049	682.7	–
1975	27.1	24.2	. .	2.220	5.447	658.1	–
1976	31.6	16.5	. .	1.805	4.552	535.4	–
1977	36.6	15.9	. .	1.746	4.050	467.7	1.527
1978	39.6	8.3	. .	1.920	3.851	402.7	1.504
1979	44.9	13.4	. .	2.123	3.887	465.5	1.548
1980	53.0	18.0	128.9	2.328	4.227	525.6	1.669
1981	59.3	11.9	130.3	2.025	4.556	444.6	1.808
1982	64.4	8.6	124.5	1.749	4.243	435.2	1.784
1983	67.4	4.6	115.3	1.516	3.870	359.9	1.704
1984	70.7	5.0	110.2	1.336	3.790	316.8	1.693
1985	75.0	6.1	109.5	1.298	3.784	307.1	1.700
1986	77.6	3.4	100.2	1.467	3.183	246.8	1.495
1987	80.8	4.1	98.7	1.639	2.941	236.5	1.420
1988	84.7	4.9	104.6	1.780	3.124	228.0	1.506
1989	91.3	7.8	101.4	1.638	3.079	225.7	1.489
1990	100.0	9.5	100.0	1.786	2.876	257.4	1.400
1991	105.9	5.9	100.7	1.769	2.925	237.6	1.428
1992	109.8	3.7	96.9	1.767	2.751	223.7	1.362
1993	111.5	1.6	88.9	1.502	2.483	166.7	1.285
1994	114.5	2.4	89.2	1.533	2.481	156.4	1.292
1995[1,2]	117.0	3.6	84.4	1.568	2.264	148.3	1.211

Notes: [1] Average values over each period. [2] As to August 1995.
Sources: Central Statistical Office – Financial Statistics, Monthly Digest of Statistics.

UK MAIN ECONOMIC INDICATORS: 1988–1994

		1988	1989	1990	1991	1992	1993	1994
Gross Domestic Product[1]								
at current prices	£billion	471.4	516.0	551.1	575.3	597.2	630.7	668.9
	% change	+11.3	+9.4	+6.8	+4.4	+3.8	+5.6	+6.1
at 1990 prices	£billion	537.2	548.9	551.1	540.3	537.4	549.6	570.7
	% change	+5.0	+2.2	+0.4	–2.0	–0.5	+2.3	+3.8
Gross Domestic Product[1] per Capita								
at current prices	£	8,248	8,995	9,575	9,952	10,296	10,839	11,454
	% change	+11.1	+9.1	+6.4	+3.9	+3.5	+5.3	+5.7
at 1990 prices	£	9,399	9,570	9,575	9,347	9,265	9,445	9,774
	% change	+4.7	+1.8	+0.0	–2.4	–0.9	+1.9	+3.5
Consumers' Expenditure								
at current prices	£billion	299.4	327.4	347.5	365.0	381.7	405.5	428.1
	% change	+12.9	+9.3	+6.2	+5.0	+4.6	+6.2	+5.6
at 1990 prices	£billion	334.6	345.4	347.5	339.9	339.5	348.4	358.9
	% change	+7.5	+3.2	+0.6	–2.2	–0.1	+2.6	+3.0
Retail Sales	Index	97.3	99.3	100.0	98.9	99.5	103.0	106.4
	% change	+5.8	+2.1	+0.7	–1.1	+0.6	+3.5	+3.3
Retail Prices	Index	84.7	91.3	100.0	105.9	109.8	111.5	114.3
	% change	+4.9	+7.8	+9.5	+5.9	+3.7	+1.6	+2.5
Population (Mid-Year Est.)	million	57.2	57.4	57.6	57.8	58.0	58.2	58.4
Average Earnings	Index	83.6	91.2	100.0	108.0	114.6	118.5	123.2
	% change	+8.7	+9.1	+9.7	+8.0	+6.1	+3.4	+3.9
Industrial Production (Total)	Index	98.2	100.3	100.0	96.1	95.9	98.1	103.2
	% change	+4.8	+2.1	–0.3	–3.9	–0.2	+2.3	+5.3
Unemployment (% of Labour Force)[2]		8.0	6.3	5.8	8.1	9.8	10.3	9.3
Vacancies at JobCentres[3]	Thousands	248.6	219.5	173.6	117.9	117.2	127.9	157.8
	% change	+5.6	–11.7	–20.9	–32.1	–0.6	+9.1	+23.4
Interest Rate (Bank Base Rate)[4]	%	10.09	13.85	14.77	11.70	9.56	6.01	5.46
Gross Domestic Fixed Capital Formation								
at 1990 prices	£billion	105.2	111.5	107.6	97.4	96.0	96.5	100.1
	% change	+13.9	+6.0	–3.5	–9.5	–1.5	+0.6	+3.7
Gross Fixed Investment by Manu. Industry								
at 1990 prices	£billion	13.8	15.0	14.2	12.8	11.8	11.1	11.8
	% change	+9.5	+8.2	–5.1	–10.0	–7.6	–6.1	+6.5
Gross Trading Profits[5]								
North Sea Oil Companies								
at current prices	£billion	7.0	6.8	7.1	6.4	6.7	8.1	9.7
	% change	–26.5	–3.1	+4.6	–9.6	+4.3	+20.9	+20.0
Other Companies								
at current prices	£billion	62.3	67.5	68.0	67.9	68.3	77.0	88.8
	% change	+19.3	+8.5	+0.7	–0.1	+0.5	+12.7	+15.3
at 1990 prices	£billion	73.5	73.9	68.0	64.2	62.2	69.1	77.7
	% change	+13.7	+0.6	–8.0	–5.7	–3.1	+11.0	+12.5
Balance of Payments								
at current prices	£billion	–16.5	–22.4	–19.3	–8.5	–9.5	–11.0	–1.7

Notes: All Indices 1990 = 100. [1] Gross Domestic Product is at market prices.
[2] Unemployment percentage is the total number of unemployed (excluding school leavers) expressed as a percentage of the estimated total workforce (the sum of unemployed claimants, employees in employment, self employed, HM forces and work related Government training programmes).
[3] Vacancies at JobCentres excluding Community Programme vacancies from 1980.
[4] Selected Retail Banks Base Rate. [5] Net of stock appreciation.

Sources: Central Statistical Office – Economic Trends, Monthly Digest of Statistics, and Financial Statistics.

RETAIL PRICES INDEX

Index based on January 1987 = 100

	Jan.	Feb.	Mar.	Apr.	May	Jun.	Jul.	Aug.	Sep.	Oct.	Nov.	Dec.
1968	16.1	16.2	16.2	16.5	16.5	16.6	16.6	16.6	16.6	16.7	16.7	17.0
1969	17.1	17.2	17.2	17.4	17.4	17.5	17.5	17.4	17.5	17.6	17.6	17.8
1970	17.9	18.0	18.1	18.4	18.4	18.5	18.6	18.6	18.7	18.9	19.0	19.2
1971	19.4	19.5	19.7	20.1	20.2	20.4	20.5	20.5	20.6	20.7	20.8	20.9
1972	21.0	21.1	21.2	21.4	21.5	21.6	21.7	21.9	22.0	22.3	22.4	22.5
1973	22.6	22.8	22.9	23.4	23.5	23.6	23.7	23.8	24.0	24.5	24.7	24.9
1974	25.3	25.8	26.0	26.9	27.3	27.6	27.8	27.8	28.1	28.7	29.2	29.6
1975	30.4	30.9	31.5	32.7	34.1	34.8	35.1	35.3	35.6	36.1	36.6	37.0
1976	37.5	38.0	38.2	38.9	39.3	39.5	39.6	40.2	40.7	41.4	42.0	42.6
1977	43.7	44.1	44.6	45.7	46.1	46.5	46.6	46.8	47.1	47.3	47.5	47.8
1978	48.0	48.3	48.6	49.3	49.6	50.0	50.2	50.5	50.7	51.0	51.3	51.8
1979	52.5	53.0	53.4	54.3	54.7	55.7	58.1	58.5	59.1	59.7	60.3	60.7
1980	62.2	63.1	63.9	66.1	66.7	67.4	67.9	68.1	68.5	68.9	69.5	69.9
1981	70.3	70.9	72.0	74.1	74.6	75.0	75.3	75.9	76.3	77.0	77.8	78.3
1982	78.7	78.8	79.4	81.0	81.6	81.9	81.9	81.9	81.9	82.3	82.7	82.5
1983	82.6	83.0	83.1	84.3	84.6	84.8	85.3	85.7	86.1	86.4	86.7	86.9
1984	86.8	87.2	87.5	88.6	89.0	89.2	89.1	89.9	90.1	90.7	91.0	90.9
1985	91.2	91.9	92.8	94.8	95.2	95.4	95.2	95.5	95.4	95.6	95.9	96.0
1986	96.2	96.6	96.7	97.7	97.8	97.8	97.5	97.8	98.3	98.5	99.3	99.6
1987	100.0	100.4	100.6	101.8	101.9	101.9	101.8	102.1	102.4	102.9	103.4	103.3
1988	103.3	103.7	104.1	105.8	106.2	106.6	106.7	107.9	108.4	109.5	110.0	110.3
1989	111.0	111.8	112.3	114.3	115.0	115.4	115.5	115.8	116.6	117.5	118.5	118.8
1990	119.5	120.2	121.4	125.1	126.2	126.7	126.8	128.1	129.3	130.3	130.0	129.9
1991	130.2	130.9	131.4	133.1	133.5	134.1	133.8	134.1	134.6	135.1	135.6	135.7
1992	135.6	136.3	136.7	138.8	139.3	139.3	138.8	138.9	139.4	139.9	139.7	139.2
1993	137.9	138.8	139.3	140.6	141.1	141.0	140.7	141.3	141.9	141.8	141.6	141.9
1994	141.3	142.1	142.5	144.2	144.7	144.7	144.0	144.7	145.0	145.2	145.3	146.0
1995	146.0	146.9	147.5	149.0	149.6	149.8	149.1	149.9				

RETAIL PRICES INFLATION

Percentage increase in the Retail Prices Index over previous 12 months

	Jan. %	Feb. %	Mar. %	Apr. %	May %	Jun. %	Jul. %	Aug. %	Sep. %	Oct. %	Nov. %	Dec. %
1984	5.1	5.1	5.2	5.2	5.1	5.1	4.5	5.0	4.7	5.0	4.9	4.6
1985	5.0	5.4	6.1	6.9	7.0	7.0	6.9	6.2	5.9	5.4	5.5	5.7
1986	5.5	5.1	4.2	3.0	2.8	2.5	2.4	2.4	3.0	3.0	3.5	3.7
1987	3.9	3.9	4.0	4.2	4.1	4.2	4.4	4.4	4.2	4.5	4.1	3.7
1988	3.3	3.3	3.5	3.9	4.2	4.6	4.8	5.7	5.9	6.4	6.4	6.8
1989	7.5	7.8	7.9	8.0	8.3	8.3	8.2	7.3	7.6	7.3	7.7	7.7
1990	7.7	7.5	8.1	9.4	9.7	9.8	9.8	10.6	10.9	10.9	9.7	9.3
1991	9.0	8.9	8.2	6.4	5.8	5.8	5.5	4.7	4.1	3.7	4.3	4.5
1992	4.1	4.1	4.0	4.3	4.3	3.9	3.7	3.6	3.6	3.6	3.0	2.6
1993	1.7	1.8	1.9	1.3	1.3	1.2	1.4	1.7	1.8	1.4	1.4	1.9
1994	2.5	2.4	2.3	2.6	2.6	2.6	2.3	2.4	2.2	2.4	2.6	2.9
1995	3.3	3.4	3.5	3.3	3.4	3.5	3.5	3.6				

Source: Bacon & Woodrow, compiled from Government information.

TRENDS IN AVERAGE EARNINGS PER PERSON[1]
PER WEEK, GB

	at Current Prices		at Constant 1994 Prices[2]	
	Average Earnings[3] Per Week (£)	Annual Percentage Change (%)	Average Earnings[3] Per Week (£)	Annual Percentage Change (%)
1951	13.7	–	215.7	–
1956	17.6	7.8	221.1	3.4
1966	23.8	5.0	222.4	1.1
1967	24.4	2.4	222.2	–0.1
1968	24.9	2.3	217.0	–2.4
1969	26.3	5.7	218.1	0.5
1970	29.0	10.2	225.7	3.5
1971	31.4	8.3	223.8	–0.8
1972	34.3	9.0	227.0	1.4
1973	37.4	9.1	226.9	0.0
1974	44.7	19.7	234.3	3.2
1975	59.0	32.0	249.2	6.4
1976	64.8	9.8	234.5	–5.9
1977	70.6	9.0	220.6	–5.9
1978	79.7	12.8	229.9	4.2
1979	92.0	15.5	234.0	1.8
1980	111.2	20.8	239.7	2.4
1981	125.3	12.8	241.6	0.8
1982	137.1	9.4	243.4	0.8
1983	148.8	8.5	252.4	3.7
1984	157.7	6.0	254.9	1.0
1985	171.0	8.5	260.6	2.2
1986	181.2	6.0	267.0	2.5
1987	194.9	7.6	275.8	3.3
1988	213.6	9.6	288.1	4.5
1989	234.3	9.7	293.1	1.8
1990	258.0	10.1	294.9	0.6
1991	278.9	8.1	301.1	2.1
1992	298.5	7.0	310.7	3.2
1993	310.9	4.2	318.6	2.5
1994	319.3	2.7	319.3	0.2

Notes: [1] Wages and salaries of those in employment, excluding those whose pay is affected by absence.
[2] Deflated by the Retail Prices Index (1994 = 100).
[3] Prior to 1971, data is derived from average salaries per unit of output. Subsequent data is derived from the earnings index of all adults in employment.

Sources: CSO; Employment Gazette; NTC.

DEMOGRAPHIC AND EMPLOYMENT DATA

RESIDENT POPULATION OF THE UK: MID 1981, 1991 AND 1994

	1981		1991		1994	
	'000s	%	'000s	%	'000s	%
England	46,821	83.1	48,208	83.4	48,707	83.4
Scotland	5,180	9.2	5,107	8.8	5,132	8.8
Wales	2,813	5.0	2,891	5.0	2,913	5.0
GB	**54,815**	**97.3**	**56,207**	**97.2**	**56,753**	**97.2**
N. Ireland	1,538	2.7	1,601	2.8	1,642	2.8
UK	**56,352**	**100.0**	**57,808**	**100.0**	**58,395**	**100.0**

Note: Figures may not add due to rounding.
Sources: OPCS; General Register Offices for Scotland and Northern Ireland.

RESIDENT POPULATION OT THE UK BY SEX & AGE: ESTIMATE MID 1993

	Total		Males		Females	
Years of age	'000s	%	'000s	%	'000s	%
under 1	759	1.3	389	1.4	370	1.2
1– 4	3,117	5.3	1,596	5.6	1,521	5.1
5–14	7,483	12.8	3,840	13.4	3,643	12.2
15–24	7,554	12.9	3,879	13.6	3,674	12.3
25–34	9,375	16.1	4,767	16.7	4,608	15.5
35–44	7,837	13.4	3,929	13.7	3,908	13.1
45–59	10,277	17.6	5,118	17.9	5,159	17.3
60–64	2,808	4.8	1,363	4.8	1,444	4.8
65–74	5,223	8.9	2,363	8.3	2,861	9.6
75–84	2,952	5.1	1,096	3.8	1,856	6.2
over 85	1,011	1.7	251	0.9	759	2.5
Total	**58,395**	**100.0**	**28,592**	**100.0**	**29,803**	**100.0**
of whom						
under 16	12,075	20.7	6,194	10.6	5,881	10.1
over 65/60	10,630	18.2	3,710	13.0	6,920	23.2

Note: Figures may not add due to rounding.
Sources: OPCS; General Register Offices for Scotland and Northern Ireland.

NRS ADULT POPULATION PROFILE OF GB: 1994/95

		Adult Population '000s	%
All Adults:		45,750	100.0
Sex:	Male	22,127	48.4
	Female	23,623	51.6
Age Group:	15 – 24	7,251	15.8
	25 – 34	9,051	19.8
	35 – 44	7,631	16.7
	45 – 54	7,161	15.7
	55 – 64	5,660	12.4
	65 or over	8,995	19.7
Marital Status:	Single	10,264	22.4
	Married/co-habiting	28,965	63.3
	Widowed	4,065	8.9
	Divorced/separated	2,422	5.3
	Not stated	34	0.1
Occupational Status:	Full-time (30+ hours)	19,083	41.7
	Part-time (8–29 hours)	4,663	10.2
	Part-time (less than 8 hours)	392	0.9
	Unemployed	2,070	4.5
	Retired	8,004	17.5
	Others	11,530	25.2
	Not stated	7	..
ACORN Categories:	A Thriving	9,519	20.8
	B Expanding	5,044	11.0
	C Rising	3,483	7.6
	D Settling	10,872	23.8
	E Aspiring	6,462	14.1
	F Striving	9,787	21.4
	U Unclassified	583	1.3
Social Grade of Chief Income Earner:	A	1,385	3.0
	B	8,709	19.0
	C1	12,540	27.4
	C2	10,298	22.5
	D	7,406	16.2
	E	5,412	11.8
Other Characteristics:	Chief Income Earner	25,613	56.0
	Spouse/Wife of CIE	13,192	28.8
	Neither	6,945	15.2

Base: (All 15+): 37,351.
Source: National Readership Survey (NRS Ltd.), July 1994 – June 1995.

NRS DISTRIBUTION OF THE ADULT POPULATION BY SOCIAL GRADE: 1993/94

Social Grade	All Adults 15+		Men		Women		Main Shoppers (Female)	
	'000s	%	'000s	%	'000s	%	'000s	%
A	1,385	3.0	729	3.3	656	2.8	828	2.9
B	8,709	19.0	4,511	20.4	4,198	17.8	5,453	18.8
C1	12,540	27.4	5,766	26.1	6,774	28.7	8,203	28.3
C2	10,298	22.5	5,509	24.9	4,789	20.3	5,956	20.6
D	7,406	16.2	3,579	16.2	3,828	16.2	4,458	15.4
E	5,412	11.8	2,035	9.2	3,377	14.3	4,048	14.0
Total	45,750	100.0	22,127	100.0	23,623	100.0	28,946	100.0

Notes: Figures are based on the social grade of the Chief Wage Earner.
Source: National Readership Survey (NRS Ltd.) July 1994 – June 1995.

NRS SOCIAL GRADE DEFINITIONS

Social Grade	Social Status	Occupation
A	Upper middle class	Higher managerial, administrative or professional
B	Middle class	Intermediate managerial, administrative or professional
C1	Lower middle class	Supervisory or clerical, and junior managerial, administrative or professional
C2	Skilled working class	Skilled manual workers
D	Working class	Semi and unskilled manual workers
E	Those of lowest level of subsistence	State pensioners or widows (no other earner), casual or lowest grades of workers

Source: National Readership Survey (NRS Ltd.).

PROJECTED GB POPULATION BY AGE GROUP*

Percent unless otherwise indicated

			Projections			
		1992	1995	2000	2010	2020
Population (millions)		**58.0**	**58.6**	**59.6**	**61.1**	**62.1**
	index	**100.0**	**101.0**	**102.8**	**105.4**	**107.0**
Sex distribution (%)	males	48.9	49.0	49.3	49.6	49.7
	females	51.1	51.0	50.7	50.4	50.3
Age distribution (%)	0–14	19.3	19.5	19.5	18.1	17.2
	15–29	22.0	20.6	18.9	19.1	18.5
	30–44	21.1	21.6	22.6	19.9	18.1
	45–59	16.9	17.8	18.5	20.2	20.9
	60–74	13.7	13.5	13.0	14.9	16.6
	75+	7.0	7.0	7.5	7.8	8.7

Source: 1992 based population projections by the Government Actuaries Department.

RATES OF MORTALITY (q_x) FROM ENGLISH LIFE TABLES NOS. 8-14

Age x	ELT 8 (1910-12)	ELT 9 (1920-22)	ELT 10 (1930-32)	ELT 11 (1950-52)	ELT 12 (1960-62)	ELT 13 (1970-72)	ELT 14 (1980-82)
Males							
0	.12044	.08996	.07186	.03266	.02449	.01980	.01271
10	.00193	.00181	.00146	.00052	.00039	.00034	.00024
20	.00348	.00349	.00316	.00129	.00119	.00106	.00093
30	.00478	.00434	.00340	.00157	.00115	.00097	.00088
40	.00811	.00688	.00562	.00290	.00235	.00226	.00184
50	.01482	.01179	.01128	.00850	.00728	.00739	.00615
60	.03042	.02561	.02415	.02369	.02287	.02075	.01843
70	.06470	.05997	.06035	.05651	.05566	.05546	.04703
80	.14299	.14002	.14500	.13629	.12747	.12019	.11334
90	.27395	.26752	.28614	.29255	.25593	.24077	.22693
Females							
0	.09767	.06942	.05455	.02510	.01896	.01523	.00984
10	.00196	.00180	.00134	.00035	.00024	.00023	.00018
20	.00295	.00306	.00268	.00083	.00044	.00045	.00035
30	.00411	.00392	.00319	.00127	.00075	.00060	.00052
40	.00660	.00532	.00440	.00227	.00180	.00160	.00127
50	.01140	.00915	.00816	.00524	.00439	.00449	.00378
60	.02310	.01897	.01770	.01271	.01088	.01025	.00986
70	.05259	.04646	.04451	.03532	.03104	.02784	.02443
80	.12419	.11766	.11858	.10466	.09108	.08014	.06982
90	.23826	.23852	.25061	.24146	.22128	.19805	.18468

Note: The rate of mortality shown represents the probability of a life exact age 'x' dying within the following year who is subject to the average mortality experience of England and Wales for various years as represented by the English Life Table shown. The table demonstrates the improving trend in mortality throughout this century.

Source: OPCS, *English Life Tables No.14*, published by HMSO.

RATES OF MORTALITY EXPRESSED AS PERCENTAGES OF ENGLISH LIFE TABLES NO. 8 RATES

Age x	ELT 8 (1910-12)	ELT 9 (1920-22)	ELT 10 (1930-32)	ELT 11 (1950-52)	ELT 12 (1960-62)	ELT 13 (1970-72)	ELT 14 (1980-82)
Males							
0	100	75	60	27	20	16	11
10	100	94	76	27	20	18	12
20	100	100	91	37	34	30	27
30	100	91	71	33	24	20	18
40	100	85	69	36	29	28	23
50	100	80	76	57	49	50	41
60	100	84	79	78	75	68	61
70	100	93	93	87	86	86	73
80	100	98	101	95	89	84	79
90	100	98	104	107	93	88	83
Females							
0	100	71	56	26	19	16	10
10	100	92	68	18	12	12	9
20	100	104	91	28	15	15	12
30	100	95	78	31	18	15	13
40	100	81	67	34	27	24	19
50	100	80	72	46	39	39	33
60	100	82	77	55	47	44	43
70	100	88	85	67	59	53	46
80	100	95	95	84	73	65	56
90	100	100	105	101	93	83	78

Source: OPCS, *English Life Tables No. 14,* published by HMSO.

EXPECTATIONS OF LIFE

Age x	Males Expectation	Females Expectation	Age x	Males Expectation	Females Expectation
0	71.043	77.002	55	20.135	25.025
1	70.956	76.766	56	19.353	24.178
2	70.016	75.820	57	18.586	23.342
3	69.051	74.855	58	17.836	22.515
4	68.077	73.878	59	17.101	21.698
5	67.101	72.896	60	16.383	20.890
6	66.123	71.913	61	15.681	20.093
7	65.142	70.927	62	14.995	19.307
8	64.160	69.941	63	14.326	18.530
9	63.176	68.954	64	13.672	17.765
10	62.191	67.966	65	13.036	17.010
11	61.206	66.979	66	12.417	16.266
12	60.221	65.991	67	11.815	15.533
13	59.237	65.002	68	11.232	14.813
14	58.254	64.014	69	10.668	14.106
15	57.274	63.028	70	10.123	13.414
16	56.297	62.044	71	9.597	12.737
17	55.326	61.062	72	9.092	12.077
18	54.382	60.082	73	8.607	11.435
19	53.442	59.103	74	8.143	10.811
20	52.496	58.124	75	7.699	10.207
21	51.545	57.144	76	7.275	9.622
22	50.589	56.164	77	6.872	9.059
23	49.631	55.184	78	6.489	8.516
24	48.671	54.204	79	6.126	7.994
25	47.710	53.225	80	5.782	7.495
26	46.749	52.245	81	5.458	7.020
27	45.787	51.267	82	5.152	6.570
28	44.824	50.288	83	4.865	6.146
29	43.862	49.311	84	4.596	5.749
30	42.899	48.335	85	4.345	5.381
31	41.936	47.359	86	4.112	5.042
32	40.974	46.385	87	3.895	4.731
33	40.012	45.413	88	3.693	4.446
34	39.051	44.442	89	3.506	4.186
35	38.092	43.474	90	3.331	3.949
36	37.134	42.507	91	3.167	3.733
37	36.179	41.543	92	3.012	3.534
38	35.227	40.581	93	2.863	3.352
39	34.279	39.622	94	2.718	3.182
40	33.335	38.667	95	2.574	3.020
41	32.395	37.715	96	2.431	2.864
42	31.461	36.768	97	2.288	2.706
43	30.532	35.825	98	2.145	2.545
44	29.611	34.887	99	2.004	2.380
45	28.696	33.955	100	1.865	2.210
46	27.790	33.028	101	1.729	2.038
47	26.893	32.108	102	1.597	1.866
48	26.006	31.195	103	1.471	1.698
49	25.129	30.289	104	1.350	1.535
50	24.264	29.390	105	1.236	1.380
51	23.411	28.500	106	1.129	1.234
52	22.571	27.618	107	1.029	1.100
53	21.744	26.744	108	.935	.976
54	20.932	25.880	109	–	.862
			110	–	.755

Note: The table shows the future life expectation at various ages of lives subject to the average mortality experience of England and Wales in the years 1980 to 1982. The table makes no allowance for improvement in mortality.

Source: OPCS, *English Life Tables No.14*, published by HMSO.

JOINT-LIFE EXPECTATION OF MALES AND FEMALES

Age of Woman	Age of Man														
	20	25	30	35	40	45	50	55	60	65	70	75	80	85	90
20	47.98	44.71	40.97	36.87	32.58	28.24	23.99	19.97	16.29	12.98	10.09	7.69	5.78	4.35	
25	45.97	43.26	39.97	36.22	32.17	27.99	23.85	19.89	16.25	12.96	10.08	7.68	5.78	4.35	3.35
30	43.37	41.25	38.52	35.23	31.52	27.58	23.60	19.75	16.17	12.92	10.06	7.67	5.77	4.35	3.35
35	40.21	38.67	36.53	33.80	30.55	26.95	23.21	19.51	16.03	12.84	10.02	7.65	5.76	4.34	3.34
40	36.59	35.55	33.99	31.86	29.16	26.01	22.60	19.14	15.80	12.71	9.95	7.61	5.74	4.33	3.34
45	32.67	32.01	30.95	29.39	27.29	24.68	21.71	18.57	15.45	12.50	9.83	7.54	5.70	4.31	3.33
50	28.60	28.22	27.54	26.48	24.95	22.93	20.48	17.76	14.94	12.20	9.65	7.44	5.65	4.28	3.31
55	24.55	24.33	23.93	23.25	22.21	20.75	18.86	16.64	14.22	11.75	9.39	7.29	5.57	4.23	3.28
60	20.60	20.49	20.27	19.86	19.20	18.21	16.86	15.17	13.22	11.12	9.01	7.08	5.44	4.17	3.24
65	16.83	16.78	16.67	16.44	16.04	15.42	14.52	13.34	11.89	10.23	8.46	6.75	5.26	4.06	3.18
70	13.31	13.29	13.23	13.11	12.89	12.53	11.98	11.21	10.23	9.02	7.66	6.25	4.96	3.89	3.08
75	10.15	10.14	10.11	10.06	9.94	9.74	9.43	8.97	8.36	7.57	6.61	5.56	4.52	3.62	2.91
80		7.46	7.45	7.43	7.37	7.27	7.10	6.84	6.50	6.02	5.41	4.69	3.94	3.24	2.66
85			5.37	5.35	5.33	5.27	5.19	5.05	4.86	4.59	4.23	3.77	3.27	2.77	2.34
90				3.95	3.93	3.91	3.86	3.78	3.68	3.52	3.30	3.02	2.68	2.33	2.02

Note: The table shows the joint life expectation of two people (a man and a woman) of various combinations of ages, subject to the average mortality experience of England and Wales in the years 1980 to 1982. The columns show the period for which both lives may expect to survive on average, and which ends on the death of the first of the two to die.

Source: OPCS, *English Life Tables No. 14*, published by HMSO.

WORKING POPULATION – UNITED KINGDOM*

	June 1971		June 1994		June 1995	
	'000s	%	'000s	%	'000s	%
Employees in employment						
– Male	13,722	54.4	10,921	38.8	11,047	39.4
– Female	8,391	33.2	10,717	38.1	10,844	38.7
All employees in employment	22,113	87.6	21,639	76.9	21,890	78.1
Self-employed persons	2,021	8.0	3,288	11.7	3,346	11.9
HM Forces	368	1.5	250	0.9	230	0.8
Work related government training	—	—	302	1.1	264	0.9
Total employed labour force	24,502	97.1	25,478	90.6	25,730	91.7
Unemployed**	744	2.9	2,645	9.4	2,314	8.3
Total working population	25,246	100	28,123	100	28,044	100
Index of working population	100.0		111.4		111.1	

Notes: *Seasonally adjusted. ** Including school leavers.
Source: Employment Gazette.

UK EMPLOYMENT AND UNEMPLOYMENT

	Working Population '000s	Employed Labour Force '000s	Employees in Employment '000s	Unemployed excl. School Leavers	
				'000s	% of Working Population
1975	25,894	25,050	22,723	941	3.6
1976	26,110	24,844	22,557	1,302	5.0
1977	26,224	24,865	22,631	1,403	5.4
1978	26,358	25,014	22,789	1,383	5.2
1979	26,627	25,393	23,173	1,296	4.9
1980	26,839	25,327	22,991	1,665	6.2
1981	26,741	24,345	21,892	2,520	9.4
1982	26,676	23,907	21,414	2,917	10.9
1983	26,608	23,624	21,067	3,105	11.7
1984	27,265	24,235	21,238	3,160	11.6
1985	27,718	24,539	21,423	3,271	11.8
1986	27,877	24,559	21,379	3,098	11.1
1987	28,077	25,084	21,586	2,807	10.0
1988	28,436	26,142	22,266	2,273	8.0
1989	28,725	26,939	22,670	1,782	6.2
1990	28,785	27,170	22,893	1,661	5.8
1991	28,571	26,269	22,220	2,286	8.0
1992	28,474	25,739	21,904	2,765	9.7
1993	28,287	25,367	21,606	2,901	10.3
1994	28,031	25,385	21,547	2,637	9.4

Source: Central Statistical Office – Economic Trends.

ANALYSIS BY INDUSTRY OF EMPLOYEES IN EMPLOYMENT – GREAT BRITAIN

Seasonally adjusted

Standard Industrial Classification 1992	June 1981		June 1995	
	'000s	%	'000s	%
Agriculture, hunting, forestry & fishing	368	1.7	293	1.4
Mining & quarrying, supply of electricity, gas & water	677	3.2	235	1.1
Food products, beverages & tobacco	606	2.8	429	2.0
Manufacture of clothing, textiles, leather & leather products	617	2.9	381	1.8
Wood & wood products	84	0.4	82	0.4
Paper, pulp, printing, publishing & recording media	485	2.3	469	2.2
Chemicals, chemical products & man-made fibres	362	1.7	236	1.1
Rubber & rubber products	213	1.0	197	0.9
Non-metallic mineral products, metal & metal products	1,121	5.2	686	3.2
Machinery & equipment	587	2.7	376	1.8
Electrical & optical equipment	675	3.2	445	2.1
Transport equipment	674	3.2	317	1.5
Coke, nuclear fuel & other manufacturing	238	1.1	227	1.1
Construction	1,125	5.3	818	3.8
Wholesale & retail trade & repairs	3,272	15.3	3,580	16.8
Hotels & restaurants	904	4.2	1,238	5.8
Transport & storage	953	4.5	872	4.1
Post & telecommunications	453	2.1	396	1.9
Financial intermediation	786	3.7	929	4.4
Real estate	122	0.6	237	1.1
Renting, research, computer & other business activities	1,487	7.0	2,403	11.3
Public administration & defence; compulsory social security	1,505	7.0	1,318	6.2
Education	1,523	7.1	1,770	8.3
Health activities	1,245	5.8	1,456	6.8
Social work activities	514	2.4	964	4.5
Other community social & personal activities	762	3.6	969	4.5
All industries & services	21,373	100	21,322	100

Source: Employment Gazette.

BACKGROUND TO PENSION SCHEMES

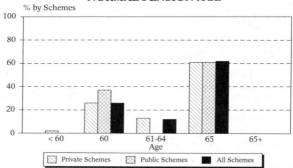

Distribution of Normal Pension Ages by number of schemes

Source: Based on data from the NAPF Annual Survey of Occupational Pension Schemes, 1994. (See note on page 16 concerning this source.)

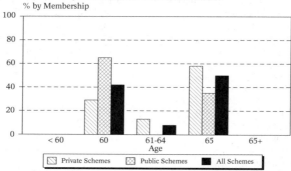

Distribution of Normal Pension Ages by number of members

Source: Based on data from the NAPF Annual Survey of Occupational Pension Schemes, 1994. (See note on page 16 concerning this source.)

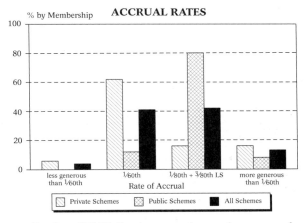

% by Membership

ACCRUAL RATES

Fraction of Eligible Earnings accrued as pension per year of pensionable service

Source: Based on data from the NAPF Annual Survey of Occupational Pension Schemes, 1994. (See note on page 16 concerning this source.)

IMMEDIATE PENSIONS ON ILL-HEALTH
Method of Calculation

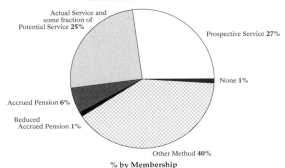

% by Membership

Method of calculation of benefits following a member's withdrawal from service due to ill-health

Source: Based on data from the NAPF Annual Survey of Occupational Pension Schemes, 1994. (See note on page 16 concerning this source.)

TYPE OF PENSION BENEFIT

	Private Schemes % %	Public Schemes % %	All Schemes % %
Money purchase	7 (3)	– (–)	7 (2)
Final salary	86 (89)	98 (100)	87 (93)
Other	7 (8)	2 (*)	6 (5)

Notes: These results, as with data from the same source appearing in other tables, are taken from the *Twentieth Annual Survey of Occupational Pension Schemes* published by The National Association of Pension Funds. On average, the information supplied applied to the year ended March 1994. About 10 million employed people in the UK are believed to be members of occupational pension schemes and the NAPF membership represents nearly two-thirds of those covered by occupational pension schemes. Some 726 companies took part in the survey representing 830 schemes covering approximately 4.0 million scheme members.

Percentage figures appearing in the NAPF tables represent proportions of schemes unless otherwise stated. Where figures appear in brackets alongside, these represent proportions of scheme members. An asterisk indicates less than 0.5%. A dash indicates zero. Percentages have been rounded to add to 100.

FINAL PAY DEFINITION

	Private Schemes % %	Public Schemes % %	All Schemes % %
Actual pensionable earnings on retirement	7 (6)	2 (*)	7 (4)
Actual pensionable earnings over last 12 months	24 (26)	14 (11)	24 (20)
Average pensionable earnings over last 3 years	7 (3)	2 (*)	6 (2)
Average pensionable earnings over best 3 consecutive years ending in last 10 years	19 (10)	– (–)	18 (6)
Average pensionable earnings over last 2 years	2 (1)	– (–)	2 (*)
Best year's pensionable earnings in last 3 years	4 (4)	68 (86)	9 (37)
Best year's pensionable earnings in last 5 years	8 (10)	4 (*)	7 (6)
Pensionable earnings at the renewal date prior to normal retirement date	4 (1)	– (–)	3 (1)
A combination of more than one of the above	12 (18)	6 (2)	11 (11)
Other definition	13 (21)	4 (1)	13 (13)

Notes: The figures in brackets represent the percentages by membership. See note above for further explanation.

Source: NAPF Annual Survey of Occupational Pension Schemes, 1994.

INTEGRATION OF BENEFITS WITH THE STATE SCHEME

	Private Schemes % %		Public Schemes % %		All Schemes % %	
No integration	52	(48)	85	(83)	54	(61)
Integration by:						
– pay adjustment	28	(30)	8	(15)	27	(24)
– benefit adjustment	10	(10)	3	(*)	10	(6)
– combination	7	(9)	2	(1)	6	(6)
– applying different pension accrual fractions to different levels of pay	2	(1)	–	(–)	2	(1)
– other method	1	(2)	2	(1)	1	(2)

Notes: The figures in brackets represent the percentages by membership.
See note on page 16 for further explanation.

Source: NAPF Annual Survey of Occupational Pension Schemes, 1994.

DISTRIBUTION OF SCHEMES AND MEMBERS BY SCHEME TYPE AND SECTOR

	Private Schemes % %		Public Schemes % %		All Schemes % %	
Staff scheme	25	(18)	8	(2)	23	(12)
Works scheme	4	(4)	5	(2)	4	(3)
Combined scheme: same benefit level	62	(72)	80	(94)	64	(81)
Combined scheme: different benefit level	3	(3)	2	(1)	3	(2)
Other	6	(3)	5	(1)	6	(2)

Notes: The figures in brackets represent the percentages by membership.
See note on page 16 for further explanation.

Source: NAPF Annual Survey of Occupational Pension Schemes, 1994.

AVERAGE NUMBER OF SCHEME MEMBERS BY GENDER AND SCHEME TYPE

	Staff Scheme	Works Scheme	Combined Scheme	
			Same Benefits	Different Benefits
Male	1,500	2,800	3,900	1,600
Female	900	500	2,500	1,200
Total	**2,400**	**3,300**	**6,400**	**2,800**

Source: NAPF Annual Survey of Occupational Pension Schemes, 1994.

AVERAGE NUMBER OF EMPLOYEES, SCHEME MEMBERS, PENSIONERS AND DEFERRED PENSIONERS BY SECTOR

Average No. of	Private	Public	All Employers
Employees			
Male	3,400	18,300	4,300
Female	2,700	19,600	3,800
Total	6,100	37,900	8,100
Scheme members			
Male	2,200	14,500	3,100
Female	1,100	11,600	1,900
Total	3,300	26,100	5,000
Pensioners	3,100	28,600	5,000
Deferred pensioners	2,300	11,500	2,900

Note: See note on page 16 for further explanation.
Source: NAPF Annual Survey of Occupational Pension Schemes, 1994.

TYPE OF POST RETIREMENT INCREASES

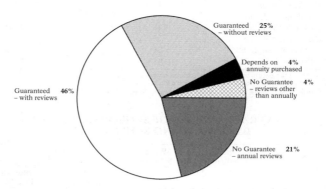

Percentage of schemes providing increases to pensions in payment on a guaranteed basis or with reviews

Note: See note on page 16 for further explanation.
Source: Based on data from the NAPF Annual Survey of Occupational Pension Schemes, 1994.

LUMP SUM PAYABLE ON DEATH-IN-SERVICE
(as a multiple of salary)

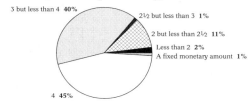

3 but less than 4 **40%**

2½ but less than 3 **1%**

2 but less than 2½ **11%**

Less than 2 **2%**
A fixed monetary amount **1%**

4 **45%**

Percentage of schemes showing the range of lump sum benefit payable on the death-in-service of a married member

Note: See note on page 16 for further explanation.
Source: Based on data from the NAPF Annual Survey of Occupational Pension Schemes, 1994.

PERCENTAGE OF MEMBERS OF DEFINED BENEFIT SCHEMES PAYING VARIOUS CONTRIBUTION RATES

(1991)

Percentage of Salary	Private Sector		Public Sector	All Combined
	Contracted-Out	Contracted-In	Contracted-Out	
Under 2%	0.4	0.9	15.5	6.9
2% and under 3%	3.0	4.5	–	1.8
3% and under 4%	5.5	18.7	–	3.9
4% and under 5%	14.5	5.4	0.1	7.8
5% and under 6%	33.5	15.2	5.7	20.5
6% and under 7%	22.3	12.5	66.8	40.8
7% and over	2.1	6.2	5.0	3.6
Non-contributory or other basis	18.7	36.6	6.9	14.7
Totals	100.0	100.0	100.0	100.0

Source: Occupational Pension Schemes 1991: Ninth Survey by the Government Actuary.

PERCENTAGE OF MEMBERS PAYING VARIOUS PROPORTIONS OF TOTAL CONTRIBUTIONS

(1991)

Proportion of Contributions Paid by the Members (%)	Private Sector
n/a	2.9
nil	15.2
1 – 9	3.1
10 – 19	4.8
20 – 29	14.8
30 – 39	20.6
40 – 49	8.3
50 – 99	20.1
100	10.2
Total	100.0

Note: 'n/a' indicates that neither employers nor members were contributing in 1991.
Source: Occupational Pension Schemes 1991: Ninth Survey by the Government Actuary.

THE LARGER UK PENSION FUNDS
Pension funds estimated to be in excess of £700m in 1994

£ million		£ million	
17,197	British Telecommunications plc	1,093	Co-operative Wholesale Soc. Ltd
15,806	CMT Pensions (British Coal)	1,090	NFC plc
12,899	Electricity Supply	1,084	Hampshire County Council
10,250	Post Office	1,071	Water Pension Scheme
9,679	Railways Pensions Fund	1,071	Welsh Water plc
9,512	Universities Superannuation Scheme	1,048	Guinness plc
		1,046	Reed International plc
8,213	British Gas plc	1,040	Co-operative Insurance Soc. Ltd
6,846	Barclays Bank plc	1,034	Scottish Power plc
6,729	The British Petroleum Co. plc	1,015	The Royal Bank of Scotland plc
6,550	Shell	1,003	Commercial Union Group
6,473	National Westminster Bank	992	The Shipbuilding Industries
5,666	British Steel	984	Northern Telecom Europe Ltd
5,417	British Airways	973	Essex County Council
4,603	Imperial Chemicals Industries plc	959	Bank of Scotland
4,263	Lloyds Bank plc	954	Courtaulds plc
3,961	British Broadcasting Corp.	943	Carnaud MetalBox Group UK Ltd
3,800	General Electric Company plc		
3,706	Midland Bank plc	939	The Wellcome Foundation Ltd
3,543	Greater Manchester County	930	Coats Viyella plc
3,434	Strathclyde Regional Council	909	Lothian Regional Council
3,092	Unilever plc/NV	908	Blue Circle Industries plc
2,833	Prudential Corporation plc	887	Avon County Council
2,630	British Aerospace	879	Esso UK plc
2,483	West Yorkshire	876	Vauxhall & Associated Cos.
2,450	West Midlands	871	Staffordshire County Council
2,434	Ford Motor Company Ltd	861	TI Group plc
2,376	TSB Group plc	859	Kent County Council
2,374	Lucas Industries plc	854	Pilkington plc
2,339	IBM United Kingdom Ltd	842	Royal Insurance plc
2,296	London Regional Transport	833	Grand Metropolitan plc
2,228	Merchant Navy Pensions	828	Cadbury Schweppes plc
2,202	The Rover Group Ltd	828	Eagle Star Group
2,035	London Pensions Fund Authority	827	BICC Group
2,000	BTR plc	826	T&N plc
1,894	Rolls-Royce plc	821	P. & O.
1,876	Civil Aviation Authority	817	BAA plc
1,851	Imperial Tobacco	803	Glaxo Group
1,725	Merseyside	795	Ranks Hovis McDougall Ltd
1,602	Sun Alliance Group plc	795	Cheshire County Council
1,435	J. Sainsbury plc	794	Associated British Foods
1,426	Marks & Spencer plc	787	Halifax Building Society
1,410	THORN EMI	786	Trafalgar House
1,384	The Boots Company plc	778	Guardian Royal Exchange Assurance plc
1,375	Lancashire County Council		
1,369	Philips Electronics UK Ltd	774	Rank Xerox Ltd
1,352	Allied Domecq plc	757	Whitbread plc
1,343	Zeneca Group plc	755	General Accident Fire & Life Assurance
1,325	Northern Ireland Local Govt.		
1,292	South Yorkshire	752	Mars
1,282	Bank of England	746	The BOC Group plc
1,280	Nestlé UK Ltd	743	RTZ Ltd
1,228	National Rivers Authority	729	Nottinghamshire Cty. Council
1,175	Tyne & Wear	715	Norwich Union Ins. Group
1,115	Pearl Assurance plc	710	Cable & Wireless plc
1,104	Bass plc	704	GKN Ltd

Notes: 1. Certain figures relate to the total of several funds within a group.
2. Some figures are estimates not necessarily supplied by the fund.

Source: Based on information derived from *Pension Funds and their Advisers, 1995,*
A.P. Information Services.

NUMBER OF COMPANIES ANALYSED BY REGION AND NUMBER OF EMPLOYEES

	Number of Employees per Company in 1994								
Region	0–499	500–999	1,000–1,999	2,000–4,999	5,000–9,999	10,000–24,999	25,000–99,999	100,000+	Total
London	80	99	82	74	40	24	21	6	**426**
South East	110	122	98	97	61	31	13	0	**532**
East Anglia	20	26	17	22	11	8	1	0	**105**
Midlands	67	76	66	51	27	14	10	0	**311**
South West	21	33	20	21	11	6	6	0	**118**
North East	39	54	47	45	13	11	7	0	**216**
North West	39	47	28	33	8	12	6	0	**173**
Wales	7	6	8	6	6	5	2	0	**40**
Scotland/ N. Ireland	23	38	35	33	11	12	6	1	**159**
Total	**406**	**501**	**401**	**382**	**188**	**123**	**72**	**7**	**2,080**

Note: Figures derived from pension funds with a membership estimated to be in excess of 500 members in 1994.

Source: *Pension Funds and their Advisers, 1995*, A.P.Information Services.

NUMBER OF PENSION FUNDS WITH CAPITAL VALUES OF VARIOUS SIZES, ANALYSED BY REGION AND SIZE OF FUNDS

	Estimated Size of Fund in 1994, £ Million								
Region	0–4.9	5–9.9	10–19.9	20–49.9	50–99.9	100–249.9	250–1,000	1,000+	Total
London	109	25	46	65	54	57	50	20	**426**
South East	136	28	63	100	56	75	61	13	**532**
East Anglia	33	8	16	17	8	8	13	2	**105**
Midlands	136	21	29	52	26	13	26	8	**311**
South West	37	10	6	17	14	10	19	5	**118**
North East	110	8	17	33	18	12	12	6	**216**
North West	63	12	24	22	19	9	17	7	**173**
Wales	13	2	6	5	4	0	9	1	**40**
Scotland/ N. Ireland	60	5	21	23	13	14	17	6	**159**
Total	**697**	**119**	**228**	**334**	**212**	**198**	**224**	**68**	**2,080**

Note: Figures derived from pension funds with a membership estimated to be in excess of 500 members in 1994.

Source: *Pension Funds and their Advisers, 1995*, A.P. Information Services.

VALUE OF TOTAL PENSION FUND ASSETS ANALYSED BY REGION AND SIZE OF FUNDS

Region	Estimated Size of Fund in 1994, £ Million								Total
	0–4.9	5–9.9	10–19.9	20–49.9	50–99.9	100–249.9	250–1,000	1,000+	
London	41	189	654	2064	3710	10162	22910	95095	134824
South East	73	200	915	3276	3901	11722	31211	38997	90296
East Anglia	29	55	222	609	487	1306	6178	2205	11091
Midlands	44	153	429	1629	1769	1868	13677	20120	39689
South West	38	80	85	542	1013	1521	8193	15540	27011
North East	45	59	238	1183	1284	2137	5697	23827	34469
North West	32	82	337	644	1395	1206	9074	19324	32093
Wales	4	17	89	150	295	0	3330	1071	4956
Scotland/ N. Ireland	47	34	291	702	810	2191	9087	13521	26682
Total	352	869	3259	10798	14664	32113	109357	229699	401111

Note: Figures derived from pension funds with a membership estimated to be in excess of 500 members in 1994.

Source: Pension Funds and their Advisers, 1995, A.P. Information Services.

SUMMARY OF INVESTMENTS BY SIZE OF PENSION FUND
(all figures refer to percentages)

Type of Investment	Estimated Size of Fund in 1994, £ Million								Av.
	0–4.9	5–9.9	10–24.9	25–49.9	50–99.9	100–249.9	250–1,000	1,000+	
Equities									
UK	50.9	50.5	56.2	54.9	57.0	54.2	54.9	52.8	**53.7**
Overseas	16.3	17.8	19.4	21.4	20.7	21.6	23.1	23.1	**22.8**
Fixed Interest									
UK	10.0	10.5	6.6	5.8	6.3	5.9	4.3	4.4	**4.6**
Overseas	1.9	2.2	2.8	3.7	3.2	2.9	3.4	2.6	**2.9**
Property									
UK	4.5	3.4	2.4	2.7	2.1	3.0	4.5	7.7	**6.2**
Overseas	0.1	0.1	0.1	0.1	0.1	0.3	0.2	0.7	**0.5**
Index-Linked Gilts	1.2	1.3	2.8	2.4	2.8	3.2	3.1	4.0	**3.6**
Cash and Deposits	6.2	4.4	4.9	4.1	3.6	4.3	4.0	3.3	**3.6**
Others	9.4	10.3	5.2	5.5	4.7	5.2	3.0	1.8	**2.6**

Note: Figures derived from pension funds with a membership estimated to be in excess of 500 members in 1994.

Source: Pension Funds and their Advisers, 1995, A.P. Information Services.

MEMBERSHIP OF PENSION SCHEMES

	UK Adult Population ('000s)	Scheme Membership ('000s)	Scheme Membership (%)	Membership/ Pop'n Group (%)	Index[1]
COMPANY PENSION SCHEMES, MID 1991					
All adults	**46,743**	**10,700**	**100.0**	**22.9**	**100**
Men	22,560	6,800	63.6	30.1	132
Women	24,182	3,900	36.4	16.1	70
Ages					
15–19	3,740	200	1.9	5.3	23
20–24	4,510	1,020	9.5	22.6	99
25–29	4,789	1,540	14.4	32.2	140
30–34	4,266	1,440	13.5	33.8	147
35–44	7,954	2,850	26.6	35.8	156
45–54	6,582	2,380	22.2	36.2	158
55–64	5,805	1,250	11.7	21.5	94
65+	9,098	20	0.2	0.2	1
PERSONAL PENSION SCHEMES[2], 1992/93					
All adults	**46,800**	**5,667**	**100.0**	**12.1**	**100**
Men	22,610	3,553	62.7	15.7	130
Women	24,190	2,114	37.3	8.7	72
Ages					
15–19	3,556	121	2.1	3.4	28
20–24	4,416	1,174	20.7	26.6	220
25–29	4,801	1,470	25.9	30.6	253
30–34	4,396	1,077	19.0	24.5	202
35–44	7,815	1,377	24.3	17.6	145
45–54	6,891	440	7.8	6.4	53
55–64	5,787	7	0.1	0.1	1
65+	9,138	–	–	–	–

Notes: [1] The index is based on the proportion of scheme membership by population group relative to the proportion of scheme membership by the population as a whole.
[2] Figures relate to schemes to which the DSS pay minimum contributions. There are approximately 2.5 million other personal pension schemes.
Source: Bacon & Woodrow, compiled from Government information.

ENTITLEMENT TO SERPS, 1992/93

	All ('000s)	16-24 ('000s)	25-34 ('000s)	35-44 ('000s)	45-54 ('000s)	55+ ('000s)
EARNINGS BAND						
All amounts	**7,827**	**2,267**	**1,537**	**1,362**	**1,611**	**1,050**
£2,999 or less	2,566	1,134	505	400	310	217
£3,000– £5,999	1,782	525	318	367	381	191
£6,000– £8,999	1,354	369	253	233	311	188
£9,000–£11,999	885	155	184	149	225	174
£12,000–£14,999	537	59	131	90	146	112
£15,000–£17,999	319	18	77	52	100	73
£18,000–£19,999	140	5	30	27	46	32
£20,000 or more	244	2	40	45	93	64

Note: Figures are based on the numbers of people paying National Insurance Contributions in 1992/93 at the not contracted-out rate, who could potentially accrue SERPS pension.
Source: Bacon & Woodrow, compiled from Government information.

PENSION SCHEME SURPLUS, 1987/88 TO 1993/94

Since 1987 pension schemes seeking full tax relief have not been allowed to accumulate funds significantly in excess of their liabilities. The following figures come from returns made to the Pension Schemes Office by scheme administrators.

1. Schemes which have reported more than once

3,253 schemes reported more than once. The pie chart below shows whether or not these schemes reported a surplus of more or less than 5% at the first, and then the most recent, valuation.

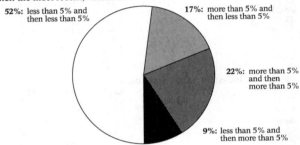

52%: less than 5% and then less than 5%

17%: more than 5% and then less than 5%

22%: more than 5% and then more than 5%

9%: less than 5% and then more than 5%

2. Aggregate surplus

1,987 schemes disclosed a surplus in excess of 5% of their liabilities in their most recent valuation. The aggregate value of surplus disclosed was £10,701m compared with an aggregate value of corresponding liabilities of £55,001m.

3. Method of reducing surplus

The following figures represent the total surplus eliminated or to be eliminated by each method. The amounts shown are based on the scheme actuary's estimated cost for each category reported in the seven year period. The figures will therefore contain some surplus and schemes counted more than once.

Method of reduction	Number of Schemes	Amount of Reduction (£million)
Contribution holiday (e'er)	2,283	100,046
Contribution holiday (e'ee)	123	218
Contribution reduction (e'er)	1,182	3,903
Contribution reduction (e'ee)	172	628
Refund to employer[1]	309	1,161
Increase in benefits	1,666	7,994
New benefits	185	148

Note: [1] Excludes amounts paid over by schemes reported to be wound up in each year.

Source: Bacon & Woodrow, compiled from Government information.

UK SOCIAL SECURITY BENEFITS

SOCIAL SECURITY BENEFIT RATES AND ELIGIBILITY RULES

The following table outlines the main Social Security benefits, giving the rates for 1995/96 and setting out the main eligibility rules. Receipt of some benefits affects entitlement to other benefits. (Rates for 1996/97 were not available at the time of going to press, therefore a blank column has been incorporated for these rates to be inserted when known.)

All rates are weekly unless otherwise specified

Benefit	Rates, 1995/96	1996/97	Eligibility
CHILDREN			
Child Benefit	Eldest child for whom benefit is payable: £10.40 Each subsequent child: £8.45 *tax free*		Responsible for a child who is: (i) under the age of 16; *or* (ii) aged 16-18 in full-time, but not further, education; *or* (iii) aged 16 or 17 and registered for work or training. Paid to wife unless she agrees otherwise.
Guardian's Allowance	Child for whom **Child Benefit** is payable:– higher rate: £9.85 lower rate: £11.05 *tax free*		Must look after a child who is orphaned or parent(s) unknown and be entitled to **Child Benefit**. Need not be the child's legal guardian.
One Parent Benefit	First or only child: £6.30 *tax free*		Must be receiving **Child Benefit** and bringing up child alone. Need not be the child's parent.
DISABILITY			
Disability Living Allowance	Care component:– lower: £12.40 middle: £31.20 higher: £46.70 Mobility component:– lower: £12.40 higher: £32.65 *tax free*		Under 66; *and* (i) have needed help with personal care or getting around before 65th birthday and for previous 3 months and likely to need help for a further 6 months; *or* (ii) is not expected to live more than 6 months.
Disability Working Allowance	Single people: £46.85 Couple/lone parent: £73.40 Child allowance[1]: £11.40 to £32.80 *tax free* *NIC credits*		(i) Aged 16 or over; *&* (ii) work 16+ hours a week; *&* (iii) illness/disability which disadvantages getting a job; *&* (iv) savings less than £16,000; *&* (v) have received other invalidity or disability benefits.

All rates are weekly unless otherwise specified

Benefit	Rates, 1995/96	1996/97	Eligiblity
Attendance Allowance	Higher: £46.70 Lower: £31.20 *tax free*		(i) Aged 65 or over; & (ii) has needed help with personal care for 6 months.
Severe Disablement Allowance	Allowance: £35.55 Addition if age first unable to work was: Under 40 £12.40 40–49 £7.80 50–59 £3.90 *tax free*		(i) Aged 16 to 64[2]; & (ii) initially have been incapable of work for a continuous period of 196 days; & (iii) assessed as at least 80% disabled if aged 20 or over; & (iv) resident in Great Britain. Voluntary work for up to 16 hours per week will not result in disqualification.
Invalid Care Allowance	Allowance: £35.25 *(Earnings limit £50)* *taxable*		(i) Caring (for at least 35 hrs per week) for a person receiving **Disability Living Allowance** at the middle or higher rate, **Attendance Allowance** or **Constant Attendance Allowance**; & (ii) aged 16 to 64[2].

INDUSTRIAL INJURIES & DISEASE

Benefit	Rates, 1995/96	1996/97	Eligiblity
Industrial Injuries Disablement Benefit	100% assessment: £95.30 (person aged over 18) *tax free*		(i) Injured/diseased on or after 5 July 1948 because of work; & (ii) accident occurred in GB; & (iii) at least 14% disabled.
Reduced Earnings Allowance	Maximum: £38.12 *tax free*		(i) Accident happened or disease started before Oct. 1990; & (ii) incapable of doing regular job (or job of same standard) due to industrial injury or disease.
Retirement Allowance	25% of **REA**, subject to a maximum rate of: £9.53 *tax free*		Replaces **Reduced Earnings Allowance (REA)** when claimant reaches State Pension Age (SPA) and ceases employment.
Constant Attendance Allowance	Part-time: £19.10 Normal maximum: £38.20 Intermediate rate: £57.30 Exceptional rate: £76.40 *tax free*		Seriously handicapped due to industrial injury or disease such that constant care and attention is needed.
Exceptionally Severe Disablement Allowance	Standard: £38.20 *tax free*		(i) Exceptionally severely disabled; & (ii) entitled to the **Constant Attendance Allowance** at one of two higher rates; & (iii) needs permanent attendance.

All rates are weekly unless otherwise specified

Benefit	Rates, 1995/96	1996/97	Eligiblity

LOW INCOME

Benefit	Rates, 1995/96	1996/97	Eligiblity
Housing Benefit	Up to full eligible rent if receiving **Income Support**, otherwise *means tested*. *tax free*		(i) Low income; & (ii) paying rent; & (iii) savings less than £16,000.
Income Support	Personal allowances vary with age, marital status, or dependent children. Basic rate for a couple both aged at least 18: £73.00 Additional premiums vary with number of children, whether disabled, carer, or whether over 60. Some housing costs not covered by **Housing Benefit**, including mortgage interest. *taxable unless unavailable for work*		Generally: (i) aged 18 and over; & (ii) resident in Great Britain; & (iii) works less than 16 hours per week; & (iv) available for work (unless disabled or caring); & (v) joint capital less than £8,000. *means tested*
Family Credit	Adult payment for one parent or a couple: £45.10 Addition for each child:– aged under 11 £11.40 aged 11-15 £18.90 aged 16-17 £23.45 aged 18 £32.80 *tax free*		(i) Working 16+ hours a week; & (ii) bringing up one or more children; & (iii) capital less than £8,000; & (iv) resident in Great Britain. *means tested*
Council Tax Benefit	Maximum help is 100%. *tax free*		*means tested*

MATERNITY

Benefit	Rates, 1995/96	1996/97	Eligiblity
Maternity Allowance	Allowance:– Working during qualifying week: £52.50 Not working or self-employed during qualifying week: £45.55 Dependant allowance: £27.50 *tax free*		(i) Not eligible for **Statutory Maternity Pay**; & (ii) employed/self-employed; & (iii) full rate NICs paid for at least 6 months in the 66 weeks ending 15 weeks before the baby is due.

All rates are weekly unless otherwise specified

Benefit	Rates, 1995/96	1996/97	Eligiblity
Statutory Maternity Pay	Higher: 90% of person's average earnings Lower: £52.50 *taxable subject to NICs*		(i) Continuously employed with same employer for at least 6 months, 15 weeks before the baby is due; & (ii) paid Class 1 National Insurance Contributions (NICs).

RETIREMENT PENSION

Benefit	Rates, 1995/96	1996/97	Eligiblity
Basic State Pension	Based on own or late spouse's NICs: £58.85 Based on spouse's NICs: £35.25 Over 80s pension: £35.25 Over 80s addition: £0.25 *taxable*		(i) Reached State Pension Age; & (ii) paid sufficient NICs. The Over 80s pension is non-contributory and subject to residence conditions.
Additional Pension	Percentage of revalued qualifying earnings from 1978. Reduced by GMP if contracted-out. *taxable*		(i) Reached State Pension Age; & (ii) paid Class 1 NICs. Widow(er)s may receive a pension based on their spouse's NICs.
Graduated Retirement Benefit	Per unit: 7.64p Employees may be contracted-out and receive EPBs instead. *taxable*		Based on NICs paid between April 1961 and April 1975.

SICKNESS

Benefit	Rates, 1995/96	1996/97	Eligiblity
Incapacity Benefit[3]	**Short Term:–** Under pension age:– basic rate (up to 28 weeks): £44.40 adult dependant: £27.50 higher rate (29-52 wks): £52.50 adult dependant: £27.50 child dependants *first child*: £9.85 *each other child*: £11.05 Over pension age:– basic rate (up to 52 weeks): £56.45 adult dependant: £33.85 child dependants *first child*: £9.85 *each other child*: £11.05		Sufficient NICs paid. Up to 28 weeks: (i) employees excluded from **Statutory Sick Pay** and others who meet contribution conditions; & (ii) unable to work for at least 4 consecutive working days because of sickness. From 29th week, must pass an objective medical assessment based on capacity to do any work, covering various categories of abilities.

All rates are weekly unless otherwise specified

Benefit	Rates, 1995/96	1996/97	Eligiblity

Incapacity Benefit[3] **(continued)**	**Long Term:–**
	Under pension age:–
	basic rate
	(after 52 weeks): £58.85
	  adult dependant: £35.25
	  child dependants
	    first child: £9.85
	    each other child: £11.05
	Over pension age:–
	retirement pension
	becomes payable
	Age additions:–
	incapacity began
	  aged under 35: £12.40
	  aged 35–44 £6.20
	
	Invalidity Allowance (transitional):–
	  lower: £3.90
	  middle: £7.80
	  higher: £12.40
	
	higher and long term rates taxable (unless previously on Invalidity Benefit)
			Payable with some exemptions to:
			(i) new claimants of **Incapacity Benefit** or **Severe Disablement Allowance**;
			(ii) existing claimant of Sickness Benefit or Invalidity Benefit;
			(iii) people receiving disability premium paid with **Income Support**, **Housing Benefit** and **Council Tax Benefit**; &
			(iv) people receiving NIC credits because of incapacity.
			
			For existing claimants of Invalidity Benefit a transitional Invalidity Allowance is paid in addition. The level depends on age on the first day of incapacity.

Statutory Sick Pay	Per week: £52.50 *taxable*		(i) Employee paying NICs; & (ii) incapable of work on the day concerned; & (iii) earnings more than £58 pw.

SOCIAL FUND

Benefit	Rates, 1995/96	1996/97	Eligiblity
Maternity Payments	Lump sum: £100 Reduced by savings over £500. Non-repayable. *tax free*		(i) Receiving **Income Support**, **Disability Working Allowance** or **Family Credit**; & (ii) having or adopting a baby not more than 12 months old.
Funeral Payments	Cost of a simple funeral to a maximum of £875. Reduced by savings over £500 (£1,000 for those aged 60 or over). Repayable from dead person's estate if assets available. *tax free*		Individual or partner is: (i) arranging a funeral and does not have enough money to pay for it; & (ii) is in receipt of **Income Support**, **Family Credit**, **Disability Working Allowance**, **Housing Benefit** or **Council Tax Benefit**.
Budget/Crisis Loans and Community Care Grant	Varies. *tax free*		Depends on merits of case and budget of Social Security office.

All rates are weekly unless otherwise specified

Benefit	Rates, 1995/96	1996/97	Eligiblity
Cold Weather Payment	Payment: £8.50 *tax free*		Receiving **Income Support** including premium for being either over 60, disabled or long-term sick, or for a child under 5.

UNEMPLOYMENT

Benefit	Rates, 1995/96	1996/97	Eligiblity
Unemploy-ment Benefit	Under SPA: £46.45 dependent partner: £28.65 Over SPA: £58.85 dependent partner: £35.25 *taxable NIC credits*		(i) Capable of, available for and actively seeking work; & (ii) sufficient Class 1 NICs.

WIDOW'S BENFITS

Benefit	Rates, 1995/96	1996/97	Eligiblity
Widow's Payment	Lump sum: £1,000 *tax free*		(i) Husband's NICs sufficient; *or* (ii) his death caused by his job and he was either not entitled to a **Retirement Pension**, or widow under 60 at his death.
Widow's Pension	Pension: £58.85 Plus SERPS pension. *taxable*		Either: (i) husband's NICs sufficient; *or* (ii) his death was caused by his job and he was 45 or over when he died; *or* (iii) 45 or over when **Widowed Mother's Allowance** ends.
Widowed Mother's Allowance	Allowance: £58.85 Additional child allowance:– first child: £9.85 each other child: £11.05 Plus SERPS pension. *children's allowance tax free*		Has child for whom entitled to **Child Benefit** or is pregnant, and either: (i) husband's NICs sufficient; *or* (ii) his death was caused by his job.

Notes: [1] Amount varies with age of child and is adjusted for income and savings.
[2] Age limits apply at date of claim.
[3] Incapacity Benefit replaced both Sickness Benefit and Invalidity Benefit for new claimants from April 1995.
Source: Bacon & Woodrow.

BASIC STATE RETIREMENT PENSIONS

From		Single Person		Married Couple	
		£ per Week	£ per Year	£ per Week	£ per Year
1948	(July)	1.30	67.60	2.10	109.20
1951	(October)	1.50	78.00	2.50	130.00
1952	(September)	1.62½	84.50	2.70	140.40
1955	(April)	2.00	104.00	3.25	169.00
1958	(January)	2.50	130.00	4.00	208.00
1961	(April)	2.87½	149.50	4.62½	240.50
1963	(May)	3.37½	175.50	5.45	283.40
1965	(March)	4.00	208.00	6.50	338.00
1967	(October)	4.50	234.00	7.30	379.60
1969	(November)	5.00	260.00	8.10	421.20
1971	(September)	6.00	312.00	9.70	504.40
1972	(October)	6.75	351.00	10.90	566.80
1973	(October)	7.75	403.00	12.50	650.00
1974	(July)	10.00	520.00	16.00	832.00
1975	(April)	11.60	603.20	18.50	962.00
1975	(November)	13.30	691.60	21.20	1,102.40
1976	(November)	15.30	795.60	24.50	1,274.00
1977	(November)	17.50	910.00	28.00	1,456.00
1978	(November)	19.50	1,014.00	31.20	1,622.40
1979	(November)	23.30	1,211.60	37.30	1,939.60
1980	(November)	27.15	1,411.80	43.45	2,259.40
1981	(November)	29.60	1,539.20	47.35	2,462.20
1982	(November)	32.85	1,708.20	52.55	2,732.60
1983	(November)	34.05	1,770.60	54.50	2,834.00
1984	(November)	35.80	1,861.60	57.30	2,979.60
1985	(November)	38.30	1,991.60	61.30	3,187.60
1986	(July)	38.70	2,012.40	61.95	3,221.40
1987	(April)	39.50	2,054.00	63.25	3,289.00
1988	(April)	41.15	2,139.80	65.90	3,426.80
1989	(April)	43.60	2,267.20	69.80	3,629.60
1990	(April)	46.90	2,438.80	75.10	3,905.20
1991	(April)	52.00	2,704.00	83.25	4,329.00
1992	(April)	54.15	2,815.80	86.70	4,508.40
1993	(April)	56.10	2,917.20	89.80	4,669.60
1994	(April)	57.60	2,995.20	92.10	4,789.20
1995	(April)	58.85	3,060.20	94.10	4,893.20

Source: Compiled from Government information.

NATIONAL INSURANCE CONTRIBUTION RATES AND STATE SCHEME EARNINGS LIMITS

| | National Insurance Contribution Rates | | | | | State Scheme Earnings Limits | | | |
| | Employer | | | Employee | | Lower Earnings Limit (LEL) | | Upper Earnings Limit (UEL) | |
Tax Year	Contracted-Out %	Not Contracted-Out %	Initial	Contracted-Out %	Not Contracted-Out %	Per Week £	Per Annum £	Per Week £	Per Annum £
1989/90 from 5.10.89									
Earnings pw									
LEL – £74.99	1.20	5.00	2.00	7.00	9.00	43.00	2,236	325.00	16,900
£75 – £114.99	3.20	7.00	2.00	7.00	9.00				
£115 – £164.99	5.20	9.00	2.00	7.00	9.00				
£165 – UEL	6.65	10.45	2.00	7.00	9.00				
1990/91									
Earnings pw									
LEL – £79.99	1.20	5.00	2.00	7.00	9.00	46.00	2,392	350.00	18,200
£80 – £124.99	3.20	7.00	2.00	7.00	9.00				
£125 – £174.99	5.20	9.00	2.00	7.00	9.00				
£175 – UEL	6.65	10.45	2.00	7.00	9.00				
1991/92									
Earnings pw									
LEL – £84.99	0.80	4.60	2.00	7.00	9.00	52.00	2,704	390.00	20,280
£85 – £129.99	2.80	6.60	2.00	7.00	9.00				
£130 – £184.99	4.80	8.60	2.00	7.00	9.00				
£185 – UEL	6.60	10.40	2.00	7.00	9.00				
1992/93									
Earnings pw									
LEL – £89.99	0.80	4.60	2.00	7.00	9.00	54.00	2,808	405.00	21,060
£90 – £134.99	2.80	6.60	2.00	7.00	9.00				
£135 – £189.99	4.80	8.60	2.00	7.00	9.00				
£190 – UEL	6.60	10.40	2.00	7.00	9.00				

| | National Insurance Contribution Rates | | | | | State Scheme Earnings Limits | | | |
| | Employer | | Initial | Employee | | Lower Earnings Limit (LEL) | | Upper Earnings Limit (UEL) | |
Tax Year	Contracted-Out %	Not Contracted-Out %		Contracted-Out %	Not Contracted-Out %	Per Week £	Per Annum £	Per Week £	Per Annum £
1993/94									
Earnings pw									
LEL – £94.99	1.60	4.60	2.00	7.20	9.00	56.00	2,912	420.00	21,840
£95 – £139.99	3.60	6.60	2.00	7.20	9.00				
£140 – £194.99	5.60	8.60	2.00	7.20	9.00				
£195 – UEL	7.40	10.40	2.00	7.20	9.00				
1994/95									
Earnings pw									
LEL – £99.99	0.60	3.60	2.00	8.20	10.00	57.00	2,964	430.00	22,360
£85 – £144.99	2.60	5.60	2.00	8.20	10.00				
£130 – £199.99	4.60	7.60	2.00	8.20	10.00				
£200 – UEL	7.20	10.20	2.00	8.20	10.00				
1995/96									
Earnings pw									
LEL – £104.99	0.00	3.00	2.00	8.20	10.00	58.00	3,016	440.00	22,880
£105 – £149.99	2.00	5.00	2.00	8.20	10.00				
£150 – £204.99	4.00	7.00	2.00	8.20	10.00				
£205 – UEL	7.20	10.20	2.00	8.20	10.00				

Note: The table shows the rates payable according to the band in which the employee's earnings fall. No contributions are payable by either employee or employer if the employee's earnings are below LEL. If the employee's earnings exceed the LEL, contributions are paid by the employer at the rate applicable to the band on all earnings between the LEL and the UEL and at the corresponding not contracted-out rate for earnings both below the LEL and above the UEL. If the employee's earnings exceed the LEL, contributions are payable by the employee at the initial rate on earnings below the LEL and at the main rate on all earnings between the LEL and the UEL. No contributions are required from employees above the UEL.

Source: Bacon & Woodrow. Summary compiled from Government information.

SECTION 148 ORDERS:
REVALUATION OF EARNINGS FACTORS

Tax Year of Earnings	Tax Year of Termination							
	1995/96 (%)	1994/95 (%)	1993/94 (%)	1992/93 (%)	1991/92 (%)	1990/91 (%)	1989/90 (%)	1988/89 (%)
1978/79	341.9	323.1	310.4	291.0	267.1	233.4	211.5	181.2
1979/80	289.7	273.1	262.0	244.8	223.8	194.0	174.9	148.1
1980/81	225.7	211.9	202.5	188.2	170.6	145.8	129.7	107.3
1981/82	173.1	161.5	153.7	141.6	126.9	106.1	92.3	73.6
1982/83	147.9	137.3	130.2	119.3	105.9	87.0	74.7	57.7
1983/84	129.8	120.0	113.4	103.3	90.9	73.4	62.3	46.4
1984/85	112.7	103.7	97.6	88.2	76.7	60.5	50.2	35.6
1985/86	99.6	91.1	85.4	76.6	65.8	50.6	41.0	27.2
1986/87	83.4	75.6	70.3	62.2	52.3	38.3	29.4	16.8
1987/88	70.8	63.5	58.6	51.1	41.9	28.9	20.5	8.7
1988/89	57.0	50.3	45.8	38.9	30.4	18.4	10.8	
1989/90	42.2	36.2	32.1	25.8	18.2	7.3		
1990/91	32.5	26.9	23.1	17.3	10.1			
1991/92	20.4	15.3	11.8	6.5				
1992/93	13.1	8.3	5.0					
1993/94	7.7	3.1						
1994/95	4.4							

Note: Previously known as 'Section 21 Orders'.
Source: Bacon & Woodrow, compiled from Government information.

CONTRACTING-OUT REBATE

Tax Years	Employee (%)	Employer (%)
78/79 to 82/83	2.50	4.50
83/84 to 87/88	2.15	4.10
88/89 to 92/93	2.00	3.80
93/94 to 96/97	1.80	3.00

Source: Bacon & Woodrow, compiled from Government information.

DEFERRED PENSION REVALUATION PERCENTAGES

Complete Years Since Leaving	Calendar Year of NPA					
	1995 (%)	1994 (%)	1993 (%)	1992 (%)	1991 (%)	1990 (%)
1	2.2	1.8	3.6	4.1	5.0	5.0
2	4.0	5.5	7.8	10.3	10.3	10.3
3	7.8	9.8	15.8	15.8	15.8	15.8
4	12.2	21.6	21.6	21.6	21.6	21.6
5	24.4	27.6	27.6	27.6	27.6	
6	33.9	34.0	34.0	34.0		
7	40.7	40.7	40.7			
8	47.5	47.8				
9	52.0					

Source: Bacon & Woodrow, compiled from Government information.

SOCIAL SECURITY AND OTHER RETIREMENT BENEFITS OVERSEAS

This section gives a summary of key economic indicators and Social Security information in tabular form for some of the larger world economies.

Notes to the international table overleaf

(a) Figures for 1995 not available – earlier figures used

(b) Treasury Bill Rate

(c) Flexible retirement age

(d) On all earnings

(e) Mostly funded through general taxation

(f) Including contributions to ARRCO

(g) Up to earnings ceiling

(h) Approximate, for new entrants to the system; earnings ceiling on pension contributions only

(j) Including contributions to ARRCO; excluding CSG special contribution

(k) Ceiling reduced to DM 76,800 in Eastern Länder

(l) Unless widower is disabled

(m) Up to earnings limit, but reduced to 2% on earnings below £3,016

(n) For most contributions, otherwise Fl 74,360

(o) Additional special medical care is only provided if employee earns less than Fl 58,950 p.a.

(p) Except for retirees and disabled people

(q) Assumes spouse older than 45

(r) State pension ages are gradually being equalised at 65 for men and women

(s) For new entrants to the system

(t) Gradually being raised to 67 for men and women

(u) The retirement pension for a couple is currently 42.5% of the Average Weekly Earnings for full time persons. This pension is subject to both an asset and income test, however.

(v) The amount of the Social Security pension is expressed as the approximate benefit, including mandatory supplementary plans, as a percentage of final salary for a middle manager with a full career in the country concerned. (*Source:* For EU countries and the US "Employee Benefits in Europe and the USA" edited by Howard Foster, published by Godwins.)

State pension formula:
      A: not related to earnings
      B: related to earnings below a fixed ceiling
      C: effectively related to all earnings

	AUSTRALIA	BELGIUM	CANADA	FRANCE	GERMANY	ITALY
1. Economic Indicators						
Population (1994, million)	17.5	10.0	27.9	57.3	80.5	57.8
GDP per capita (1994, local currency)	25,300	762,100	26,900	128,800	37,000	28,392,700
GDP per capita (1994, £ equivalent)	12,000	16,300	12,800	16,500	16,100	11,300
Price inflation (1994-95, % pa)	4.5	1.2	2.7	1.6	2.3	5.6
Earnings increases (1994-95, % pa)	3.8	1.6(a)	1.6	2.1	4.3	2.8
Money market rate (av. yield Q1 1995, %)	7.4	5.7	8.1	6.0	4.9	10.7(b)
Government bond yield (av. yield Q1 1995, %)	10.0	8.2	9.0	8.1	7.3	12.7
Exchange rate (£1 =, Aug. 1995)	Aus$ 2.1	BFr 46.7	Can$ 2.1	FFr 7.8	DM 2.3	Lit 2,504
2. Social Security Information (1995)						
State pension ages	65m,60.5f(r)	60-65 m&f(c)	65 m&f	60-65 m&f(c)	65 m&f	57-65 m&f(c, s)
Typical contributions (employer, %)	(e)	35(d)	3(g)	40(f)	20(g)	50(h)
Typical contributions (employee, %)	(e)	13(d)	3(g)	20(j)	20(g)	10(h)
Earnings ceiling (local currency)	n/a	1,325,550	34,400	155,940	93,600(k)	132,000,000(h)
Earnings ceiling (approx. £ equivalent)	n/a	28,400	16,400	20,000	40,700	52,700(h)
Social Security pension for middle manager (approx.)						
– type (u)	A (u)	B	A+B	B	B	B (s)
– amount (u)	(u)	30%	20%	60%	30%	70%
Survivors' benefits	60%	80%	60%	50%	60% (q)	60%
Widowers' benefits	Yes	Yes	Yes	Yes	Yes	Yes
Provision of medical care	Yes	Yes	Yes	Yes	Yes	Yes

	JAPAN	NETHERLANDS	SPAIN	UK	USA
1. Economic Indicators					
Population (1994, million)	124.3	15.1	39.1	57.7	255.4
GDP per capita (1994, local currency)	3,775,100	39,800	1,654,000	11,600	26,400
GDP per capita (1994, £ equivalent)	25,200	15,900	8,500	11,600	17,600
Price inflation (1994-95, % pa)	0.3	2.1	5.1	3.5	3.0
Earnings increases (1994-95, % pa)	3.5	0.8	4.6	3.1	3.2
Money market rate (av. yield Q1 1995, %)	2.2	4.9	9.9(b)	5.4	5.8(b)
Government bond yield (av. yield Q1 1995, %)	3.6	7.8	11.7	8.6	7.5
Exchange rate (£1 =, Aug. 1995)	¥ 150	Fl 2.5	Pta 194	£ 1.0	US$ 1.5
2. Social Security Information (1995)					
State pension ages	65 m&f	65 m&f	65 m&f	65m,60f(r)	65 m&f(t)
Typical contributions (employer, %)	8(g)	10(g)	32(g)	10(d)	14(g)
Typical contributions (employee, %)	8(g)	46(g)	7(g)	10(m)	8(g)
Earnings ceiling (local currency)	7,080,000	44,350(m)	4,346,280	22,880	61,200
Earnings ceiling (approx. £ equivalent)	47,200	17,700	22,400	22,880	40,800
Social Security pension for middle manager (approx.)					
– type (u)	A+B	A	B	A+B	B
– amount (u)	70%	20%	50%	30%	20%
Survivors' benefits	45%	70%	50%	60%	100%
Widowers' benefits	Yes	Yes	No(l)	No(l)	Yes
Provision of medical care	Yes	Yes(o)	Yes	Yes	No(p)

AUSTRALIA

Company Plans: Benefit structure

Multinational companies and medium to large local companies have traditionally sponsored final average salary related defined benefit plans. However, defined contribution plans are becoming increasingly common as a result of union-promoted industry schemes and the minimum levels of employer contributions required by legislation.

Normal retirement age is usually 65 for men and either 60 or 65 for women. Anti-discrimination legislation is bringing the retirement ages into line, generally to 65.

Benefits normally take the form of a lump sum whether on retirement, total and permanent disablement, withdrawal or death. Death and disablement benefits are generally equal to the prospective benefit payable at normal retirement age.

Benefits to early leavers generally comprise a return of their own contributions plus interest plus an amount funded by employer contributions. The employer funded benefit must currently be at least equivalent to contributions of 6% of salary. Any benefits funded by employer contributions may be required to be preserved in a plan until the member retires at or after age 55.

Company Plans: Contributions and funding methods

Existing plans are normally contributory and 5% of pensionable salary is customarily paid by members. The employer meets the balance of costs. The contribution rate may be lower for wage earners and some employees may notionally contribute to a scheme out of pre-tax remuneration.

Funding methods are generally similar to those in the UK with a mix of insured and self-administered plans.

Since 1 January 1992 employers have been obliged to contribute to a suitable pension scheme on behalf of their employees. The minimum contribution rate is 6% of salaries (from 30 June 1995), rising to 9% by 2002. Benefits equivalent in value to these contributions can be provided. Employer contributions can be funded from surplus.

The federal government has foreshadowed a minimum level of employee contributions, starting from 1% of salary in 1997/98, rising to 3% by 1999/2000. The government will match these minimum levels of employee contribution.

Taxation and regulation

Employer contributions to approved plans are tax deductible. Employee contributions to employer-sponsored plans are not generally tax-deductible. Pension plan income (including employer contributions) is taxed at 15%. The actual rate of tax paid on investment income will be less than 15% because an imputation credit is given for franked dividends and capital gains are taxed only in excess of inflation.

The first A$83,168 of a lump sum retirement benefit is paid tax-free and the balance is taxed at the reduced rate of 15% plus the Medicare levy of 1.5%. Reduced rates of tax also apply in respect of lump sum benefits deemed to have accrued for service prior to 1 July 1983 or arising from termination of employment due to redundancy, death or invalidity. Increased rates apply to lump sums paid before age 55.

Pensions from private superannuation plans are treated in the same manner as privately purchased annuities, with the pension being taxed as ordinary income; there is a basic 15% rebate from income tax plus a rebate for the deemed capital component of each payment.

From 1 July 1994, the maximum concessionally taxed lump sum benefit is A$418,000. If more than half of a benefit is a 'complying' annuity or pension, the maximum increases to A$836,000.

Regulation of superannuation plans is undertaken by the Insurance and Superannuation Commission of the Federal government. Considerable regulation exists regarding:

- the material to be provided to members;
- the investment of plans assets;
- trustees; *and*
- the financial management of funds.

Current Topics

Some of the topics currently being debated are:

- member investment choice;
- the provision of reasonable benefits to women; *and*
- increasing the proportion of benefits paid as annuities and pensions.

BELGIUM

Company Plans: Benefit structure

Multinational companies normally provide final salary related pensions with partial or full lump sum commutation. Pension formulae usually range from 1½%-2% of final average earnings per year of service, including Social Security benefits. (Defined contribution schemes are still prevalent among local companies and provide lump sum benefits.)

Normal retirement still commonly remains at age 65 for men and 60 for women, although many plans are moving towards a joint retirement age of 65 as a result of the recent ECJ rulings.

Survivors' benefits take the form of a spouse's pension on death, either before or after retirement.

Insurance policies must be fully vested immediately; in most cases, the vested benefit is a paid-up insurance policy. No specific rules exist for the vesting of the employer's contribution for non-insured schemes, but the member is always entitled to have his own contributions, increased by 4.75% p.a. interest, refunded.

Company Plans: Contributions and funding methods

Employees' contributions are customarily in the range of 5%-6% of earnings above the Social Security assessment ceiling (currently about £28,000). Some schemes require minimal contributions on earnings up to the ceiling.

Funding methods include insured schemes and privately invested funds. The latter must be established within the framework of a separate non-profit-making company (ASBL). Both methods are subject to strict control. Some insurance companies have developed forms of deposit administration or managed funds.

Taxation

If certain conditions are met, employers' contributions to approved schemes are tax deductible, but there is an 8.86% social security levy on employers' contributions to occupational plans. Employees' contributions receive a tax credit computed at an average tax rate of between 30% and 40%. A premium tax of 4.4% is levied on all contributions paid to insurance companies as well as to self-administered funds. Pensions are fully taxable as income. Lump sum benefits are normally taxed at the favourable rate of 17%.

Regulation
Insured schemes and (as from 1 January 1986) non-insured schemes are subject to specific regulations. In particular, eligibility categories and benefits must be defined and membership can be made compulsory for new employees on meeting the eligibility conditions.

In all cases, the total retirement benefit, including Social Security, may not exceed 80% of the final salary.

Current topics
In order to help the financing of the Belgian social security system, a 'solidarity' contribution of between 0.5%-2% of pensions paid has been introduced. This contribution is based on all pensions receivable and lump sum retirement payments are also subject to this tax on the equivalent pension amount.

The Colla law was published on 6 April 1995. Though the details of the law have yet to be finalised, significant features of it include the tightening of equalisation requirements and vesting law. Employees are also now entitled to transfer vested pension rights between schemes.

CANADA

Company Plans: Benefit structure
Most pension plans provide benefits for salaried employees related to final average salary, the most common pension formula being 2% per year of service, integrated with the State earnings-related scheme (CPP/QPP). Plans for unionised hourly employees typically provide a flat amount per year of service. Defined contribution schemes are prevalent among smaller employers and are often offered on an optional basis by larger ones to supplement a defined benefit plan.

Normal retirement age is usually 65 for men and women.

Survivors' pensions on death before and after retirement are unusual, although some companies provide spouses' pensions on death after retirement. Death-in-service benefits are normally paid from resources outside the pension plan, e.g. an insurance policy.

Company Plans: Contributions and funding methods
Most earnings-related schemes are contributory, with employees normally contributing 5%-6% of annual salary inclusive of contributions to CPP/QPP. Defined contribution plans may have various optional levels of contributions which attract a matching employer contribution.

Funding methods are broadly similar to those used in the UK and may involve insurance and/or direct investment.

Pensions for employees earning more than the tax-approved salary 'cap' (Senior Executive Retirement Pension Schemes – SERPS) are, if provided, normally unfunded.

Taxation and regulation
Employer and employee contributions to an approved pension scheme are deductible. For defined benefit plans, both employee and employer

contributions are deductible, although there is a limit on the pension that may be provided. For defined contribution plans, the contributions up to a specified limit are deductible.

In addition to employer-sponsored pension schemes, individuals have the opportunity to contribute voluntarily to personal arrangements such as Registered Retirement Savings Plans (RRSPs). Contributions are tax deductible within certain dollar limits.

Current topics

Corporate disclosure requirements now show that 80% or more of large employers provide SERPS (Senior Executive Retirement Pension Schemes). Changes to the Income Tax Act have resulted in a further deferral for the date when the tax approved salary will be indexed.

FRANCE

Company Plans: Benefit structure

Few employees in France are entitled to benefits other than those provided by the basic state scheme and the mandatory complementary pay-as-you-go schemes (principally affiliated to ARRCO and AGIRC), the rate of contribution to which can be selected within specified bands.

A number of companies pay defined contributions to supplementary arrangements to top up the ARRCO/AGIRC benefits; a few large companies guarantee a target pension of (typically) 50-70% of final pay after a full career, including State benefits and the proceeds from the complementary systems. These supplementary plans are usually (but not always) confined to higher-paid employees.

Normal retirement age in the ARRCO/AGIRC schemes and (generally) in supplementary arrangements is 65 for men and women, although as in the case of the basic State scheme they can retire at 60 with a full pension if 40 years' service have been completed (slightly less in the case of individuals retiring before 2003).

As spouses' and disability benefits payable from the mandatory systems tend to be inadequate (being based only on service completed and often not payable below age 55), virtually all employers provide insured death and disability benefits. Insured medical plans are also widespread, to meet part or all of the share of costs not reimbursed by the State scheme.

Company Plans: Contributions and funding methods

Supplementary plans are generally insured (external financing is required in order to obtain a tax deduction in respect of the contributions). Benefits under some defined benefit supplementary plans are paid directly by the employer and are in most cases backed by book reserves, allocations to which are not tax-deductible. There is no legal requirement to establish a book reserve in respect of a pension liability, although a reference to the liability must appear at least as a note to the accounts.

Taxation

Employee and employer contributions to social security, the complementary systems and supplementary defined contribution arrangements are not taxable as income to the employee up to a limit of 19% of 8 times the social security ceiling (the ceiling is currently about £20,000 p.a.). A similar limit exists for exemption from employee and employer social charges (which are generally more significant than income tax).

Contributions to supplementary defined benefit arrangements are not taxable as income to the employee as long as the benefits provided are not deemed excessive, although contributions in excess of an upper limit may be subject to social charges (of about 25%), which in practice is only likely to affect senior executives.

Pensions in payment are normally taxed as earned income, subject to certain concessions, and there are no tax incentives to take benefits in lump sum form.

Current topics

The seemingly never-ending debate on the subject of *fonds de pension*, a framework for the creation of private funded pension plans to supplement the compulsory systems, continues. The former finance minister Alain Madelin was pushing for their introduction early in 1996, but since his forced resignation (for suggesting that social security benefits needed to be cut back) the government is perceived to have other priorities.

The cost of the compulsory systems continues to increase; the minimum joint contribution rates to ARRCO and AGIRC are now 5% and 15% respectively and will rise to at least 7.5% and 20% respectively by 2003. Many employers, at least in the short term, may not feel able to afford to pay additional contributions to a private plan.

Despite the increase in the contribution rates, unless further action is taken ARRCO will run out of money to pay its pensioners early next century.

GERMANY

Company Plans: Benefit structure

Although career average and flat amount based pensions have grown in importance, multinational companies normally provide old age and disability pensions ranging from 1%-2% of final average salary per year of service on earnings above the social security ceiling. The rate below the ceiling is commonly one-quarter to one-half of that above the ceiling. Survivors' benefits normally take the form of spouses' (60%) and orphans' pension, on death either before or after retirement.

Normal retirement age is usually 65 for men and women, but early retirement ages following the flexible retirement ages in the social security system are legally required.

Employees become entitled to vested benefits after age 35, either after ten years' plan membership or after 12 years' employment with three years' plan participation.

Employees' contributions are not customary (and not possible under some financing methods).

The practical financing methods for German companies are:

(a) Book reserves (internal balance sheet provisions), possibly coupled with full or partial reinsurance of benefit liabilities.

(b) Support funds, which are established as separate legal entities from the employing company.

(c) Direct insurance, in which case policies are 'owned' by the employees.

(d) Pensionskassen, which are effectively 'captive' insurance companies subject to strict supervision by the insurance authorities.

About two-thirds of all employees are covered by company schemes.

Those financed through book reserves cover about 70% of employees and about 80% of the total cost of company scheme benefits. This unusual feature distinguishes Germany from most other European countries.

Taxation and regulation

Appropriations to *book reserves* are calculated by a prescribed method (which may not reflect true cost) and, together with any reinsurance premiums, are tax-deductible to the employer. (Employees cannot contribute to a book-reserve plan.) Benefits payable to employees or dependants under the book-reserve system are taxed as income subject to certain tax-free allowances.

Contributions by an employer to a *support fund* are tax-deductible but the maximum contributions and fund assets are very restricted in size. (Employees cannot contribute to support funds.) Support fund benefits are taxed in the same manner as benefits paid from a book reserve.

Employers' contributions for *direct insurance policies* or to a *Pensionskasse* are tax-deductible but constitute additional taxable income to the employee, although the employer often pays this tax. Employees' contributions to these arrangements are only tax-efficient up to a modest level. Pensions are taxed only on the interest content (e.g. 24% of a pension commencing at age 65). Lump sum benefits from direct insurance are tax-free.

Schemes financed under the book reserve or support fund system must effect insolvency insurance with a special mutual insurer (PSV).

Pensions law prescribes a triennial review of pensions in payment; these pensions must be increased in line with inflation unless the employer can demonstrate financial hardship according to labour court legislation.

The Company Pension Law was extended to the new Federal States (i.e. the former East Germany) with effect from 1 January 1992. The social security system was also extended to include the new States but the lower ceiling on contributions and benefits, reflecting the lower average earnings in those States, will not be brought into line with the ceiling applicable to the rest of Germany for some years.

Current topics

The still increasing cost of unification of the former East and West Germany is concentrating the minds of those concerned with social security, and the financial difficulties being experienced by the health insurance funds tend to overshadow the strains on the State retirement pension system. The Pension Reform Act 1992 will enable State retirement benefits to be slowly eroded in the future to counter the projected shifts in the demographic balance of the population, which will affect Germany to a much greater extent than virtually any other developed country (with the possible exception of Japan).

The deep recession which slowly bottomed out towards the beginning of 1995 has resulted in many pension schemes being cut back in terms of pension levels and employee coverage. Cost reduction and cost containment are the major goals of scheme amendments.

JAPAN

Company Plans: Benefit structure

Most company schemes provide defined benefits in lump sum form, both on normal retirement and on termination of employment for any other reason. The benefit is normally calculated by reference to years of service, final monthly basic salary (sometimes plus some of the various allowances) and whether the termination of employment is voluntary or involuntary.

Benefit levels vary but normally would be lower for voluntary than for involuntary termination, other than when the employee nears normal retirement age. Larger companies normally provide a higher level of benefits than smaller ones; typically, on involuntary termination the lump sum benefit could be in the range of one to one and a half month's salary per year of service.

Normal retirement age is usually 60 for men and women.

Separate group life insurance schemes are customary and provide benefits either at a flat rate or according to a graded table. While there are no minimum legal vesting conditions, it is customary for Japanese schemes to provide benefits on voluntary termination after not more than three years' service. For involuntary termination, the period is generally one year or less.

Company Plans: Contributions and funding methods

The majority of schemes are non-contributory.

For taxation reasons (discussed below), benefits are often expressed in pension form with a full commutation option. These schemes can be operated on a funded basis subject to a minimum of 15 employees being covered. The scheme must be insured unless there are a minimum of 100 employees, in which case a trust bank may be used.

Taxation and regulation

Appropriations to book reserves for the purposes of providing retirement or termination of employment allowances are tax deductible within certain limits. For an externally funded plan to be tax approvable, it must be established in pension form; this approach usually leads to a larger tax deductible employer contribution.

Employees' contributions are tax deductible up to a certain amount including life insurance premiums. Pensions are taxed as income. 50% of a lump-sum benefit is tax free, the remainder being subject to tax at special rates after deducting a retirement allowance which depends on length of service.

Eligibility must be non-discriminatory and the scheme must either form part of a labour agreement or be subject to rules filed with the Supervisory Authority.

Current topics

Restrictions on the management of pension funds have been eased, allowing institutions other than insurance companies and trust banks to manage assets, and the pressure for continuing liberalisation continues. However, government regulations still permit only a small portion of the total funds to be managed by outside investment managers. As a result agreements reached in trade talks between the US and Japan, further liberalisation will take place in the future.

There is also continuing pressure to revise the retirement age upwards from its current level of 60 (although many retire later). Japan is experiencing demographic changes similar to other Western countries, life expectancy there being the highest in the world.

ITALY

Company Plans: Benefit structure

Because of the generous provisions of the compulsory schemes, most companies do not operate a supplementary pension plan. (A small number of national and multinational companies introduced supplementary *dirigenti* (managers') pension plans prior to the removal of the ceiling on benefits in 1988, but many of these have been discontinued.)

In addition to the compulsory schemes, there are significant lump sum payments payable by the employer (known as 'termination indemnities') on ceasing employment in almost all circumstances.

Taxation

Employer and employee contributions to basic Social Security are tax-deductible.

The rules regarding the taxation of private pension schemes were changed in 1993 and then revised again this year. The 15% advance tax on contributions – perhaps the most controversial component of the 1995 legislation – has been withdrawn. The maximum tax deductible contribution will now be 6% of salary which will be made up of a 2% employer and employee contribution plus 2% of the amount allocated for termination indemnities. For new hires, the entire indemnity must be allocated. The maximum tax deductible contribution for the employer and employee each is limited to LIt 2.5 million.

Half the benefit from these private plans will be paid in lump sum form and this will be taxed in the same way as termination indemnities are now. The other half will be paid in pension form and 12.5% of this pension will be exempt from income tax.

Current topics

A new social security pensions law was introduced on 4 August 1995 after almost 20 years of debate. The new law represents a fundamental change from the old INPS system as benefits will be linked to the contributions made rather than being expressed as a percentage of final salary. An earnings ceiling (of LIt 132,000,000 for 1996, about £53,000) for benefits and contributions has also been introduced.

The new system will be phased in progressively: new entrants will join it straight away, those with fewer than 18 years of contributions will have their past service in the INPS system and their future service in the new system, and those with more than 18 years of contributions will continue in the INPS system.

THE NETHERLANDS

Company Plans: Benefit structure

An important feature of the Dutch pensions scene is the incidence of industry-wide schemes. These are jointly controlled by employee/employer representatives and vary considerably in scope. In general, these schemes are mandatory for all employee groups in the industry. Individual employer schemes normally include all categories of employee, although where employees are included in an industry-wide scheme, coverage would often be confined to higher-paid staff.

The majority of schemes are of the defined-benefit type. A typical pension formula is 1.75% of pensionable salary per year of service so that, together with the State pension, the maximum pension for 40 years' service is about 70% of salary at retirement. The definition of final salary is subject to wide variation; some schemes fix this at age 60, others average over periods of up to ten years.

Normal retirement age is 65 for men and women.

Survivors' benefits are in the form of spouses' pensions, on death before and after retirement.

Full vesting is obligatory after one year's scheme membership.

Company Plans: Contributions and funding methods

Employees are normally required to contribute in the range of 5%-8% of pensionable salary (after deducting the offset for the State pension), although some plans are non-contributory.

An employer has the choice of funding private scheme benefits by means of group deferred annuities or individual capital insurances (with obligatory conversion to pension), or on a self-administered basis. There is a common practice of leaving past service liabilities partially unfunded, although a tax deduction on this 'back service' liability is granted. Despite having few statutory investment controls, local practice for self-administered plans is to invest rather more heavily in local fixed-interest investments than would be common in the UK.

Taxation and regulation

Employers' and employees' contributions to approved pension schemes are tax deductible, but employers' contributions for any lump sum benefit are taxable as income to the employee. Employees can also obtain a tax deduction within certain limits for individual pension insurance policies.

Pensions are taxable as normal income. For the reasons given above, lump sum benefits are not normally provided (although a few schemes include a small lump sum death benefit).

Early leavers are entitled to 'pro rata' deferred benefits.

Current topics

In September 1995 the Dutch cabinet adopted changes recommended by a working party headed by the finance ministry's director-general for fiscal affairs. The changes included:

- Lowering the minimum retirement age from 60 to 55, though the normal retirement age must be between 60 and 65. The cut off age for accruing pension rights will continue to be 70.
- Subject to their employer's approval, individuals may retire at age 55 and continue to work part-time. Individuals who are demoted to lower positions at the end of their career may continue to build up pension rights based on their former, higher salary.
- The maximum pension accrual rate is 2% p.a. and the maximum pension benefit is now 100% of salary (including State pension benefits).

SPAIN

Company Plans: Benefit structure

Book-reserved company pension plans are relatively common, particularly among multinational, and medium and large national companies. They arose from the gradual deterioration in Social Security benefits, the need for an incentive to encourage retirement and the requirements of various industrial collective agreements. Typical pensions provided range from 60%-80% of final earnings, less the Social Security benefit, and are often independent of service.

There is no mandatory retirement age, but State pensions can be paid from age 65 (for men and women), or from age 60 in certain special cases.

Survivors' pensions are often provided.

Immediate vesting requirements are imposed for plans qualified under the 1987 law as discussed below.

Company Plans: Contributions and funding methods

Legislation enacted in 1987 encourages outside funding and denies tax deductibility in respect of book-reserved arrangements. However, it seems that several aspects of the legislation, such as employee involvement in fund management and the problems in providing differential benefits, are resulting in most companies retaining unfunded plans.

Taxation

Qualified plans now have to be funded in order to receive favourable tax treatment, including deductibility of employer contributions and zero corporation/capital transfer tax on plan assets. Employer contributions are fully imputed into the employee's taxable income, but the employee receives a corresponding tax deduction as a result of which no tax is payable.

Pensions in payment are taxed as earned income. Lump sums are taxed as 'irregular' income.

Accounting Treatment for Book Reserves

Since 1 January 1991 companies have had to show reserves in their balance sheet to cover pension commitments, with interim arrangements for past service liabilities. In addition, companies may include anticipated tax-relief on pension payments over the next 10 years as an asset in their balance sheets.

Current Topics

By 1 January 1996 a new law governing the supervision of insurance business is expected to be on the statute book. In addition to its central aims of introducing into Spanish law the requirements of various EU Insurance Directives, this law will also modify the existing 1987 pension law.

Principal amongst the changes will be a requirement for all private pension arrangements to be funded externally, either by means of an insurance contract or by a qualified pension plan. If the new law comes into practice qualified pension plans will be able to amortise the past service liabilities over ten years without incurring any additional tax liability. Details of the insurance option will be left to future regulation. However, as a minimum, insurance contracts will have the same actuarial and financial constraints as those placed on qualified pension plans.

All pension arrangements must be brought into line with the new law within three years of its publication. Exemptions to the changes introduced by the law will apply to insurance companies, stock brokers, banks and building societies.

UNITED STATES OF AMERICA

Company Plans: Benefit structure

Company plans are much influenced by ERISA (Employees' Retirement Income Security Act 1974), non-discrimination legislation and repeated tax reform. Pensions practice is constantly changing and it should also be understood that it varies considerably between different industries and geographical areas.

Union-negotiated schemes are widespread and many are based on a fixed dollar pension amount per year of service. Such schemes, which are not normally contributory, are regularly reviewed as part of normal pay bargaining negotiations. For salaried staff, retirement benefits can be included in pension, profit-sharing or savings schemes; many companies operate more than one type of scheme.

Pension schemes for salaried staff normally provide final salary related benefits, although defined contribution schemes are rapidly gaining in popularity. Pension formulae range from around 1%-2% of final average earnings per year of service, including Social Security benefits. There are rules relating to eligibility, integration with Social Security, average benefit/contribution levels etc. to ensure that the scheme does not discriminate in favour of 'highly compensated' employees.

Survivors' benefits in defined benefit plans generally take the form of a spouse's pension on death before or after retirement and this is often provided by means of a reduction in the member's pension. Lump sum survivor benefits in such plans are generally provided via a separate life insurance contract. Defined contribution plans typically only offer a lump sum survivor's benefit.

Benefits must either vest in full after five years' service or in a graded fashion from 3 to 7 years.

Company Plans: Contributions and funding methods

Most staff pension schemes are non-contributory but employees may be required to contribute to separate group insurance schemes, including death, disability and medical expenses benefits.

Pension scheme funding methods are similar to those available in the UK, although it is not essential to establish a separate trust for an insured scheme. Maximum and minimum tax-deductible funding levels are prescribed by legislation.

Taxation

Employers' contributions to a qualified pension plan are tax-deductible, subject to certain maximum benefit and contribution limitations. Supplemental benefits for more highly paid employees are generally unfunded. Obligatory employees' contributions are not tax-deductible, but contributions to profit sharing plans and personal pensions (IRA's) are deductible within defined limits.

Pensions or lump sum payments from an approved pension plan are taxable if they relate to contributions which were tax-deductible. Benefits are, however, exempt from tax to the extent that they were secured by a non-deductible contribution (e.g. employee contribution from taxed income).

Current topics

Health care reforms are still a dominant concern, although Clinton's health care reform push has clearly subsided. 'Managed Care' practices continue to develop within the industry.

Legislation has been passed to strengthen funding requirements for poorly funded plans.

Pension 'simplification' proposals are again being entertained by Congress.

Several 'flat tax' proposals are afloat, most of which affect the tax deductibility of pension plan contributions and could have significant impact in the future over employers' views of sponsoring such plans.

INVESTMENT DATA

UK ANNUAL INFLATION

UK INVESTMENT YIELDS AND INFLATION

UK INTEREST RATES AND INFLATION

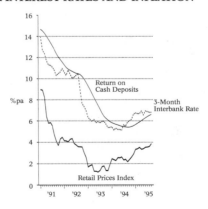

UK INVESTMENT HISTORY (1)

	Annual Increase:*		One-Year Returns on Investments:				
Year	RPI %	NAE %	Cash Deposits %	Long Gilts %	Index-Linked Gilts %	U.K. Equities %	Median Fund %
1985	5.5	8.2	12.2	11.3	1.3	20.5	15.8
1986	3.9	7.7	11.0	11.5	6.8	27.5	23.6
1987	3.3	8.7	9.8	16.3	6.6	8.0	2.3
1988	7.5	9.2	10.3	9.5	12.0	11.6	11.8
1989	7.7	9.2	14.0	5.7	14.5	36.1	31.5
1990	9.0	9.2	14.8	4.2	5.8	−9.7	−10.5
1991	4.1	7.0	11.6	18.7	5.4	20.8	18.3
1992	1.7	4.5	9.7	17.0	16.5	20.5	20.6
1993	2.5	3.6	5.9	34.5	18.9	28.4	29.2
1994	3.3	3.7	5.5	−12.2	−7.0	−5.9	−4.8

Note: * The increases shown represent the increase over the calendar year.
Source: Collated by Bacon & Woodrow.

UK INVESTMENT HISTORY (2)

		Annual Increase:		Equivalent Annual Rate of Return on Investments:				
Period	(years)	RPI %	NAE %	Cash Deposits %	Long Gilts %	Index-Linked Gilts %	U.K. Equities %	Median Fund* %
1993-94	(2)	2.9	3.6	5.7	8.7	5.2	10.0	10.9
1992-94	(3)	2.5	3.9	7.0	11.4	8.8	13.4	14.0
1991-94	(4)	2.9	4.7	8.2	13.2	7.9	15.2	15.1
1990-94	(5)	4.1	5.6	9.4	11.3	7.5	9.7	9.4
1989-94	(6)	4.7	6.2	10.2	10.4	8.6	13.7	12.8
1988-94	(7)	5.1	6.6	10.2	10.2	9.1	13.4	12.7
1987-94	(8)	4.9	6.9	10.2	11.0	8.8	12.7	11.3
1986-94	(9)	4.7	7.0	10.2	11.0	8.6	14.3	12.6
1985-94	(10)	4.8	7.1	10.4	11.1	7.8	14.9	13.0

Note: * This column shows the median rate of return achieved on pension fund portfolios which were measured in the Combined Actuarial Performance Services Ltd measurement service.
Source: Collated by Bacon & Woodrow.

UK INVESTMENT HISTORY (3)
Historic Yields and Returns (Equivalent Annual Rates)

Period	Increase in (%): RPI	NAE	Returns on Investments (%) Ind. Ord. Shares	3-Month Treasury Bills	2.5% Consols
5 years to 1945	3.7	5.9	15.5	1.0	
5 years to 1950	4.0	4.3	6.3	0.5	
5 years to 1955	4.4	6.5	16.3	2.1	
5 years to 1960	2.4	4.1	20.0	4.5	4.9
5 years to 1965	3.3	3.6	7.1	4.7	6.0
5 years to 1970	4.6	6.2	10.7	6.7	7.4
5 years to 1975	13.0	17.8	4.1	8.4	11.3
5 years to 1980	14.4	14.5	22.2	11.1	12.4
5 years to 1985	7.2	7.4*	25.0	11.0	11.3
5 years to 1990	5.9	8.6*	15.9	11.3	9.7
10 years to 1950	3.8	5.1	10.8	0.7	
10 years to 1960	3.4	5.3	18.1	3.3	
10 years to 1970	4.0	4.9	8.9	5.7	6.7
10 years to 1980	13.7	16.1	12.8	9.7	11.8
10 years to 1990	6.6	8.0*	20.4	11.2	10.5
20 years to 1950	3.6	3.4	7.5	0.9	
20 years to 1960	3.6	5.2	14.4	2.0	
20 years to 1970	3.7	5.1	13.4	4.5	
20 years to 1980	8.7	10.4	10.8	7.7	9.3
20 years to 1990	10.1	12.0*	16.5	10.4	11.2

Note: *Index used after 1983 not strictly comparable. Earlier figures use Basic Weekly Rates.
Source: Collated by Bacon & Woodrow.

UK INVESTMENT RETURNS AND INFLATION

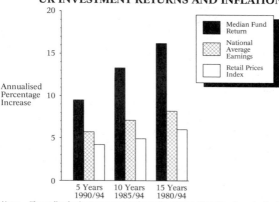

Note: The median fund return represents the median return achieved by all pension funds participating in the Combined Actuarial Performance Services Ltd performance measurement service. Returns are shown to the end of 1994.
Source: CAPS – Pension Fund Investment Performance General Report 1994.

INDEX RETURNS FOR YEARS TO 31 MARCH

	1986 %	1987 %	1988 %	1989 %	1990 %	1991 %	1992 %	1993 %	1994 %	1995 %
UK Equities	37.2	28.1	−7.0	25.5	8.8	12.5	3.4	26.1	15.2	2.8
Overseas Equities	29.1	34.1	−9.3	26.5	−0.4	−1.1	−0.9	30.5	15.1	−1.7
US Equities	13.9	15.6	−23.1	**31.1**	20.7	8.0	11.5	32.3	2.2	5.2
European (excl. UK) Equities	–	–	−25.0	26.7	**40.2**	−14.2	8.4	19.3	24.5	−1.1
Japan Equities	**48.2**	**69.3**	12.9	22.7	−26.2	−4.7	−21.9	**38.0**	24.4	−7.9
Pacific Basin (excl. Japan) Equities	–	–	–	–	–	5.4	**19.2**	31.9	**42.1**	−5.5
Canadian Equities	–	–	–	–	–	−4.8	−3.1	13.4	9.6	−4.1
Overseas Bonds	–	5.6	−6.7	12.9	8.4	7.0	13.7	30.9	8.0	2.1
UK Bonds	21.3	9.2	10.2	4.7	−0.5	**22.9**	11.0	21.5	8.9	3.0
Index-Linked Gilts	1.8	14.4	1.2	14.9	2.5	13.4	3.3	22.3	5.9	1.2
Sterling Cash	12.7	10.9	10.9	14.8	13.8	13.7	11.5	11.5	5.4	5.1
Property Assets	5.3	4.9	**29.0**	**31.1**	9.3	−11.6	3.5	−1.8	20.6	**7.1**
Retail Prices Index	4.2	4.0	3.5	7.9	8.1	8.2	4.0	1.9	2.3	3.5
Earnings Index	8.5	6.7	9.5	9.2	9.5	9.3	7.3	4.0	4.0	3.5

Note: The variation in returns on the different asset categories has been marked over the last ten years. This table details the returns achieved on representative indices in the individual years during the ten year period ending 31 March 1995 and highlights (in **bold**) the best sector in each year. Increases in the Retail Prices Index and the National Average Earnings Index are also shown for comparison.

Source: CAPS, Pension Fund Investment Performance General Report to 31 March 1995.

INDEX RETURNS OVER CUMULATIVE PERIODS ENDING 31 MARCH 1995

Annualised Returns	1Yr %	2Yrs %	3Yrs %	4Yrs %	5Yrs %	6Yrs %	7Yrs %	8Yrs %	9Yrs %	10Yrs %
UK Equities	2.8	8.8	14.3	11.5	11.7	11.2	13.1	10.4	**12.2**	**14.5**
Overseas Equities	−1.7	6.4	13.9	10.0	7.7	6.3	9.0	6.5	9.2	11.1
US Equities	5.2	3.7	12.4	12.2	11.4	12.9	15.3	9.6	10.3	10.6
European (excl. UK) Equities	−1.1	11.0	13.7	12.3	6.5	11.5	13.5	7.8	–	–
Japan Equities	−7.9	7.0	16.5	5.4	3.3	−2.3	0.9	2.3	8.2	11.7
Pacific Basin (excl. Japan) Equities	−5.5	**15.9**	**21.0**	**20.5**	**17.3**	**15.9**	**19.0**	**13.3**	–	–
UK Fixed Interest	3.0	5.9	10.9	10.9	13.2	10.8	9.9	9.9	9.9	11.0
Index-Linked Gilts	1.2	3.5	9.4	7.9	8.9	7.8	8.8	7.8	8.6	7.9
Sterling Cash	5.1	5.3	6.4	7.7	9.1	10.1	10.2	10.1	10.2	10.4
Property Assets	**7.1**	13.7	8.3	7.1	3.0	4.0	7.5	10.0	9.4	9.0
Retail Prices Index	3.5	2.9	2.6	2.9	4.0	4.6	5.1	4.9	4.8	4.7
Earnings Index	3.5	3.7	3.8	4.7	5.6	6.2	6.6	7.0	7.0	7.1

Note: The best performing sector over each period is highlighted in **bold** typeface.

Source: CAPS Survey of UK Pooled Pension Funds (Quarter ended 31/03/95).

PENSION FUND INVESTMENT PERFORMANCE FOR YEARS TO 31 MARCH

Table 1: Total Fund
Percent

	9th Decile	Lower Quartile	Median	Upper Quartile	1st Decile
1985/86	25.4	27.7	30.4	33.1	35.4
1986/87	18.4	20.5	22.4	24.1	26.4
1987/88	–10.9	–8.5	–6.5	–4.2	–2.0
1988/89	18.1	19.9	21.2	22.6	24.2
1989/90	5.2	7.1	9.0	11.2	12.7
1990/91	4.7	6.8	8.5	10.1	11.6
1991/92	1.5	2.6	4.0	5.3	6.5
1992/93	21.5	23.7	25.2	27.2	29.2
1993/94	14.7	16.1	17.2	18.9	20.3
1994/95	–1.9	–0.6	0.7	1.9	3.4

Table 2: Total Fund Excluding Property
Percent

	9th Decile	Lower Quartile	Median	Upper Quartile	1st Decile
1985/86	26.9	29.3	31.9	34.3	36.4
1986/87	18.9	21.1	23.0	24.6	26.7
1987/88	–11.3	–9.1	–7.4	–5.6	–3.1
1988/89	17.9	19.5	20.8	22.4	23.9
1989/90	4.8	6.9	9.0	11.3	12.8
1990/91	5.3	7.3	9.0	10.7	12.1
1991/92	1.6	2.8	4.1	5.3	6.5
1992/93	22.7	24.4	26.0	27.9	29.5
1993/94	14.4	15.9	17.1	18.8	20.2
1994/95	–2.0	–0.7	0.5	1.9	3.4

Table 3: UK Equities
Percent

	Lower Quartile	Median	Upper Quartile	Index
1985/86	35.2	38.1	41.3	37.2
1986/87	25.5	27.8	30.7	28.1
1987/88	–9.2	–7.4	–5.3	–7.0
1988/89	23.3	25.4	27.7	25.5
1989/90	5.0	7.1	9.0	8.8
1990/91	11.1	13.5	15.6	12.5
1991/92	0.8	2.7	4.4	3.4
1992/93	25.0	27.0	29.4	26.1
1993/94	14.6	16.1	17.8	15.2
1994/95	1.3	2.7	3.7	2.8

Table 4: Overseas Equities
Percent

	Lower Quartile	Median	Upper Quartile	Index
1985/86	23.5	29.7	34.6	29.1
1986/87	21.8	25.0	28.3	34.1
1987/88	–20.9	–17.9	–14.5	–9.3
1988/89	21.5	23.8	27.1	26.5
1989/90	14.7	20.4	24.7	–0.4
1990/91	–8.0	–4.7	–2.3	–1.1
1991/92	1.9	3.6	5.8	–0.9
1992/93	24.7	26.1	28.5	30.5
1993/94	24.4	27.7	30.3	15.1
1994/95	–7.5	–5.0	–3.4	–1.7

Table 5: US Equities
Percent

	Lower Quartile	Median	Upper Quartile	Index
1985/86	10.5	14.8	18.1	13.9
1986/87	9.1	12.4	15.3	15.6
1987/88	−27.5	−25.3	−22.8	−23.1
1988/89	23.5	26.2	28.9	31.1
1989/90	20.3	22.5	24.4	20.7
1990/91	3.4	7.8	11.2	8.0
1991/92	7.1	11.0	14.4	11.5
1992/93	28.8	32.5	35.2	32.3
1993/94	3.1	5.6	7.6	2.2
1994/95	0.5	2.2	4.1	5.2

Table 6: European (excl. UK) Equities
Percent

	Lower Quartile	Median	Upper Quartile	Index
1987/88	−29.6	−26.1	−23.0	−25.0
1988/89	24.3	28.0	31.8	26.7
1989/90	41.3	46.4	48.7	40.2
1990/91	−18.0	−14.3	−11.6	−14.2
1991/92	8.9	10.7	12.6	8.4
1992/93	16.5	18.5	20.8	19.3
1993/94	24.0	25.4	29.5	24.5
1994/95	−3.4	−1.4	−0.3	−1.1

Table 7: Japan Equities
Percent

	Lower Quartile	Median	Upper Quartile	Index
1985/86	26.4	37.0	47.0	48.2
1986/87	40.4	46.3	53.3	69.3
1987/88	1.9	8.3	20.4	12.9
1988/89	9.0	13.7	17.4	22.7
1989/90	−18.4	−13.9	−5.2	−26.2
1990/91	−6.2	−3.6	−0.1	−4.7
1991/92	−21.0	−18.9	−17.3	−21.9
1992/93	30.1	34.4	37.7	38.0
1993/94	25.6	29.1	34.0	24.4
1994/95	−16.4	−12.7	−9.7	−7.9

Table 8: Pacific Basin (excl. Japan) Equities
Percent

	Lower Quartile	Median	Upper Quartile	Index
1990/91	−6.9	−3.8	4.5	5.4
1991/92	11.1	16.1	18.9	19.2
1992/93	31.6	33.5	38.7	31.9
1993/94	40.7	44.3	47.7	42.1
1994/95	−6.9	−4.9	−4.2	−5.5

Table 9: Overseas Bonds

Percent

	Lower Quartile	Median	Upper Quartile	Index
1985/86	−2.0	20.4	28.8	–
1986/87	5.2	11.1	22.9	5.6
1987/88	−9.1	1.2	10.6	−6.7
1988/89	2.6	11.1	20.1	12.9
1989/90	11.2	13.0	16.9	8.4
1990/91	7.6	11.5	14.2	7.0
1991/92	13.4	16.1	19.0	13.7
1992/93	31.0	35.9	38.7	30.9
1993/94	7.6	8.4	10.6	8.0
1994/95	−1.8	1.6	5.7	2.1

Table 10: UK Bonds

Percent

	Lower Quartile	Median	Upper Quartile	Index
1985/86	25.7	26.3	27.1	21.3
1986/87	7.5	8.2	8.9	9.2
1987/88	9.8	10.5	11.2	10.2
1988/89	4.3	4.8	5.5	4.7
1989/90	−5.1	−3.7	−2.2	−0.5
1990/91	23.6	25.2	25.9	22.9
1991/92	11.3	12.1	13.7	11.0
1992/93	22.1	23.0	24.8	21.5
1993/94	8.5	10.8	12.7	8.9
1994/95	0.9	1.7	3.0	3.0

Table 11: Index-Linked Gilts

Percent

	Lower Quartile	Median	Upper Quartile	Index
1985/86	−0.3	0.3	1.6	1.8
1986/87	14.2	15.0	15.7	14.4
1987/88	−2.4	−0.8	1.3	1.2
1988/89	15.5	16.7	17.6	14.9
1989/90	1.0	1.5	2.0	2.5
1990/91	11.6	12.3	13.4	13.4
1991/92	1.4	2.5	4.3	3.3
1992/93	23.8	25.4	26.5	22.3
1993/94	5.4	6.6	7.2	5.9
1994/95	0.4	0.6	0.9	1.2

Table 12: Property Assets

Percent

	Lower Quartile	Median	Upper Quartile	Index
1985/86	3.3	5.8	8.6	5.3
1986/87	2.4	6.4	9.7	4.9
1987/88	18.3	22.7	27.8	29.0
1988/89	25.2	29.6	34.6	31.1
1989/90	4.8	8.7	12.7	9.3
1990/91	−9.7	−7.9	−3.1	−11.6
1991/92	−0.8	2.6	6.5	3.5
1992/93	−1.6	1.2	4.1	−1.8
1993/94	19.5	24.6	29.1	20.6
1994/95	4.5	5.8	8.8	7.1

Notes: The figures show the range of returns in each year since 1985 obtained by funds participating in the CAPS investment performance measurement service. The figures under the heading 'Index' are the annual returns on a representative index for the asset category.

Source: CAPS, Pension Fund Investment Performance General Report to 31 March 1995.

POOLED PENSION FUND PERFORMANCE

This table sets out the median returns achieved by the UK Pooled Pension Funds participating in the CAPS Survey over cumulative periods ending 31 March 1995.

Annualised Returns	1Yr %	2Yrs %	3Yrs %	4Yrs %	5Yrs %	6Yrs %	7Yrs %	8Yrs %	9Yrs %	10Yrs %
UK Equities	1.2	8.8	13.9	10.8	10.8	10.3	12.0	9.6	11.7	14.0
Overseas	−5.5	8.4	14.2	10.7	7.8	8.2	10.8	6.5	9.0	10.6
North America	1.6	3.6	12.2	12.2	10.9	12.2	12.5	8.0	8.5	8.5
Europe	−1.7	11.3	13.7	12.4	6.6	11.6	13.6	7.2	7.7	–
Japan	−13.2	6.0	14.8	5.8	4.8	0.3	3.8	3.9	9.1	12.0
Pacific Basin (excl. Japan)	−5.9	**17.1**	**23.7**	**21.3**	**16.0**	**18.1**	**19.5**	**15.0**	**20.7**	**16.2**
Fixed Interest	2.2	5.9	11.1	11.5	13.6	10.9	10.1	10.1	9.9	11.3
Index-Linked	0.8	3.5	10.0	8.2	9.0	7.9	9.1	7.9	9.0	8.1
Cash	**5.3**	5.5	6.7	7.8	9.3	10.2	10.3	10.2	10.3	10.5
Property	5.2	13.2	9.0	7.3	4.6	5.2	8.5	9.7	9.5	9.4
Non-Property Mixed	−1.2	8.0	13.1	10.7	10.2	10.4	11.5	8.7	10.0	12.3
Mixed with Property	−0.2	8.3	13.3	10.9	10.2	9.8	11.2	9.2	10.5	12.5

Note: The best performing sector over each period is highlighted in **bold** typeface.
Source: CAPS Survey of UK Pooled Pension Funds (Quarter ended 31/03/95).

METHOD OF INVESTMENT OF FUNDS BY SECTOR

	Private		Public		All Schemes	
	Schemes %	Members %	Schemes %	Members %	Schemes %	Members %
Unfunded	*	*	2	39	*	14
Insured	4	2	–	–	4	1
Managed fund or other pooled arrangement	23	5	4	1	22	4
Direct investment – external managers only	56	54	59	29	56	45
Direct investment – in-house managers only	9	23	8	5	9	17
Direct investment – external and in-house managers	6	16	27	26	7	19
Members have a choice of investments	2	*	–	–	2	*

Note: Data to year ending March 1994. See note on page 16 for further explanation.
Source: NAPF, Twentieth Annual Survey of Occupational Pension Schemes, 1994.

PENSION FUND ASSET DISTRIBUTION

This table shows the average distribution of pension fund assets between the major market sectors at the start of each year since 1 April 1985 and at the end of the most recent year, based on proportions of overall market values.

	UK Equities	Overseas Equities	Overseas Bonds	UK Fixed Interest	Index–Linked Gilts	Sterling Cash	Property
	%	%	%	%	%	%	%
1.4.85	53	18	0	16	2	5	5
1.4.86	54	21	0	15	2	4	4
1.4.87	58	22	0	10	2	4	3
1.4.88	59	16	0	13	2	7	3
1.4.89	59	20	1	7	2	8	3
1.4.90	55	24	4	4	2	8	3
1.4.91	58	22	6	4	2	6	2
1.4.92	58	25	5	3	2	5	2
1.4.93	58	24	6	3	3	4	2
1.4.94	57	26	5	3	3	4	2
31.3.95	57	22	6	6	3	5	2

Source: CAPS, Pension Fund Investment Performance General Report to 31 March 1995.

ANALYSIS OF PROPERTY INVESTMENTS

	Value			Percent		
	UK £m	Overseas £m	Total £m	UK %	Overseas %	Total %
Direct holdings						
Retail	5,811	459	6,270	33	3	36
Industrial	2,953	50	3,003	17	*	17
Office	5,336	541	5,877	30	3	33
Rural	455	2	457	3	*	3
Residential/leisure	88	3	91	1	*	1
Other	255	389	644	1	2	4
Pooled holdings						
Multiple property unit trusts/managed funds	988	82	1,070	6	*	6
Single property investments	169	5	174	1	*	1
Total			**17,586**			**100**

Note: Data to year ending March 1994. See note on page 16 for further explanation.
Source: NAPF, Twentieth Annual Survey of Occupational Pension Schemes, 1994.

PENSION SCHEMES PERMITTING SELF-INVESTMENT

This table sets out the proportion of funds where the trust deed permits self-investment.

	Private %	Public %	All Employers %
Permitting self-investment	54	33	53
Not permitting self-investment	46	67	47

Source: NAPF, Twentieth Annual Survey of Occupational Pension Schemes, 1994.
(See note on page 16 concerning this source.)

PENSION SCHEMES PRACTISING SELF-INVESTMENT

Not all funds where the trust deed permits self-investment actually have such investments. This table sets out the proportion of those funds where the trust deed permits self-investment which actually practise self-investment.

	Private %	Public %	All Employers %
Self-investment	34	33	34
No self-investment where permitted	66	67	66

Source: NAPF, Twentieth Annual Survey of Occupational Pension Schemes, 1994.
(See note on page 16 concerning this source.)

SUMMARY OF SELF-INVESTMENT BY EMPLOYERS

The following chart shows the proportion of funds where self-investment is both permitted and actually practised.

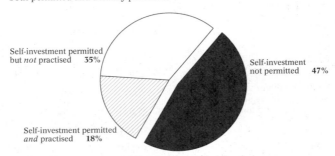

Self-investment permitted but *not* practised **35%**

Self-investment not permitted **47%**

Self-investment permitted *and* practised **18%**

Source: NAPF, Twentieth Annual Survey of Occupational Pension Schemes, 1994.
(See note on page 16 concerning this source.)

LEGAL FRAMEWORK OF PENSIONS

The existing legal framework within which pension schemes operate is extremely complicated. The present sources of pension law include trust law, tax law, Social Security law, contract law, employment law, the Financial Services Act and European Community law.

Of these, the first three have most direct impact on those charged with the oversight and administration of pension schemes. Contract and employment law govern the relationship of employee and employer and are outside the scope of this pocket book. European Community law is becoming increasingly important, for example, the European Court of Justice's ruling that pension rights are pay has necessitated the reappraisal of the rules governing many pension schemes (*see Section 14 for the effect on equal treatment of men and women*). The Financial Services Act is dealt with in more detail in *Section 18* and Social Security legislation is covered in various other sections. Trust law, which is at the heart of pension law, is considered in more detail below.

In addition, this framework is being reinforced by a new Act of Parliament, the Pensions Act 1995, which received Royal Assent on 19 July 1995 (*see Section 20*). This Act will make extensive changes to pensions law, most of which will come into effect from April 1997.

THE ROLE OF TRUSTEES

Trust law

It has been usual for many years to set up pension schemes under trust, partly because it was a legally convenient vehicle, partly because of Inland Revenue pressure.

Trust law has existed for several centuries. It is mainly judge-made: that is, there is no one statute which lays down what a trustee must or must not do. Instead, the principles have been spelt out in court cases at different times.

What is a trust?

Many of the text-books say that no one has yet succeeded in defining a trust satisfactorily, but it is worth trying to do so. One definition is that 'a trust is an equitable obligation binding a person (who is called a trustee) to deal with property over which he has control (which is called the trust property) for the benefit of persons (who are called the beneficiaries) of whom he may himself be one, and any of whom may enforce the obligation'.

So the first important principle is that one person is holding assets for the benefit of other persons. In the case of a pension scheme, the trustees are holding the pension fund assets for the benefit of the members, and their first duty is to them – not to their employer, their trade union, or any outside body. 'Members' for this purpose include not just those currently employed and paying into the scheme, but also people with deferred pensions and those who are drawing benefits.

Who can be a trustee?

At present, the trustees of a scheme can be either individuals (as long as they are over 18 and not insane) or corporations, or a combination of both.

Historically, the first trustees have generally been appointed by the employer when setting up the trust and often the employer will retain the power to remove or replace them. It is becoming increasingly common nowadays for members of a fund to have some degree of involvement in the selection and appointment of a proportion of the trustees. The Pensions Act 1995 will give members the right to select at least one-third of their trustees if they wish. This Act will also prevent certain people from becoming trustees (*see Section 20*).

The new trustee

The first job of newly appointed trustees is to find out as much as possible about the scheme, and how it is run at present. New trustees must become familiar with the scheme's working documents as quickly as possible. These will include:

- the trust deed and rules;
- the scheme booklet;
- the most recent accounts;
- the most recent actuarial valuation;
- any undertakings that have been given to the Inland Revenue;
- the scheme's contacting-out certificate;
- minutes of recent trustee meetings, and of any sub-committees.

The trustee should ask for copies of all these, and if necessary for explanations of what they mean.

A new trustee should also be aware of relevant legislation, together with the Inland Revenue's discretionary practice in relation to pension schemes. Much of this is explained in various official Memoranda, Announcements, Updates and Practice Notes issued by the Occupational Pensions Board and/or the Pension Schemes Office of the Inland Revenue.

All trustees should make sure that they read the Occupational Pensions Board guide for pension trustees called 'Pensions Trust Principles'.

Tax

The Inland Revenue can grant 'Exempt Approval' to a pension scheme. This is valuable because it means that the employee pays no tax on the employer's contributions and obtains tax-relief on his or her own contributions; also no tax is paid on the investment income of the fund, nor on the lump sums paid by most schemes at retirement. But this does not mean that pension schemes are immune from all effects of taxation. For example, in 1993 the tax credit on share dividends was changed from 25% to 20%, reducing the amount of tax reclaimable by pension schemes per £1 of declared dividend.

One requirement for Exempt Approval is that the scheme must be established under an irrevocable trust. This does not prevent a fund being wound-up, or the employer stopping contributions. What it means is that the assets of the fund must be set aside from those of the employer, and must be held by the trustees on terms which ensure that they are used for the benefit of the members. In general, these assets must not be returned to the employer, although they may be returned on the winding-up of the fund or where the Inland Revenue requires action to be taken over a scheme surplus which they regard as excessive.

The trust deed and rules

The trust deed and rules describe the trustees' powers and duties. Generally, when a scheme is first set up, a temporary trust deed is used to make the administrative arrangements and to obtain the interim approval of the Inland Revenue and the Occupational Pensions Board. This is called the Interim Deed. It will be in outline terms and will refer to the more permanent deed which will be written later, in which fuller details will be given.

The longer term version is called the Definitive Deed, and is far more detailed. The Inland Revenue says that this must be completed within two years. In the meantime, announcements to scheme members about scheme changes have the same legal force.

The Definitive Deed usually has two main parts. The trust clauses normally define the powers and duties of the trustees and employer, and the duties of trustees to the members.

The rules normally say who is eligible to be a scheme member and cover details of the benefits promised, the areas where the trustees have discretion, the employer's commitment on contributions, and the level of members' contributions.

If there is any question about what is to be done, the trust documents must govern the trustees' actions. Generally speaking, only when the deed and rules do not deal with a point is it necessary to think about the general principles of trust law.

A Supplemental Deed extends a Definitive Deed, perhaps by introducing new powers. An Amending Deed changes it. Trustees may find they have to refer to several different documents, if recent sets of amendments have not yet been incorporated into the main deed. In addition, several Acts of Parliament now 'override' trust deeds. This means that they change the rules of the scheme whether the deed is amended or not. It is good practice to try to keep everything in one place by having a single consolidated deed which is amended as necessary.

Who is covered by the scheme?

In a small scheme, it will be clear from the beginning who is entitled to be a member and who is not. However, in the larger company, or one with large numbers of subsidiaries, it may not always be apparent. The trust deed, and the contracting-out certificate, will list the subsidiaries which are covered and the new trustee should check these and ask for further details where necessary. It is also wise to check in the trust deed what happens when a new subsidiary is bought or created, or an existing one leaves the holding company's ownership.

What about the investments?

Every pension fund trust deed will have a statement about what investments are permitted, and who holds them. Most modern trust deeds give pension fund trustees wide powers of investment but there may well be some limitations, for example the pension fund may be completely prohibited from investing in shares of the sponsoring employer. Trustees should make sure that they do not break their own rules inadvertently.

Are trustees responsible for what their predecessors did?

A new trustee is not usually liable for breaches of trust committed by earlier trustees. Unless there is a reason to believe otherwise, the trustees are entitled to assume that their predecessors performed their duties correctly. However, if they found that something had gone wrong they would need to take action to put it right.

THE ROLE OF THE EMPLOYER

The employer is a party to the trust and retains certain duties and powers which may be specified in the trust deed. One of the conditions of Inland Revenue approval of a scheme is that the employer must contribute to the scheme: this does not preclude the possibility of a contribution holiday when a surplus exists, but means that the employer must carry a substantial burden of the cost of the scheme benefits or its administration or both. The employer would expect to retain certain powers, especially in areas where there is a cost element, for example the power to augment benefits or to amend the scheme. They have the ultimate power to cease contributions to the scheme which will lead to the scheme either winding-up or ceasing to provide any further benefit accrual, according to the provisions of the trust deed. Beyond these bounds, the employer should act in a reasonable manner to ensure that the trustees can operate the scheme satisfactorily: this includes providing information on members, paying contributions when due, and meeting any obligations imposed on them by the trust deed or by legislation.

THE ROLE OF THE ACTUARY

The main statutory duties of the actuary to a pension scheme at present are:

- to carry out valuations and advise on the funding of the scheme;
- to provide the certificates required by the Pension Schemes Office (PSO) and Occupational Pensions Board (OPB);
- to approve the basis of calculation of individual transfer values and to certify transfers where the members' consents have not been obtained;
- to certify any debt on the employer in the event of the scheme winding-up.

In future the Pensions Act 1995 will require trustees to appoint a 'scheme actuary' to report to them on the new funding and contribution requirements being introduced from 1997. Under the Act, the scheme actuary will be obliged to notify OPRA (see 'Role of the OPB' below) if he/she believes that anyone else is failing to perform their proper duties to the scheme (see Section 20).

In addition, most schemes require the trustees to take actuarial advice before taking decisions, on such matters as augmentations and bulk transfers, which will affect the finances of the scheme.

Actuaries also provide expert advice in benefit design and implementation, and assist both employers and trustees in ensuring that the pension provision offered to employees is both appropriate and soundly based.

The actuarial valuation

Under the Disclosure Regulations, trustees are required to obtain actuarial valuations at intervals not exceeding 3 years 6 months. The valuation report describes the level of funding of the scheme, and recommends a future contribution rate.

Actuarial statements and certificates

The actuary is also required to provide the following statements and certificates:

    (i)   an actuarial statement, to be included in the annual report issued by the trustees;

(ii) a certificate to the Inland Revenue, concerning the extent of any excess of the value of the assets of the fund over the value of its liabilities on a prescribed basis;

(iii) if the scheme is contracted-out on a salary-related basis, a certificate to the OPB concerning the security of the Guaranteed Minimum Pensions (GMPs).

Transfer values

Members of occupational pension schemes have a right to a 'cash equivalent' transfer value on leaving service. The cash equivalent must be calculated on methods and assumptions certified by an actuary.

An actuarial certificate is normally a necessary condition for a transfer without the consent of the transferring member. An exception is made where the scheme is winding-up and the new scheme relates to employment with the same employer.

Debt on employer

When a pension scheme is wound-up, any deficiency is treated as a debt due from the employer. Regulations require that the deficiency should be calculated by the actuary.

THE ROLE OF THE INVESTMENT MANAGER

The investment manager directs the day-to-day dealings of the fund. The degree of involvement of the trustees in these decisions varies, but normally the investment manager is given wide discretion within guidelines set by the trustees. The Pensions Act 1995 set out certain requirements with which trustees must comply in setting their guidelines and ensuring that the investment manager complies (*see Section 20*).

THE ROLE OF THE AUDITOR

The Disclosure Regulations require occupational pension schemes to obtain audited accounts. The audit report states whether the scheme accounts show a true and fair view of the financial transactions during the year and the disposition of the assets and current liabilities at the end of the year. The auditor also confirms whether or not contributions have been paid in accordance with the scheme rules and the recommendations of the actuary. Under the Pensions Act 1995, the scheme auditor appointed by the trustee will (like the scheme actuary) be required to notify OPRA if he/she believes that anyone else is failing in their proper duties to the scheme.

THE ROLE OF THE PSO

Since pension benefits are often costly, employers will generally wish to take advantage of the tax reliefs which are available to schemes which can meet certain criteria. These criteria are set by the PSO, part of the Inland Revenue, which will then approve schemes for tax relief if the necessary conditions are met (*see Section 9 for a summary of approvable benefit limits*).

Following approval, the PSO monitors schemes to ensure that the limits referred to above are not exceeded. The PSO is responsible for approval of schemes' proposals for disposal of excess surplus (*see Section 15*). Scheme administrators are, as a condition of approval, required to supply it with the information necessary to enable its monitoring to be effective, e.g. copies of actuarial reports or certificates, details of directors' benefits and changes in the scheme's provisions etc.

THE ROLE OF THE OPB

The OPB has as its main functions:

(i) ensuring that schemes satisfy various requirements under Social Security legislation (e.g. preservation);

(ii) monitoring schemes that are contracted-out of the State Earnings Related Pension Scheme (SERPS) to ensure that the necessary procedures for obtaining a contracted-out certificate have been followed and that the schemes remain adequately funded; *and*

(iii) acting as Registrar of Occupational and Personal Pension Schemes.

The OPB is to be replaced by a new body, the Occupational Pensions Regulatory Authority (OPRA), which is established under the Pensions Act 1995.

UK LEGISLATION RELEVANT TO PENSIONS

ACTS OF PARLIAMENT

Finance Act 1971
Financial Services Act 1986
Income and Corporation Taxes Act 1988
Social Security Act 1989
Finance Act 1989
Finance Act 1991
Social Security Contributions and Benefits Act 1992
Social Security Administration Act 1992
Trade Union Reform and Employment Rights Act 1993
Pension Schemes Act 1993
Finance Act 1994
Finance Act 1995
Pensions Act 1995

MAIN STATUTORY INSTRUMENTS MADE SINCE 1 JANUARY 1994

(For earlier Statutory Instruments see previous editions of this pocket book)

Occupational Pension Schemes (Deficiency on Winding Up etc) Regulations 1994 (SI 1994/895)

Occupational and Personal Pension Schemes (Consequential Amendments) Regulations 1994 (SI 1994/1062)

Social Security Act 1989 (Commencement No. 5) Order 1994 (SI 1994/1661)

Protected Rights (Transfer Payment) Amendment Regulations 1994 (SI 1994/1751)

Occupational Pensions (Revaluation) Order 1994 (SI 1994/2891)

Retirement Benefits Schemes (Indexation of Earnings Cap) Order 1994 (SI 1994/3009)

Occupational and Personal Pension Schemes (Miscellaneous Amendments) Regulations 1995 (SI 1995/35)

Guaranteed Minimum Pensions Increase Order 1995 (SI 1995/515)

Occupational and Personal Pension Schemes (Levy) Regulations 1995 (SI 1995/524)

Pensions Increase (Review) Order 1995 (SI 1995/708)

Personal and Occupational Pension Schemes (Pensions Ombudsman) (Procedure) Rules 1995 (SI 1995/1053)

Social Security Revaluation of Earnings Factors Order 1995
(SI 1995/1070)

Occupational Pension Schemes (Equal Access to Membership)
Amendment Regulations 1995 (1995/1215)

Personal Pension Schemes (Appropriate Schemes) Amendment
Regulations 1995 (SI 1995/1612)

INLAND REVENUE MATERIALS

Occupational Pension Schemes: Practice Notes:
IR 12 (1979) & IR 12 (1991) 2nd Edition

Free-Standing Additional Voluntary Contributions:
IR 12 (1979) Supplement 8/89 3rd Edition

Personal Pension Schemes: Guidance Notes:
IR 76 (May 1991)

The Tax Treatment of Top-Up Pension Schemes:
(August 1991)

CURRENT PSO UPDATES

This is a new series replacing the PSO Memoranda series. Memoranda relating
to Personal Pension Schemes and Free Standing Additional Voluntary
Contribution Schemes are still current and should be retained.

No. 1:	PSO Updates
	Practice Notes
	New Forms
No. 2:	Relocation
	Customer Survey
	Service Standards
No. 3:	Approval of Policies
No. 4:	Reciprocal Transfer Arrangements with the Isle of Man and the Republic of Ireland
	Practice Notes
No. 5:	Customer Service
	Schemes at Interim Stage
	1987 and 1989 Overriding Legislation
	AVC Regulations
	Profit Related Pay
No. 6:	Retirement Benefit Schemes: Tax Charge on Cessation of Approval
No. 7:	Small Self-Administered Schemes: Annuity Purchase Requirements
No. 8:	Personal Pension Schemes:
	• Annuity Deferral and Income Withdrawal
	• Inheritance Tax on Lump Sum Death Benefit
	• Definition of 'Insurer'
No. 9:	Selective In-Depth Examination of Small Self-Administered Schemes

CURRENT OPB/PSO MEMORANDA

No. 32 (OPB): Equal access for men and women

No. 50 (OPB): Interim Documentation – Paragraphs 20 and 21 only

No. 66 (OPB): Contracting-Out: Elections and related procedures

No. 74 (OPB): Schemes which cease to be contracted-out

No. 75 (PSO/ OPB): Preservation, equal access and contracting-out requirements for schemes with an overseas element; transfers to overseas schemes

No. 76 (OPB): Contracting-Out: Supervision of scheme resources

No. 77 (OPB): Contracting-Out: Salary related schemes

No. 78 (OPB): Preservation, Voluntary Contributions, Revaluation and Transfer Values

No. 84 (OPB): Disclosure of Information by Occupational Pension Schemes

No. 92 (OPB): Social Security Act 1986 and Personal Pension Schemes

No. 93 (OPB): Money Purchase Contracting-Out: Scheme Rule Requirements

No. 95 (PSO): Personal Pension Schemes and Retirement Annuity Contracts

No. 101 (PSO): Personal Pension Schemes:
Part I   Investment of Members' Contributions
Part II   Use of Scheme Funds

No. 103 (OPB): Operation of the Register and Collection of the Levy

No. 106 (PSO/ OPB): Relocation of PSO and OPB

No. 118 (PSO): Additional Voluntary Contributions
Amending Regulations (1987 and 1989 Overrides)

APPROVED OCCUPATIONAL PENSION SCHEMES – INLAND REVENUE LIMITS

Generally, a member may always be provided with a pension of 1/60 x final remuneration and, by commuting some of this pension, a lump sum of 3/80 x final remuneration for each year of service with the company (to a maximum of 40) regardless of retained benefits. However, higher benefits may often be provided, as shown in the table.

	Pre-1987 Limits	1987 Limits	1989 Limits
Employees covered (subject to exceptions under the transitional regulations)	Members of schemes who joined before 17 March 1987.	Members of schemes established before 14 March 1989 who joined between 17 March 1987 and 31 May 1989 inclusive.	All members of schemes established on or after 14 March 1989 and members of other schemes who joined on or after 1 June 1989 or who have opted to be subject to these limits.
Normal retirement date	The date of attaining a specified age within the range of 60 to 75. Lower ages may be possible subject to Inland Revenue approval.		

Final remuneration	Generally, either:
	  (i) basic pay, plus fluctuating pay averaged over the preceding 3 or more years, for any year in the 5 years preceding exit; *or*
	
	  (ii) the average of total pay over any 3 or more consecutive years ending not more than 10 years preceding exit.
	
	May include most taxable remuneration and earlier years' pay may usually be increased to allow for inflation.		

	No cash limit applies.	Limited to £100,000 for calculating maximum lump sum on retirement.	Limited to earnings cap: £78,600 for tax year 1995/96 (normally increased each year in line with the Retail Prices Index).
Employee contributions (including any additional voluntary contributions)	15% of remuneration.		15% of capped remuneration.

	Pre-1987 Limits	1987 Limits	1989 Limits
Member's pension at normal retirement age (including pension equivalent of any lump sum)	2/3 x final remuneration after 10 years' service. If service is less than 10 years, a fraction of final remuneration from the following table: **Service (Years)** / **Fraction (1/60ths)** 1–5 — 1 each year 6 — 8 7 — 16 8 — 24 9 — 32 10 — 40	2/3 x final remuneration after 20 years' service. If service is less than 20 years, 1/30 x final remuneration for each year.	
Lump sum at normal retirement age	1½ x final remuneration after 20 years' service. If service is less than 20 years, a fraction of final remuneration from the following table: **Service (Years)** / **Fraction (1/80ths)** 1–8 — 3 each year 9 — 30 10 — 36 11 — 42 12 — 48 13 — 54 14 — 63 15 — 72 16 — 81 17 — 90 18 — 99 19 — 108 20 — 120	Lump sum may be enhanced above 3/80ths accrual (up to 'uplifted 1/80ths' level) in proportion to pension enhancement above 1/60ths accrual.	2¼ x the initial annual rate of actual pension (including pension secured by AVCs and FSAVCs paid during the period of membership of the scheme) before commutation or any allocation to dependants' benefits.
Early retirement benefits: ill-health retirement	The maximum potential pension that could have been provided at normal retirement date.		
	The maximum potential lump sum that could have been provided at normal retirement.		A lump sum of the greater of: (a) 3/80 x potential total service (max. 40 years) x final remuneration, *and* (b) 2¼ x initial annual rate of actual pension (before commutation or allocation

	Pre-1987 Limits	1987 Limits	1989 Limits
Early retirement benefits (other than on ill-health)	A proportion of the maximum permissible pension assuming the member had continued in service to normal retirement date ('maximum potential pension') based on the ratio of completed to potential service, and on final remuneration at actual retirement.		A pension of 1/30 x final remuneration for each year of service, subject to a maximum pension of 2/3 x final remuneration on retirement at any age between 50 and 75, irrespective of normal retirement date. A lump sum of 2¼ x initial annual rate of actual pension (before commutation or allocation).
	A corresponding proportion of the maximum permissible lump sum assuming the member had continued in service to normal retirement date.	Lump sum may be enhanced above 3/80ths accrual (up to 'uplifted 1/80ths' level) in proportion to pension enhancement above 1/60ths accrual.	
Leaving service benefits	A deferred pension equal to a proportion of the maximum potential pension, based on the ratio of completed to potential service, and on final remuneration at date of leaving service.		A deferred pension of 1/30 x final remuneration for each year of service, subject to a maximum deferred pension of 2/3 x final remuneration. A deferred lump sum of 2¼ x initial annual rate of actual pension (before commutation or allocation).
	A deferred lump sum calculated as for early retirement in good health.	A deferred lump sum calculated as for early retirement in good health.	
Death-in-service lump sum	4 x final remuneration plus return of employee's contributions (with interest).		
Death-in-service pension	2/3 x the maximum potential pension which could have been provided for the member at normal retirement date.		
Death after retirement pension	2/3 x the maximum pension which could have been provided for the member at retirement, increased in line with the RPI.		
Additional voluntary contributions (AVCs)	Retirement lump sum from proceeds of AVCs allowed only if the employee had entered into arrangements to pay AVCs prior to 8 April 1987. Surplus AVCs may be repaid to the employee after tax, at 35%, has been deducted. This equates to a tax credit at the basic rate only.		
Retained benefits (i.e. benefits from previous employers)	Generally, benefits must be aggregated with any retained benefits to assess whether the '2/3rds' pension limit is exceeded.		
	Retained benefits test required for lump sum calculation.	Retained benefits test not required for lump sum calculation.	
	No retained benefits tests required for dependants' benefits.		
	No retained benefits need to be taken into account for new entrants on or after 31 August 1991 who earn less than ¼ of the earnings cap in their first year of membership.		

Source: Bacon & Woodrow.

UNAPPROVED ARRANGEMENTS

Prior to the Finance Act 1989, an employer with an approved pension scheme could not provide scheme members with further pension benefits via unapproved arrangements. The scope for providing such benefits was therefore limited (*see Section 9*). The Act introduced a cap on earnings for benefits from approved arrangements, but also allowed unlimited benefits to be provided through unapproved arrangements without affecting the tax status of approved schemes.

The most important tax consequences of providing benefits through a UK unapproved arrangement, as compared with an approved scheme, are as follows:

(a) the arrangement's investment income and capital gains are subject to tax;

(b) income tax is payable by the employee either on the contributions or on the benefits (or, in some instances, both) – there is thus no equivalent to the tax-free retirement lump sum which is available from an approved scheme; *and*

(c) relief from corporation tax cannot be claimed by the employer until income tax is paid by the employee.

Unapproved arrangements may be *funded* or *unfunded*. The tax consequences of the two approaches are significantly different: in a *funded* scheme, contributions are taxed but lump sum benefits are tax-free; in an *unfunded* scheme, the member pays tax on all benefits when received.

Tax treatment of retirement benefit arrangements

A brief summary comparing the tax treatment of unapproved and approved retirement benefit arrangements is set out in the following table.

	Funded Arrangement (External Fund)		Unfunded Arrangement (Book-Reserves)	
	Approved	Unapproved[1]	Approved	Unapproved
Employer's contributions/allocations to reserves:				
– corporation tax relief for employer	yes	yes	maybe[2]	no[3]
– income tax charge on employee	no	yes	no	no
Investment returns/growth in reserves	tax-free	income tax & capital gains tax payable	corporation tax relief may be given[2]	no corporation tax relief
Tax paid by beneficiary on:				
– pension	income tax payable[4]	income tax payable[4]	income tax payable[4]	income tax payable[4]
– lump sum	tax-free (amount of lump sum is limited)	tax-free	tax-free (amount of lump sum is limited)	income tax payable

Notes: [1] The funded unapproved arrangement is assumed to be established as an 'accumulation trust' with UK resident trustees. [2] Corporation tax relief may be given if book reserves are calculated on the basis of actuarial advice. [3] Corporation tax relief may however be claimed when benefits are paid. [4] All pensions, regardless of the type of arrangement, are taxed at source under Schedule E via the PAYE system.

Tax treatment of death benefit arrangements

Pensions

Pensions payable on death-in-service, whether from unfunded, funded or insured arrangements, are fully assessable to income tax in the hands of the beneficiary. This is despite the fact that contributions to funded and insured arrangements will already have been subject to income tax. In view of this adverse tax treatment, the most efficient way of providing a pension on a funded or insured basis is to provide an additional tax-free lump sum, which the beneficiary may use to secure a purchased life annuity: such an annuity is taxed only on the interest element of each instalment. When the pension is paid on an unfunded basis each instalment will be an allowable expense to the employer for corporation tax purposes.

Lump sums

The following table gives a brief summary of the tax treatment of arrangements for providing unapproved lump sum benefits on death-in-service.

	Funded[1]	Insured	Unfunded	Additional Salary & Individual Insurance
Employer's contributions/ allocations to reserves:				
– corporation tax relief for employer	yes	yes	no[2]	yes but NICs[3] due
– income tax charge on employee	yes[4]	yes[4]	no	yes and NICs[3] due
Investment returns/ growth in reserves:	income tax and capital gains tax payable	corporation tax payable (by insurance company)	no corporation tax relief on interest allocation to reserves	corporation tax payable (by insurance company)
Tax paid by beneficiary				
– income tax charge	no[5]	no[5,6]	yes[5]	no[5]

Notes: [1] The funded arrangement is assumed to be established as an 'accumulation trust' with UK resident trustees.

[2] Corporation tax relief may however be claimed when benefits are paid.

[3] National Insurance contributions. For the employee, these are payable only on earnings up to the upper earnings limit.

[4] Special conditions apply in respect of a group arrangement so that the cost of each individual's benefits can be calculated.

[5] Inheritance tax is potentially payable but is avoidable in most cases. For unfunded schemes the governing document should clearly state that any lump sum death benefit is payable at the sole discretion of the person paying the benefit.

[6] Corporation tax may be payable if chargeable gains arise, but these are avoidable.

The tax treatment of unapproved arrangements is covered in the booklet, 'The Tax Treatment of Top-Up Pension Schemes', published by the Inland Revenue.

PERSONAL PENSIONS

Personal pensions have been available since July 1988. All personal pensions are based on the 'money purchase' principle: pension contributions accumulate with interest and capital appreciation within an individual fund, which is used to purchase a pension on retirement. The amount of the eventual benefit is thus dependent upon the contributions paid, the investment performance of the fund, expense deductions, and the financial conditions at the time benefits are secured.

Contributions to a personal pension may be made by anyone under the age of 75 with taxable income from employment or self-employment. However, individuals cannot be members of an occupational scheme as well as having a personal pension in respect of the same source of earnings, unless:

- the occupational scheme provides only a lump sum benefit on death-in-service or pensions for spouses and/or dependants; *or*
- the personal pension is to be used by a member of a contracted-in occupational pension scheme for the sole purpose of contracting-out of SERPS.

A member of an occupational scheme may nevertheless take out a personal pension for the sole purpose of accepting transfer payments.

The Inland Revenue have issued guidance notes referred to as IR 76 on the tax approval of personal pension schemes. Occupational Pensions Board Memorandum No 92 gives further details of the requirements of the Social Security legislation.

Contracting-out

A personal pension scheme which is used for the purpose of contracting-out of SERPS is known as an 'Appropriate Personal Pension'. Pension rights accumulating from the minimum contributions paid by the Department of Social Security (DSS) to the scheme where the member is contracted-out are known as protected rights. The main features of contracting-out are set out in *Section 12*.

Contributions and tax relief

Contributions to a personal pension are restricted by reference to 'net relevant earnings', which means broadly taxable income from employment or self-employment. The maximum percentage of net relevant earnings which may be paid as a personal pension contribution varies with age. The following table shows the maximum percentages. In addition, the amount of net relevant earnings which may be taken into account for the purpose of calculating contributions in any tax year is restricted to the amount of the 'earnings cap' in that year. The earnings cap for 1995/96 is £78,600.

Payments to personal pension schemes attract tax relief. Contributions by employed persons are made net of basic rate tax. The personal pension provider recovers from the Inland Revenue an amount equal to basic rate tax on the grossed-up contributions. If the individual pays income tax at the higher rate, he may obtain the extra tax relief by submitting a claim to his Inspector of Taxes.

Age at start of tax year:	Maximum Percentage of Net Relevant Earnings	
	1987/88– 1988/89	1989/90 onwards
35 or less	17.5	17.5
36–45	17.5	20.0
46–50	17.5	25.0
51–55	20.0	30.0
56–60	22.5	35.0
61–74	27.5	40.0

Self-employed persons are not permitted to deduct tax from contributions paid: all tax relief must be claimed directly from the Inspector of Taxes.

Carry forward of unused relief

If contributions in any tax year are less than the maximum allowed the balance may be carried forward as 'unused relief'. Unused relief may generally be carried forward to any of the following six tax years, to permit contributions above the maximum percentage in that tax year.

Carry back of contributions

'Carry back' is another system which makes use of unused relief. This enables members to have part or all of a contribution counted, for tax purposes, as being paid in the previous tax year, provided there is unused relief for that year. Contributions can be carried back by one year only, unless there were no net relevant earnings in that year, in which case the year before that may be used. Contributions by an employer may not be carried back. An election to carry back contributions must be made not later than three months after the end of the tax year in which the contribution was paid.

Limits on lump sum at retirement

There are no limits on the pension benefit which may be paid on retirement: this depends on the value of the accumulated fund and the financial conditions applying at the time benefits are secured. However, there are limits on the proportion of the accumulated fund which may be taken in the form of a tax-free lump sum.

For arrangements entered into on or after 27 July 1989 the maximum lump sum is 25% of the total fund excluding the value of protected rights.

For arrangements made before 27 July 1989, the maximum lump sum is 25% of the total fund excluding the value of any spouse's or dependant's pension. Protected rights may be *included* in the total fund, but the lump sum calculated in this way must be paid from that part of the fund not constituting protected rights: the protected rights must be paid in pension form.

Group personal pensions

A group personal pension scheme is an arrangement tailored for the needs of the employees of a particular employer. The group arrangement may achieve economies of scale which can make it more cost-effective than individual personal pension arrangements.

Annuity purchase

Before the Finance Act 1995, an annuity had to be purchased with the proceeds of a personal pension at the time of retirement, regardless of the state of the annuity market at the time. From 30 June 1995 it became possible to defer purchasing an annuity, while withdrawing income from the funds. Initially, only funds in excess of Protected Rights may be treated in this way, but it is expected that Protected Rights will be subject to similar rules from April 1996.

The following main conditions currently apply:

- Withdrawals may be made between ages 50 and 75, with an annuity being purchased at or before age 75 (withdrawals before 50 are permitted for incapacity retirements and for certain occupations).

- The amount of income withdrawn must be in a range calculated according to published tables, and must be reviewed every 3 years.

- On the member's death during the deferral period, the surviving spouse or dependant may continue to make income withdrawals until age 75 (or until the member would have been 75, if earlier), or may purchase an annuity, or may take the fund as cash (subject to a 35% tax charge). The existing option for a surviving spouse to defer annuity purchase until age 60 continues, but income withdrawals would not then be permitted.

Income withdrawals are subject to tax under PAYE, while the investment returns on the remaining funds continue to be tax-free. The ability to take part of the funds as a lump sum on retirement is unaffected.

CONTRACTING-OUT

The opportunity for final salary schemes to contract-out of SERPS has been available to employers since April 1978. To qualify, an employer must have a good quality occupational pension scheme which promises to pay at least a minimum pension (the GMP) to each employee. The employee's SERPS pension from the State is reduced by the amount of the GMP and, in return, both employer and employee pay lower rates of National Insurance (NI) contributions. The reduction in NI contributions is called the contracting-out rebate. For the period April 1993 to April 1997 the rebate is 4.8% of band earnings: 1.8% for the employee and 3% for the employer.

From April 1988, the contracting-out choice was widened to allow what is known as money purchase contracting-out. This may be done in two ways. Firstly, employees may be contracted-out of SERPS if their employer guarantees to pay contributions equal to the contracted-out rebate to his scheme. The scheme must then provide each employee with benefits based on the payments actually made and the investment return achieved, rather than with benefits calculated according to a pre-determined formula. Secondly, as an alternative to a company scheme, employees may elect to contract-out on an individual basis by taking out an Appropriate Personal Pension (APP) or a Free-Standing Additional Voluntary Contribution Scheme (FSAVC).

If the employee decides to contract-out by way of an APP or a FSAVC, the employer and employee continue to pay the full rate of NI contributions. The DSS then pay a 'minimum contribution' equal to the contracting-out rebate directly to the APP or FSAVC.

Until April 1993 the DSS also paid an 'incentive' of 2% of band earnings to most APPs. From April 1993 a new incentive, amounting to 1% of band earnings, is being paid to APPs of all contributors aged 30 or over at the start of each tax year. (It is not paid for younger APP contributors or to occupational schemes.) For APPs, an amount equal to the equivalent of tax relief at the basic rate on the employee's share of the contracting-out rebate is added. This tax relief is not available where the payments are made to a FSAVC.

The State pays the same reduced SERPS pension to an individual, regardless of the method by which he has been contracted-out. The contracting-out rebate is equivalent to an estimate of the cost of the GMP, under particular financial assumptions, for an employee of average age. But the benefit provided by a money purchase arrangement will not necessarily match the GMP deducted from State benefits, because the benefits emerging will depend on the investment return actually achieved, the employee's age and on financial conditions at the time the pension is secured.

MAIN FEATURES

CONTRACTED-OUT SALARY RELATED SCHEME (COSR)

* Contract-out by providing GMPs.

* Employer must contribute.

* Scheme should be set up under irrevocable trust or by Statute.

* GMPs accrue at rates corresponding to the SERPS 20% target, must be increased in payment by 3% (or RPI if less) each year and are payable from current State pension age (age 65 for males and 60 for females). Pre 6 April 1988 GMPs accrued at rates corresponding to a SERPS 25% target and no increases in payment are required.

* Widows and widowers who have children or who are over 45 must have a widow's or widower's GMP payable at the level of 50% of the GMP (only contracted-out service post 5 April 1988 qualifies for widower's GMP).

* On withdrawal prior to State pension age the accrued GMP and widow(er)'s GMP may be transferred back to the State, to another scheme or to an individual policy; alternatively the benefits may remain with the scheme, where they must be revalued up to State pension age either:

  (i) in line with national average earnings (Section 148 Orders (previously Section 21 Orders) – *see page 34); or*

  (ii) at a fixed rate of $8\frac{1}{2}$% pa (leavers before 6 April 1988), $7\frac{1}{2}$% pa (leavers 6 April 1988 to 5 April 1993), or 7% pa (leavers after 5 April 1993); *or*

  (iii) if a limited revaluation premium is paid to the State, at the lesser of 5% pa and the increase in national average earnings.

CONTRACTED-OUT MONEY PURCHASE SCHEME (COMP)

* Contract-out by providing 'protected rights'. Protected rights are a member's rights to benefits derived from the accumulation of minimum payments (i.e. the joint contracting-out rebate paid to a COMP scheme) including any incentive to which the member may have been entitled prior to April 1993 and any benefits derived from the transfer of protected rights or GMPs from another arrangement.

* Scheme should be set up under irrevocable trust or by Statute.

* Employer must contribute.

* Protected rights pensions must not commence before age 60 (except on death), must increase at 3% (or RPI if less) each year and must continue at half rate to a widow or widower who has children or who is aged 45 or over. Terms to purchase the pension must not vary according to sex.

CONTRACTED-OUT SIMPLIFIED DEFINED CONTRIBUTION SCHEME (COSDC)

- Contract-out by providing protected rights (*see COMP above*).
- Employer must contribute.
- Scheme should be set up under irrevocable trust or by Statute.
- Total contributions made by or on behalf of the employee must not exceed 17½% of remuneration.
- Further restrictions apply where scheme is self-administered.

FREE-STANDING ADDITIONAL VOLUNTARY CONTRIBUTIONS SCHEME (FSAVC)

- Contract-out by providing protected rights (equal to 'minimum contributions' paid by DSS and subject to similar conditions as for a COMP).
- Employer must not contribute and employee need not contribute.
- Scheme must be tax approved or provisionally tax approved by the Inland Revenue under Chapter I Part XIV ICTA 1988.
- 'Minimum contribution' scheme benefits count against Revenue limits.
- 'Minimum contributions' do not count against 15% limit on member's contributions.
- Tax relief is not available against any part of 'minimum contributions'.
- Exchange of information required between employer and provider to minimise the possibility of Revenue maximum benefit limits being exceeded and to observe procedures concerning surplus AVCs.

APPROPRIATE PERSONAL PENSION (APP)

- Contract-out by providing protected rights (equal to 'minimum contributions' paid by DSS, including the tax rebate at basic rate on the member's minimum contribution, and subject to similar conditions as for a COMP except that payment must not commence before State pension age, or death if earlier).
- Employer and employee need not contribute.
- The 1% incentive is payable from April 1993 for contributors aged 30 or over.
- Scheme must be tax approved or provisionally tax approved by the Inland Revenue under Chapter IV Part XIV ICTA 1988.
- Scheme should be set up under irrevocable trust or under an insurance contract.
- 'Minimum contribution' scheme benefits do not count against Revenue maximum limits.
- 'Minimum contributions' do not count against maximum employer/employee contributions.

VEHICLES FOR CONTRACTING-OUT

	COSR	COMP Full Tax Approval	COSDC Simplified Tax Approval	FSAVC	APP
Set up by	Employer	Employer	Employer	Insurance Co., Building Society etc. (Provider)	Insurance Co., Building Society etc. (Provider)
Form	Occupational Scheme	Occupational Scheme	Occupational Scheme	Individual 'Policy'	Individual 'Policy'
Responsibility for administration	Trustees	Trustees	Trustees	Trustees of main scheme and Provider	Provider
May employee also be in (another) occupational scheme?	YES	YES	NO (except death-in-service or widow(er)'s scheme)	Compulsory	NO[1]
Scheme portable from job to job?	NO	NO	NO	YES[2]	YES
Employer contributions	Compulsory	Compulsory	Compulsory	Not Allowed	Optional
Contracting-out rebate paid to Scheme by	Employer	Employer	Employer	DSS	DSS
Tax-free lump sum at retirement	YES	YES	YES	NO	YES
Other Inland Revenue benefit limits at retirement	Final Salary Type	Final Salary Type	Maximum Contribution Only	Final Salary Type	Maximum Contribution Only

Notes: [1] Unless the occupational scheme is contracted-in and 'minimum contributions' only are paid to the APP or the occupational scheme provides only death-in-service or widow(er)s' benefits.

[2] But must be concurrent with membership of an employer's pension scheme. Contributions must stop if the employee leaves the scheme or joins an employer without an occupational scheme.

Source: Bacon & Woodrow.

THE FUTURE FOR CONTRACTING-OUT

The Pensions Act 1995 (*see Section 20*), makes radical changes to the present system for contracting-out of SERPS from April 1997.

COSR schemes

- No GMPs will accrue from April 1997.

- In order to be contracted-out after April 1997, the scheme actuary must certify that the scheme provides pensions for members which considered as a whole are broadly equivalent to, or better than, those under a **Reference Scheme**:

Pension age	65
Pension accrual rate	1/80th
Pensionable Salary	90% of Band Earnings
Final Pensionable Salary	Average of Pensionable Salary over last 3 tax years
Pensionable Service	Actual service up to 40 years
Spouse's pension	50% of member's pension

- The scheme must be re-tested at regular, three-yearly intervals to remain contracted-out.

- Limited Rate revaluation and most State Scheme premium options will be removed in respect of accrued GMPs.

- The contracted-out rebate will continue to be a universal flat rate.

APPs and COMP schemes

- Age-related rebates will be introduced.

- State Scheme Premium options on winding-up will be removed.

All schemes

- **No** SERPS benefit will accrue whilst contracted-out – this removes the effective index-linking of substitute benefits by the State.

- **All** post-1997 salary-related benefits and Protected Rights must carry LPI increases.

LEAVING SERVICE BENEFITS

PRESERVATION

The preservation legislation provides members of an occupational pension scheme with a legal right to short service benefit (SSB) if they leave pensionable service before normal pension age (NPA). The essential principle is that an early leaver's benefits should be calculated on a consistent basis with those of a member who remains in service to NPA. Entitlement to SSB is dependent upon the member either having at least two years' 'qualifying service' or having transferred benefits from a personal pension into the scheme. 'Qualifying service' is the sum of all actual pensionable service under the scheme plus pensionable service in any scheme from which a transfer payment has been received. Members who do not satisfy the preservation conditions may nevertheless be provided with deferred benefits if scheme rules so permit. Alternatively, the scheme may provide for them to receive a refund of their own contributions, if any, less tax and their share of any premium required to re-instate contracted-out service back into the State scheme.

In money purchase schemes, early leavers must normally be entitled to whatever benefit derives from contributions paid by or in respect of them.

Payment of short service benefits

Preserved benefits must normally be payable not later than the member's NPA. However, the preservation legislation defines NPA as the earliest age at which a member is entitled to receive benefits on retirement from the relevant employment, disregarding any special provisions for early retirement. Therefore, even if scheme rules define retirement age as 65, NPA could be earlier if members have an unqualified right to retire on an unreduced pension from an earlier age. Benefits need not be paid before age 60, however, if scheme rules contain a specific provision to this effect.

REVALUATION

The position of early leavers from final salary occupational pension schemes has in recent years been progressively improved. Before 1986, with the exception of GMPs, there was no legal requirement for preserved benefits to be increased during the period of deferment until the pension came into payment. Consequently, the purchasing power of the eventual pension could be seriously eroded by the effects of inflation.

The Social Security Act 1985 introduced the requirement to increase (or 'revalue') the part of a preserved pension in excess of GMP which related to service completed on or after 1 January 1985, for a member who left pensionable service on or after 1 January 1986. The Social Security Act 1990 further extended the revaluation requirement to cover the whole of the member's pension in excess of GMP for members leaving pensionable service after 1 January 1991. The revaluation percentage is the lesser of the increase in the Retail Prices Index and 5% per annum compound over the whole period of deferment.

GMPs

In addition to the revaluation requirements on the excess of the member's pension over any GMP, members of contracted-out schemes must also have their GMP revalued between leaving service and State pension age either:

    (i)   in line with national average earnings (section 148 orders – previously known as section 21 orders) – *see page 34*); *or*

   (ii)   by fixed revaluation at the rate of 7% pa, 7½% pa or 8½% pa for leavers after 5 April 1993, leavers after 5 April 1988 but before 6 April 1993, and leavers before 6 April 1988 respectively; *or*

  (iii)   if a limited revaluation premium is paid, at the lesser of 5% pa and section 148 orders. (This option is being withdrawn from April 1997.)

    For members who leave pensionable service after 31 December 1984, the revaluations on the GMP cannot be 'franked' against the excess pension over the GMP, or against revaluation on the excess.

TRANSFER VALUES

Rights to cash equivalent

Generally, members of occupational pension schemes whose pensionable service ends on or after 1 January 1986 have the right to the cash equivalent of all or part of their benefits to be paid as a transfer value to another approved arrangement (*but see 'Recent Developments' below*). This right is normally subject to there being a period of at least one year between the termination of the member's pensionable service and NPA, although where NPA is earlier than 60 the right arises on termination of service at any time before NPA.

When giving advice on the calculation of a transfer value the actuary has to make sure that it will not only be calculated in accordance with the rules of the scheme but will comply with the law concerning cash equivalents. The manner of calculation of the statutory cash equivalent is laid down in legislation. It must generally represent the actuarial value of the accrued benefits which the member will be giving up.

Members who opt out of pension schemes without leaving their jobs also have the right to transfer at least part of their benefits. This transfer only entitles the member to a 'partial' cash equivalent, related to service completed after 6 April 1988 – when members generally first had the right to opt out.

Transfers of contracted-out benefit

Since 6 April 1990, transfers of contracted-out benefit can be made freely between most arrangements contracted-out on either the GMP or the protected rights basis, in which case the nature of the contracted-out benefit may alter from GMP to protected rights or vice versa, depending on the circumstances of the transfer.

When a transfer is being made from a scheme contracted-out on a GMP basis to one contracted-out on a protected rights basis – such as an appropriate personal pension – it is necessary for the administrator to identify that part of the transfer which relates to the GMP. It is this part which then becomes protected rights in the new arrangement. On a transfer in the opposite direction, protected rights disappear and the new arrangement has to provide a GMP as if the member had been contracted-out on a GMP basis for the period of service to which the protected rights relate.

Whenever there is a transfer of contracted-out benefit the scheme needs to identify the benefit being transferred and notify the DSS accordingly.

Inland Revenue rules

The benefits to be provided by the receiving scheme will be commensurate with the amount of the transfer payment. The amount which can be taken in the form of a tax-free lump sum at retirement is limited by the Inland Revenue, and a certificate may be needed from the transferring scheme in some cases to enable any part of the transferred benefits to be paid in this way (*see page 85*). The Inland Revenue also require a certificate to be given confirming that the transfer payment is not more than a prescribed value whenever a high earner or controlling director wishes to transfer from an occupational scheme to a personal pension arrangement.

A NIL certificate is required to enable a transfer to be made from a scheme where retirement benefits are restricted to non-commutable pension only (*see JOM 104, para. 5*). The certificate will indicate to the receiving scheme that the transfer payment is not to be used to provide lump sum retirement benefits. On a subsequent transfer, a further NIL certificate must be provided specifying that part of the transfer payment to which this further certificate applies.

Overseas transfers

Transfers *to* (but not *from*) overseas schemes require the consent of the OPB.

Transfers to and from overseas schemes require the consent of the PSO unless a reciprocal or special arrangement is in force. The reciprocal arrangements in force at the time of writing are between the UK and the Republic of Ireland, the Isle of Man, Jersey and Guernsey. Special arrangements exist for transfers to the pension scheme for staff of the European Communities.

Recent developments

The Pensions Act 1995 (*see section 20*) introduces a number of new provisions relating to transfer values:

- the right to a cash equivalent will be extended to those whose pensionable service ended before 1 January 1986. However, under proposed regulations, schemes (such as most public sector schemes) which fully protect pensions from inflation both before and after retirement will be exempted from the requirement;

- a 3-month window, in which the cash equivalent from a salary-related scheme will be guaranteed not to be subject to recalculation, will apply.

These provisions are expected to be effective from April 1997.

WHAT TYPES OF TRANSFER ARE PERMITTED BETWEEN APPROVED UK ARRANGEMENTS?

Transferring Arrangement	Receiving Arrangement								
	OPS COSR	OPS COMP	OPS C-IN	APP (1,2)	PP (2)	FSAVC C-O	FSAVC C-IN	S226 Policy	S32 Policy
OPS/COSR	✓	✓	(3)	✓	(3)	✗	✗	✗	✓
OPS/COMP	✓	✓	(4)	✓	(4)	✗	✗	✗	(4)
OPS/C-IN	✓	✓	✓	✓	✓	✗	✗	✗	✓
APP		✓	(4)	(5)	(4,5)	✗	✗	✗	✗
PP		✓	✓	(5)	(5)	✗	✗	✗	✗
FSAVC/C-O	✓	✓	(4)	(6)	(4,6)	✓	(4)	✗	(4)
FSAVC/C-IN	✓	✓	✓	(6)	(6)	✓	✓	✗	✓
S226 Policy (7)	✓	✓	✓	✓	✓	✗	✗	✓	✗
S32 Policy (7)	✓	✓	(8)	✓	(8)	✗	✗	✗	✓

Notes:
(1) Transfers to 'minimum contribution' APPs can only be made from other 'minimum contribution' APPs.
(2) For high earners and controlling directors, a transfer from an OPS, a FSAVC scheme or a S32 policy can only be made if the transfer value does not exceed an amount calculated according to special regulations.
(3) Only the excess over the GMP can be transferred. The GMP must be retained in the scheme, bought-out, paid back into SERPS or transferred to an APP or to a contracted-out occupational scheme.
(4) Only the excess over the PRs can be transferred. The PRs must be retained in the scheme or transferred to an APP or to a contracted-out occupational scheme.
(5) Permitted apart from transfers from post 26.7.89 PPs to pre 27.7.89 PPs.
(6) Permitted only if the member is no longer accruing benefits, other than death benefits, in an employer's scheme.
(7) Policy must contain an appropriate provision or be appropriately endorsed before any transfer is permitted.
(8) Only the excess over the GMP can be transferred. The GMP must be transferred to another S32 policy, to an APP or to a contracted-out occupational scheme.

Key:
APP	Appropriate Personal Pension
C-IN	Contracted-In
C-O	Contracted-Out
COMP	Contracted-Out Money Purchase
COSR	Contracted-Out Salary Related
FSAVC	Free-Standing Additional Voluntary Contribution Scheme
OPS	Occupational Pension Scheme
PP	Personal Pension
PR	Protected Rights
S226	Insurance Policy for self-employed under Section 226 of ICTA 1970 (now Chapter III of Part XIV, ICTA 1988)
S32	Insurance buy-out policy under Section 32 of Finance Act 1981 (now incorporated in Chapter I of Part XIV, ICTA 1988)

TRANSFERS FROM APPROVED UK OCCUPATIONAL PENSION SCHEMES TO APPROVED UK ARRANGEMENTS

Is a lump sum certificate needed ?

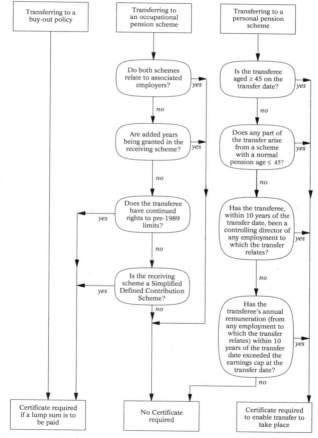

Source: Bacon & Woodrow.

MAXIMUM LUMP SUM PAYABLE IN RESPECT OF A TRANSFER FROM AN OCCUPATIONAL PENSION SCHEME

Receiving Scheme	'1989 Regime' Member[1]	'Pre-1989 Regime' Member[2]
Occupational pension scheme[3]	2.25 × pension[4] from the transfer; *or* 3 × pension[4] if lump sum is not provided via commutation; *or* for transfers before 1 March 1991, if greater[5]: the certified lump sum[6] increased in line with the RPI[7]	The greater of: (a) The certified lump sum[6] increased in line with the RPI[7]; *and* (b) 3/80 × final remuneration in receiving scheme × no. of added years *(if added years are granted)*
Personal pension scheme[3]	25% of the accumulated transfer payment in excess of protected rights subject to a maximum of the certified lump sum[6], if any, increased in line with the RPI[7]	
Buy-out policy[3]	The greater of: (a) 3/80 × final remuneration in transferring scheme × no. of years service with transferring employer increased in line with the RPI[8]; *and* (b) 2.25 × the emerging pension[4]	The certified lump sum[6], increased in line with the RPI[7]

Notes: [1] Members joining a scheme established on or after 14 March 1989 or joining a scheme existing before that date on or after 1 June 1989 where they are not covered by transitional arrangements and members who have 'opted' for the 1989 regime.

[2] Members who before 1 June 1989 joined a scheme established before 14 March 1989 or joined a scheme as in (1) above but who are covered by transitional arrangements.

[3] No part of a transfer payment subject to a NIL certificate may be used to provide benefit in lump sum form.

[4] This is the initial pension before commutation (if appropriate) or allocation.

[5] Specific PSO agreement to pay this greater amount is required where the transfer was to a scheme approved on or after 29 November 1991.

[6] This is the lump sum certified by the transferring scheme.

[7] This is the proportionate increase in the retail prices index from the date of transfer to the date of retirement.

[8] This is the proportionate increase in the retail prices index from the date of termination of pensionable service to the date of retirement.

Source: Bacon & Woodrow.

EQUAL TREATMENT

Laws to enforce equal treatment of men and women, particularly in the areas of pay and employment conditions, have been strengthened over recent years. The driving force, as far as the UK is concerned, has been the attitude within the European Union. Article 119 of the Treaty of Rome, which states that men and women must receive equal pay for equal work, has had a major influence on benefits such as pensions. This has been mainly through the widening of interpretation of its scope by the courts, in particular by the judgments of the European Court of Justice (ECJ) in several cases. The UK has had to enact its own legislation on equal pay and benefit provision in order to comply with European Council Directives, and the Pensions Act 1995 contains a number of provisions aimed at enforcing equal treatment for men and women in both State and Private pension arrangements.

A summary of the general principles of equal treatment, established by the ECJ rulings, is given below.

GENERAL PRINCIPLES OF EQUAL TREATMENT

Equal benefits

Occupational pension schemes must provide equal benefits for men and women. In this respect, equality is only required for benefits in respect of service after 17 May 1990, except for claims initiated earlier.

Equal access

Men and women must have equal rights to join their employer's scheme. The exclusion of part-timers may thus constitute sex discrimination, if the exclusion affects a much greater number of one sex than the other, *unless* the employer shows that it may be explained by objectively justified factors unrelated to sex. The right to join a scheme may be claimed in respect of service back to 8 April 1976, although time limits for bringing actions under national laws may be applied (*see below*).

Role of trustees, employers and the courts

Trustees must observe the principle of equal treatment in performing their duties. Both trustees and employers are bound to use all the means available under national laws in order to eliminate discrimination. National courts must apply the principle of Article 119 in the context of domestic laws, taking due account of the respective liabilities of employers and trustees. Article 119 may be relied on in claims against trustees as well as against employers.

APPLICATION OF EQUAL TREATMENT PRINCIPLES TO OCCUPATIONAL AND STATE PENSIONS

Member contributions

The equal treatment principle of Article 119 applies to the whole benefit paid by an occupational pension scheme, and no distinction need be made between the parts derived from the employer's and from the employee's contractual contributions. However, benefits derived from members' additional voluntary contributions are not pay and so do not fall within the scope of Article 119.

Pension age and benefit accrual

Normal pension ages for men and women must not be discriminatory for benefits accrued since 17 May 1990. In respect of service from 17 May 1990 up to the date of equalisation (the equalisation date), the provisions applying to the less favoured sex must be levelled up to those of the more favoured sex, whatever the difficulties of the occupational scheme or the employer may be. For periods of service after the equalisation date, Article 119 does not preclude equal treatment being achieved by levelling benefits down, e.g. by raising pension age. (There may, however, be contract law and/or trust law obstacles to doing this in the UK). For service before 17 May 1990, there is nothing in EU law that would justify benefits being levelled-down retrospectively (and in the UK, contract law and/or trust law problems are likely). If members have a right to retire early, this right must not be discriminatory for benefits accrued since 17 May 1990.

Benefit accrual for service since 17 May 1990 must be equalised not only for scheme members, but also for their dependants. For benefits not linked to length of service, e.g. lump sum benefits on death in service, equal benefits must be provided for men and women when the event triggering payment of the benefit occurs on or after 17 May 1990. In schemes where members have always been all of one sex, there is no need to equalise the respective benefits to those of a hypothetical member of the other sex. Where the funds held by the trustees are insufficient, any decision on how equalisation of benefits should be achieved must be resolved on the basis of national law.

Under the provisions of the Pensions Act 1995, all occupational pension schemes will be deemed to have an "equal treatment rule" covering both admission of members and benefits. The rule will effectively level up any unequal terms relating to service after 17 May 1990.

Bridging pensions and State pension offsets

Bridging pensions which allow for differences in the commencement dates of State pensions for men and women were ruled to be permissible in one case brought before the ECJ. State pension offsets which commence at differing State pension ages should, on the same principle, also be permissible. Offsets which differ in amount for men and women are not allowed.

Transfers

Funded schemes may, if they wish, calculate transfers out using actuarial factors which vary according to sex. The benefits to which the factors are applied should, of course, be equalised for service since 17 May 1990. Where a transfer value has in fact been based on unequal benefits for a period of service after 17 May 1990, the transfer value might be lower than it would have been if it had been based on equalised benefits. In such circumstances the **receiving** scheme must increase the benefits provided to those which could have been bought by the higher transfer value that should have been paid.

Actuarial factors

Actuarial factors for commutation, early retirement and surrender of pension for a dependant may all vary according to sex in a funded scheme. (No case has yet addressed the question of unequal factors in unfunded schemes.)

Money purchase schemes

No case has yet addressed the issue of equality as it applies to money purchase schemes. It therefore remains unclear whether, on buying-out benefits from a money purchase scheme, trustees may apply identical cash sums to purchase different pensions for men and women.

Contracting-out problems

Contracted-out schemes have particular difficulties in equalising the benefits they provide because GMPs accrue at different rates and are required to come into payment at different ages for men and women. This issue was not resolved in the Pensions Act 1995, and as the law stands at the time of writing, it seems that, for service since 17 May 1990, members may now be entitled to receive overall pension payments (including any GMP) equal to the greater of the amounts that would be payable to either a man or a woman in identical circumstances.

Time limits for bringing claims

The equality provisions in the Pensions Act 1995 will mean that members and prospective members of occupational pension schemes will be able to bring claims under the Equal Pay Act 1970 against pension scheme trustees via industrial tribunals. Claims under this Act must be made not later than 6 months after leaving and up to 2 years' damages may be awarded.

On 31 May 1995, regulations were laid which effectively brought into immediate effect these time limitations insofar as they will apply to persons unfairly excluded from pension scheme membership. The regulations also require the employer to pay the full cost for service between 31 May 1995 (or the deemed date of entry if later) and the actual date of entry. This is a more stringent requirement on employers than that in a 1994 ECJ case where it was ruled that the employee could be required to pay full arrears of member contributions.

Statutory occupational pension schemes

Schemes for Government employees are subject to the equal treatment requirements of Article 119 even though they are established by statute.

Maternity leave

The Trade Union Reform and Employment Rights Act 1993 requires *all* benefits in kind, including pension accrual, to be maintained during the *statutory* 14 week period of maternity leave (whether paid or unpaid). Details of how pension rights should be maintained are contained in the Social Security Act 1989 which requires *paid* maternity absence to be treated as a period of normal service as far as an employer-related benefit scheme is concerned. When assessing benefits it should be assumed that the normal pay for the job was received. However, the member is required to pay contributions only on the actual remuneration received.

State pension ages

State pension age is to be equalised at 65 for men and women. The change is to be phased in over a 10 year period from April 2010. From that date, State pension age for women will increase by one month for every two months elapsed (*see table below*). Women born before 6 April 1950 will not be affected by the change; women born after 5 April 1955 will have a new State pension age of 65.

Female pension ages during phasing-in period

Date of Birth	Pension Date	Date of Birth	Pension Date
Before 6.4.50	60th b'day	6.3.53–5.4.53	6.3.2016
6.4.50–5.5.50	6.5.2010	. . .	. . .
6.5.50–5.6.50	6.7.2010	6.3.54–5.4.54	6.3.2018
6.6.50–5.7.50	6.9.2010	. . .	. . .
. . .	. . .	6.3.55–5.4.55	6.3.2020
6.3.51–5.4.51	6.3.2012	6.4.55 and after	65th b'day
. . .	. . .		
6.3.52–5.4.52	6.3.2014		

PENSION FUND SURPLUSES

The Finance Act 1986 (now consolidated into Income and Corporation Taxes Act 1988) requires schemes to eliminate surpluses in excess of a statutory level, as calculated on a statutory basis. The requirement took effect from 6 April 1987 for actuarial valuations submitted to the Revenue after that date.

For most schemes, an actuarial report or a certificate must be submitted to the Pension Schemes Office (PSO) at regular intervals. The report or certificate must either state that there is no surplus over 5% of the value of the past service liabilities or show the extent of any surplus over 5%.

The actuarial values of assets and liabilities used to assess the surplus must be calculated employing an actuarial method and assumptions laid down by the government. The liabilities take account of accrued service to the date of the valuation and projected pay increases up to retirement.

Any surplus of assets in excess of 105% of these liabilities has to be eliminated in one or more of the following ways:

(i) benefit improvements (e.g. pension increases);

(ii) a reduction in employer and/or employee contributions, to eliminate it within 5 years;

(iii) a payment from the scheme to the employer.

If action is not taken to reduce surplus to the 5% level the scheme will lose part of its tax exemptions.

No refund to the employer may be made unless full Limited Price Indexation (LPI) increases have already been guaranteed for all service. Refunds must be agreed in advance with the PSO and must not reduce surplus below the 5% level.

Tax at 40% must be deducted by the scheme administrator from payments to employers who are not tax exempt (e.g. charities): the tax is paid direct to the Inland Revenue. There are no allowances against this tax charge, which is described as 'free-standing'. The tax is regarded as income tax (Schedule D, case VI) or corporation tax as appropriate. The payment will not then be treated as employer's income or a trading receipt for tax purposes.

The requirements to produce a report or certificate on the statutory basis do not apply to:

(a) a self-administered scheme with less than 12 members (including those in service, deferred pensioners and pensioners); *or*

(b) an insured scheme, the policies in respect of which require levels of contribution to take account of surpluses; *or*

(c) an insured scheme, the policies in respect of which provide only for lump sum benefits for members on death before normal retirement age; *or*

(d) a simplified defined contribution scheme (SDCS).

If overfunding does occur in any of the first three cases, however, any refund of surplus will be subject to the 40% tax charge. The funding of SDCSs is controlled by limits on the contributions so surpluses cannot arise.

WHEN AND WHAT THE SCHEME ADMINISTRATOR MUST TELL THE PSO

Event	Information Required by PSO	Timescale
(1) **Normal valuation of scheme**	Valuation report on prescribed basis or certificate	Within 3 months of date of signing report on prescribed basis or certificate
If an excess surplus is disclosed by report on prescribed basis or certificate	Proposals for reducing surplus including their cost shown on a completed SF290	Within 6 months of date of signing report or certificate
(2) **A change is made to prescribed basis from assumptions for previous valuation**	Changes made and justification in writing	At or before the time the valuation report or certificate is submitted
Whenever a certificate is produced	Information relating to prescribed basis required under Guidance Notes	When issuing the certificate
(3) **PSO not satisfied with content of certificate**	A signed valuation report on the prescribed basis	Within 60 days of PSO's request
(4) **PSO not satisfied with valuation on prescribed basis produced under either (1) or (3) above**	Further particulars specified by PSO	Within 30 days of PSO's request
(5) **PSO makes an estimate of assets and liabilities**	Whether administrator wishes to appeal	Within 30 days of PSO's 'estimate letter'
(6) **If an excess surplus is disclosed under (3) – (5) above**	Proposals for reducing surplus including their cost shown on a completed SF290	Within 3 months of date of PSO estimate or acceptance of report; or within 30 days of determination of appeal
(7) **Administrator makes refund to employer(s)**	Amount of cash payment Apportionment between employers	Within 6 month period permitted for refund

Source: Bacon & Woodrow.

DISCLOSURE OF PENSION SCHEME INFORMATION

The Pension Schemes Act 1993 requires the trustees of occupational pension schemes to disclose actuarial and accounting information, as well as details of his or her benefits to each member. These rules override any provisions in schemes' trust documents if the two are in conflict.

The disclosure regulations apply to money purchase schemes as well as to defined benefit schemes, but there are some differences. The most significant is the requirement for money purchase schemes to provide annual benefit statements automatically, rather than just on request.

The Pensions Act 1995 (*see Section 20*) will make a number of changes to the disclosure requirements through regulations. In particular, more information about the funding position of the scheme and about the management of its investments is likely to have to be disclosed to members. The proposed changes are **not** reflected in the summary below.

SUMMARY OF DISCLOSURE REQUIREMENTS

Information	To Be Disclosed to	In What Circumstances	Time Limits and Other Information
Trust Deed and Rules or other documents constituting the scheme, including names and addresses of participating employers.	**Members, Prospective Members** and their **Spouses.** **Beneficiaries.** Recognised independent **Trade Unions.**	**For inspection once a year,** free of charge. **A copy to keep** on request, for a reasonable fee.	Within a reasonable time of the request being made.
Scheme Details, including an address for enquiries.	**Members, Prospective Members** and their **Spouses.** **Beneficiaries.** Recognised independent **Trade Unions.**	**Automatically within 13 weeks of joining.** **To others,** on request no more than **once a year.**	Within one month of request. A change in the address for enquiries must be notified to members and beneficiaries within one month. Other changes must be notified to active members, in advance where feasible and in any case within one month.
Estimates of Transfer Values.	**Members.**	On request, no more than **once a year.**	Within two months of request. Leavers need not be told the amount of the transfer value unless they ask for it.

Information	To Be Disclosed to	In What Circumstances	Time Limits and Other Information
Benefit Statements.	**Members.** **Beneficiaries.** **Prospective Members.**	**Automatically** when benefit is due, or changes other than as described in a previous statement. **To Members** of **money purchase schemes automatically** once a year. **To Members**, on request no more than **once a year.**	When benefits become due or are changed, other than as described in a previous statement, within one month. Leavers must be told their rights and options automatically within two months of leaving service. Beneficiaries must be notified of rights and options within two months of trustees being notified of death. Personal representatives of members who have died may request information, which must be provided within two months. Most other information must be provided within two months of request. Prospective members may only request information about the effect of a transfer-in.
Availability of Trustees' Annual Report.	**Members, Prospective Members.** **Beneficiaries.** Recognised independent **Trade Unions.**	**Automatically.**	To active members and trade unions, within one month of the report becoming available. To others, within three months.
Trustees' Annual Report containing: – audited accounts – actuarial statement – trustees' review – investment report.	**Members, Prospective Members.** **Beneficiaries.** Recognised independent **Trade Unions.**	**For inspection, once every 3 years.** (The 5 most recent reports must be available.) **A copy** of the most recent report **to keep** free of charge on request.	Within one month of request. The report must be available within 12 months of the end of the scheme year. The report should include a statement that other information is available and from where it may be obtained.
Actuarial Valuation Report.	**Members, Prospective Members.** **Beneficiaries.** Recognised independent **Trade Unions.**	**For inspection, once every 3 years,** free of charge. **A copy to keep** on request, for a reasonable fee.	As soon as practicable following request. Reports must be obtained within two years of their effective dates and available to members within three months of receipt.

Source: Bacon & Woodrow.

SCHEME DETAILS

Scheme details must include:

- Eligibility and conditions for membership.
- The period of notice which a member must give to leave pensionable service.
- Whether re-entry to pensionable service is permitted, and if so upon what conditions.
- How members' and employer's contributions are calculated, and the extent of the employer's commitment to pay benefits if the scheme has insufficient resources.
- Tax approval and contracted-out status.
- Normal pension age (other than for SDCSs).
- The benefits payable (including discretionary pension increases), how they are calculated, the conditions for payment, and which benefits are funded.
- Details of how any discretions to grant pension increases have been exercised over the past 10 years.
- Whether the trustees accept transfers into the scheme.
- Whether cash equivalents take into account discretionary additional benefits.
- Whether information about the scheme has been given to the registrar of occupational and personal pension schemes.
- The functions and address of the Pensions Ombudsman and the Occupational Pensions Advisory Service (OPAS).
- A statement that further information is available and an address for enquiries.

BENEFIT STATEMENTS

Active members of salary related schemes

If he asks, the member must be given:

- a statement of accrued benefits, or benefits allowing for service up to normal pension age, based on current salary (or, if the trustees prefer, sufficient information to calculate them);
- a statement of the benefits payable if the member were to die in service within one month of the date of receipt of the information (if the scheme is not a SDCS);

the information must include:

(i) the date on which the member's pensionable service commenced;

(ii) the accrual rate or formula for calculating the member's own benefits and any survivors' benefits;

(iii) the amount of the member's current pensionable salary; *and*

(iv) details of how any deduction from benefits (e.g. offset for State pension) is calculated;

- a statement of the rights and options available if the member were to leave pensionable service;
- an estimate of the transfer value available if he were to leave service with an indication of whether an allowance for discretionary benefits (e.g. future pension increases) has been included;
- whether a refund of contributions is available and an estimate of its amount.

All members of money purchase schemes

Statements must be given automatically at least once a year and must show:

- contributions credited to the member before deductions during the immediately preceding scheme year;
- if the scheme was contracted-out during the year, the contributions in respect of the member attributable to:
  - (i) minimum payments made by the employer;
  - (ii) any incentive payments made to the trustees by the DSS;
- premiums paid to insure death before retirement benefits (if the scheme is a SDCS);
- value of protected rights (if any) as at a specified date;
- value of other accrued rights (if any) at a specified date;
- cash equivalents of protected rights and other accrued rights as at the specified dates, if they differ from the values of these rights.

Members and deferred pensioners in other types of scheme which include money purchase benefits are entitled to request the last three items in the list. The trustees need not comply with a request made within a year of providing the information, so if they provide benefit statements automatically once a year, there is no need to respond to one-off requests.

Contracted-out money purchase (COMP) schemes have a special responsibility to members who have used the scheme to contract-out. Members must be told the options they have in respect of all accrued rights, including protected rights, between four and six months before State pension age. If a member's protected rights have not begun to be paid as benefits by six months before his 75th birthday, the scheme must again tell him what options he has.

TRUSTEES' ANNUAL REPORT

The report must include:

- Audited accounts, including auditor's report.
- Actuarial statement and whether or not it is a revised statement.
- Trustees' financial review, reflecting the accounts and actuarial report.
- Names of trustees (and the rules for changing trustees) and names of actuaries, auditors, solicitors, banks and other organisations acting for the trustees. Changes during the year.
- A statement whether each trustee has access to a copy of the statement on pension trust principles issued by the OPB.
- Changes during the year in any of the scheme details.
- Numbers of members and beneficiaries at a date during the year.
- Increases made during the year to pensions and deferred pensions, in excess of those required by law. The extent to which increases were discretionary is to be stated.
- Confirmation that transfer values paid during the year were calculated in accordance with the law, whether any were less than the full value of the member's preserved benefits and, if so, why and when full values are likely to be available.
- Name of investment manager, the extent to which the trustees delegate to him and the basis of his remuneration if all or part of it is paid by the scheme.

- Statement of investment policy and changes made during the year.
- Review of investment performance and of the scheme's assets.
- Self-investment details and steps taken or proposed to reduce excessive self-investment.
- Address for enquiries.
- A copy of the statement which any auditor of the scheme has made on resignation or removal as auditor in the year.
- If there is a discrepancy between contributions paid into the scheme and the amount set out in the rules or recommended by the actuary, how this will be resolved.

AUDITED ACCOUNTS

The trustees must prepare accounts and have them audited by an auditor who is independent of the trustees, the employer and the scheme. Audited accounts must be obtained by the trustees within one year of the scheme year end.

The requirements are similar to those of the Statement of Recommended Practice (SORP) No. 1 on Pension Scheme Accounts, although less detailed. The regulations require it to be stated whether the SORP has been followed.

AUTOMATIC DISCLOSURES IN SPECIAL CIRCUMSTANCES

Trustees must disclose information automatically, rather than on request, in the following circumstances:

- **If any member's contributions have not been passed to the trustees** by three months of the due date, the member must be informed within one month of the information coming to the attention of the trustees.

- **Details of any proposed transfer without the member's consent,** including the value of the rights being transferred, must be provided at least one month before the proposed date of the transfer.

- **If a scheme is being wound-up,** all members (including deferred pensioners) and beneficiaries must be told within one month of the winding-up having commenced. Once the assets have been applied in accordance with the winding-up rules, members and beneficiaries must be told the amounts of their benefits within three months. Information concerning independent trustees must be given to members and beneficiaries on request.

- **If a COMP scheme ceases to be contracted-out** with respect to one or more employments, members must be told within four weeks and certain further information must be given within four months.

DEFINITIONS

Beneficiary. Anyone (other than a member) currently entitled to payment of benefits from the scheme.

COMP Scheme. Contracted-out money purchase scheme.

Members. Active members and former members, including pensioners, who remain entitled to benefits.

Money purchase benefit. Any benefit which is calculated by reference to payments made by or in respect of the member, except average salary benefits.

Money purchase scheme. A scheme providing money purchase benefits only, or money purchase benefits and salary related death-in-service benefits only.

Prospective member. An employee who is not a member but who has the option to become one, or will have the option if he continues in the same employment.

Protected rights. Benefit rights derived from the accumulation of minimum payments (i.e. the joint contracting-out rebate paid to a COMP scheme) and any incentive (if applicable) including any benefits derived from the transfer of protected rights or GMPs from another arrangement *and also* rights to any other money purchase benefits under the scheme unless they are specifically excluded from protected rights by the scheme rules.

Request. A request in writing.

Scheme year. A year specified in the rules of the scheme. If the rules do not specify a scheme year, a period of 12 months commencing on 1 April or such other date as the trustees select.

It can include, where the trustees have selected a new scheme year, a period of more than 6 months but not more than 18 months.

SDCS. Simplified defined contribution scheme.

Trustees. In relation to a scheme which is not established under a trust, means the managers of the scheme. In relation to a scheme established outside the United Kingdom, means the person or body treated by the Board of Inland Revenue for the time being as the administrator of the scheme for the purposes of UK tax approval.

EXEMPTIONS

- Schemes with less than 2 members.
- Schemes providing only death-in-service benefits.
- Schemes neither established in the UK nor with a trustee resident in the UK.
- Unapproved schemes for which approval is not being sought.
- Unfunded schemes and public service pension schemes are not required to obtain audited accounts or an actuarial valuation and statement.
- Public service pension schemes are not required to publish an annual report.

SMALL SELF-ADMINISTERED SCHEMES

Small self-administered schemes (SSASs) were introduced for company controlling directors following the repeal in 1973 of the legislation which disallowed such directors being members of approved occupational pension schemes.

Because of the close relationship between the employer, the trustees and the members of these schemes, often all being the same people, the Pensions Schemes Office (PSO) of the Board of Inland Revenue imposed special requirements. As the popularity of SSASs grew, further restrictions were introduced under the Board's discretionary powers of approval. It was decided in 1987 to limit this discretion by specifying certain requirements in statutory legislation. The result was the Retirement Benefits Schemes (Restriction on Discretion to Approve) (Small Self-administered Schemes) Regulations 1991 which came into force on 5 August 1991.

The Government intends to exempt SSASs where all the members are trustees from the requirement of the Pensions Act 1995 to have internal dispute resolution procedures and, if all trustee decisions have to be made by unanimous agreement, they will also be exempt from the Compensation Scheme requirements (*see Section 20*).

Definition of a SSAS

The Regulations define a SSAS as a scheme which is not invested solely in insurance policies and which has less than 12 members, at least one of whom is related to:

- another member of the scheme; or
- a trustee of the scheme; or
- a partner (if a partnership); or
- if the employer is a company, a member or a person connected with that member who has been a controlling director of the company at any time during the preceding 10 years.

A director of a company is a controlling director if he on his own or with one or more associates beneficially owns or is able to control directly or indirectly 20% or more of the ordinary share capital of the company. An associate in this context is very wide and includes any relative or partner or a trustee of any settlement in which the director or a relative was the settlor.

The Inland Revenue may also treat a scheme with 12 or more members as a SSAS if, for example, some employees on low levels of benefit were included merely to make up numbers.

Trustees

It is a condition of approval of a SSAS that the trustees must include a 'pensioneer trustee'. A pensioneer trustee is an individual or body widely involved with occupational pension schemes, approved by the Inland Revenue to act in such a capacity and who has given the PSO an undertaking not to agree to the termination of the scheme except within the terms of the winding-up rule.

The Government intends to exempt all SSASs from the Pensions Act 1995 requirements to appoint member-nominated trustees, to restrict the scheme actuary from acting as a trustee and, where all the members are trustees, to appoint an independent trustee on employer insolvency (*see Section 20*).

Funding

The funding of a SSAS is closely monitored by the PSO, actuarial reports being required every three years. The PSO will not permit contributions to be paid to a SSAS which are not within the needs of the scheme, as justified in the report. The PSO are, at the time of writing, reconsidering permissible funding arrangements for SSASs.

Death benefits which exceed the value of the member's interest in the SSAS must be separately insured and when a pension becomes payable it must be secured by the purchase of a non-commutable, non-assignable annuity from a life office. Purchase of the annuity for a member can be deferred up to age 75, with the pension being paid directly from the scheme in the interim. In the case of a spouse's or other dependant's pension, the purchase of an annuity may similarly be deferred up to the recipient's 75th birthday or until the deceased member would have reached age 75 if earlier. Where deferral of annuity purchase takes place, further restrictions on the investments apply so as to ensure that the pensions can be maintained.

Investment and borrowing restrictions

In addition to the Regulations restricting the PSO's discretionary powers in respect of SSAS investment and borrowing, Section 20 of the PSO's Practice Notes sets out aspects remaining under PSO discretionary practice in relation to SSASs.

The Regulations also contain the transitional provisions set out below for a SSAS established before, but not approved by, 5 August 1991 and these transitional arrangements also apply to schemes already approved before that date in respect of investments made before 15 July 1991:

- it may retain otherwise disallowed assets if acquired before 15 July 1991;
- it may sell to a scheme member assets acquired before 15 July 1991.

The Occupational Pension Schemes (Investment of Scheme's Resources) Regulations 1992 generally restrict a scheme's investments in 'employer-related investments' to 5% of its assets. These regulations apply to SSASs unless all the members are trustees and the rules of the scheme require written consent of all the members of the scheme to any 'employer-related investments'.

'Employer-related investments' are:

- shares or other securities (including debentures, loan stock, bonds and related certificates) issued by the employer;
- land occupied by, used by or leased to the employer;
- other property used in carrying on the business of the employer;
- loans to the employer, including any contributions due but unpaid.

The table on the following page shows the limits placed on scheme investment and borrowing. Under the SSAS Regulations, the administrators of a scheme are required to notify the PSO and supply relevant documentation within 90 days of certain specified transactions by the trustees.

Loss of approval

The Finance Act 1995 introduced a special tax charge on SSASs which lose their tax approval on or after 2 November 1994. The new tax charge is set at 40% of the value of the funds at the date approval is withdrawn. The legislation does not differentiate between schemes which deliberately lose their approval and unintentional cases. However, the Inland Revenue will give advance warning of the consequences of loss of approval and will give trustees the opportunity and assistance to rectify the matter in all cases.

Type of Investment/Borrowing	Restrictions Under Regulations
Trustee borrowing for investment	3 x aggregate of employer and employee ordinary annual contributions, plus 45% of assets
Any employer-related investment	5% of assets (subject to transitional provisions)[1]
Loans to employer and/or the purchase of shares in the employer[2]	25% of assets, exclusive of transfers-in, for first two years. 50% thereafter[3]
Shares in private company	Must not exceed 30% of the voting rights or entitlement to more than 30% of the dividends
Loans to a member[4]	Not allowed
Purchase or sale of property from or to a member[4]	Not allowed
Purchase or sale of property from or to an employer	Allowable subject to independent professional advice
Personal chattels	Generally, not allowed
Residential property	Allowable only if required for employee to perform duties or if occupied by a person who also occupies connected business premises leased from the trustees[5]

Notes: [1] Unless all the members are trustees and the rules of the scheme require the written consent of all the members of the scheme to any employer-related investments.

[2] Includes associated employers. The Regulations state that a loan may only be made if it is:
    (a) necessary for the employer's business;
    (b) for a fixed term;
    (c) at a commercial rate of interest; *and*
    (d) contains a written agreement to the effect that it will be repaid if the borrower is in breach of the conditions of the loan, ceases to carry on business or becomes insolvent.

[3] The percentages represent the limit applicable to the sum of any outstanding loan and the market value of the shares.

[4] Includes connected persons.

[5] Employee or occupier must not be a connected person.

THE FINANCIAL SERVICES ACT AND PENSION SCHEMES

Introduction

The Act provides that no person shall carry on investment business in the UK unless he is authorised or exempt. Authorisation is generally granted either by the Securities and Investments Board (SIB) or by a Self-Regulating Organisation (SRO). The intention is that those providing any form of investment service should be 'fit and proper' to do so and, in particular, that they should meet standards of honesty, competence and solvency.

Pension schemes

Pension scheme trustees and administrators are clearly concerned with investments in various ways. They may be:

- responsible for the management of the scheme's assets (whether in insurance policies or self-managed investments);
- involved in giving financial advice to scheme members and prospective members;
- involved in arranging investments for individual members, such as insurance company buy-outs.

Each of these activities can be investment business requiring authorisation which will not be a mere formality of registration with an appropriate body. Whether a certain action constitutes investment advice for which authorisation is required can be a complicated issue, particularly when considering relationships between trustees and individual members.

Management of investments

The Act specifically provides (in Section 191) that those engaged in the activity of managing the assets of occupational pension schemes will have to be authorised or exempt, even if (as is the case with many trustees) they are not doing so as a business. But the Act goes on to provide that authorisation will not be required if all day-to-day decisions about the management of investments are taken on their behalf by a person who is himself authorised or exempt.

The Pensions Act 1995 will reinforce these provisions by imposing a requirement on pension scheme trustees to appoint a fund manager who is authorised or exempt. It also defines certain matters on which trustees will be required to obtain investment advice.

DEFINITIONS

Authorised

A person can be authorised by the SIB or by a recognised SRO to carry on investment business if it appears that the applicant is a fit and proper person to carry on the investment business and provide the relevant services.

Exempt

Exempted persons include the Bank of England, Lloyd's and recognised investment exchanges and clearing houses acting in certain respects.

Securities and Investments Board (SIB)

The special body which has substantial regulatory powers delegated to it by the Government under the terms of the Act. It comprises practitioners from a wide variety of investment activities together with independent 'lay members', all appointed jointly by the Government and the Bank of England. They are responsible for the rules putting the principles of investor protection into practice and will apply sanctions to those who break the rules.

Self-Regulating Organisation (SRO)

Bodies set up to provide proper regulation for areas of investment activity. Their rules provide investors with equivalent protection to that provided by the SIB. An authorised member of an SRO recognised by the SIB must act within limits prescribed by that SRO's rules. The SRO for firms with investment management as their activity (including pension funds) is the Investment Management Regulatory Organisation (IMRO). The SRO for the retail sector of the financial services industry is the Personal Investment Authority (PIA).

Investments

For the purposes of the Act, investments include shares, debentures, Government and public securities, options and futures, units in unit trust schemes and long-term insurance contracts. They do not include property or cash deposits held with a bank, building society or licensed deposit taker.

A scheme member's rights under the trusts of an occupational pension scheme are not investments, but his rights under a personal pension scheme will be if the underlying assets include assets which are classified as investments.

Investment business

According to the Act the following activities constitute investment business:

- dealing in investments;
- managing investments;
- arranging deals in investments;
- offering investment advice.

The Act requires authorisation for these activities if they are carried out as a business but it does not, however, define 'business'. Dictionary definitions of business give as normal meanings 'trade, profession, habitual occupation or commercial activity'. Legal definitions are as varied as they are frequent.

PENSION COSTS IN COMPANY ACCOUNTS

ACCOUNTING FOR PENSION COSTS: SSAP 24

Statement of Standard Accounting Practice No. 24: 'Accounting for Pension Costs' (SSAP 24) was issued in May 1988 by the Accounting Standards Committee. Copies are available from Accountancy Books, PO Box 620, Central Milton Keynes, MK9 2JX.

The main purpose of the Standard is to ensure that a company's accounts show a 'true and fair' figure for the cost to the company of providing pension benefits. Prior to the Standard, normal practice was simply to charge the amount of contributions paid, which may not always have been a true reflection of pension cost.

In 1995 the Accounting Standards Board issued a discussion paper outlining proposed changes to SSAP 24 (*see 'Proposals for Change' below*).

A summary of the Standard is set out below.

SCHEMES COVERED

The Standard applies to all schemes, both legal or contractual arrangements and others, where, as a result of established custom and practice, there is an implicit commitment by the employer to provide pensions. It applies to both unfunded and funded arrangements, whether insured or self-administered. The Standard mainly addresses pension schemes, but its principles have also been extended to other post-retirement benefits (e.g. medical expenses cover) for accounting periods ending on or after 23 December 1994.

EFFECTIVE DATE

As far as pension costs of UK companies are concerned, the Standard has applied to accounting periods beginning on or after 1 July 1988.

PENSION COST

The pension cost charged in the company accounts must meet the accounting objective set by the Standard:

> "*the employer should recognise the expected cost of providing pensions on a systematic and rational basis over the period during which he derives benefit from the employees' services.*"

For defined contribution schemes, the charge against profits must be the amount of contributions due in respect of the accounting period.

For defined benefit schemes, the charge against profits is intended to be a best estimate of the cost of pension benefits for the current employees. Because these benefits will be paid many years hence, this estimate (or **'regular cost'**) will need to be revised from time to time to take account both of actual past experience, where this differed from the basis of the estimate, and of changed expectations about the future. These revisions (or **'variations'**) are reflected not by changing past figures retrospectively, but by adjusting current and future pension cost.

The Standard requires the effect of most variations to be spread over future service lives with the company of the present members of the scheme.

There are some adjustments to regular cost, such as the effect of a refund of surplus or a redundancy exercise which are, however, treated differently. In particular, full credit may be taken for a refund of surplus in the accounting period in which it is received. The table below gives details.

SUMMARY OF TREATMENT OF VARIATION FROM REGULAR COST

Source of Variation	Immediate Credit	Spread Over Future Service Lives
Changes in actuarial assumptions or valuation method	No	Yes
Retrospective benefit improvements (other than pension increases)	No	Yes
Refund of surplus subject to 40% tax under Finance Act 1986	If desired, credit may be taken for the net refund in the period received	If desired
Events allowed for in the actuarial assumptions differ in magnitude from those assumed (e.g. better than expected investment return)	No	Yes
* Pension increases for which no allowance has been made in the actuarial assumptions used for accounting purposes; ex gratia pensions	Capital cost accounted for in the period in which increase granted (to the extent that the cost is not covered by surplus)	No
A major event, outside the normal scope of the actuarial assumptions, giving rise to a deficiency	May account for over a short period but only if prudence dictates this and significant extra contributions to the scheme are actually paid	If no significant extra contributions are paid to the scheme
Sale or termination of an operation	Immediate recognition aggregating with other financial effects of that event	No
Other significant reduction in workforce resulting in a surplus (or deficiency) which is reflected in a change to the actual contributions being paid	Accounted for over the period over which the contributions actually change (e.g. over the period of contribution holiday); pension augmentations to be treated as pension increases (*see above*)	No

Note: *The preferred treatment of pension increases is to allow for them in the actuarial assumptions used for accounting purposes if they are likely to be granted on a regular basis.

Source: Bacon & Woodrow.

DISCLOSURE

The Standard requires companies to disclose a range of information about their pension schemes in their accounts. The objective is to provide an accurate picture of the financial impact of the pension arrangements.

The information to be given about a particular pension scheme depends on whether it is a defined contribution scheme or a defined benefit scheme. A defined benefit scheme is a scheme in which the rules specify the benefits to be paid and the scheme is financed accordingly. A defined contribution scheme is a scheme in which the benefits are directly determined by the value of contributions paid in respect of each member.

The accounts must say which of these two kinds of scheme is being operated. Schemes which are a mixture of both types should be treated according to the underlying substance of the scheme; i.e. a limited money purchase guarantee in a final salary scheme would not justify its treatment as a defined contribution scheme.

Defined contribution schemes

For a defined contribution scheme (for example, a COMP scheme) the disclosures are relatively simple:

- the accounting policy;
- the amount of contributions due for the accounting period (which may differ from those actually paid);
- any outstanding or prepaid contributions at the balance sheet date.

Defined benefit schemes

For a defined benefit scheme, the information to be disclosed is more extensive:

Accounting policy

A statement of accounting policy is required, which would be expected to remain unchanged for a number of years. The accounting treatment adopted for certain events (such as refunds of surplus) must also be disclosed.

Funding policy

Whether or not the scheme is funded must be stated. If the funding policy differs from the accounting policy (for example, by making no allowance for discretionary pension increases or by spreading variations over a different period) the funding policy should be disclosed.

Pension cost charge for the period

The pension cost must be determined under the principles set out in the Standard, which may lead to a charge different from the actual contributions paid. Explanations should be given of significant changes in the charge compared with that shown for the previous accounting period. An indication should also be given of any significant changes in future pension cost expected under the particular actuarial approach used.

Provisions or prepayments

These balance sheet items arise if there has been any difference between the pension cost charged in the accounts and the contributions (and/or direct pension payments) actually made in the present or previous accounting periods.

Actuarial advice

It should be stated whether the pension cost and any prepayment or provision are assessed in accordance with the advice of an actuary and, if so, when the most recent actuarial review used to calculate them was carried out. (Reviews need not be carried out every year.) If the actuary is an employee or officer of the company, this must be disclosed.

Actuarial method and assumptions

The actuarial valuation method and significant assumptions used in the calculation of pension cost must be disclosed and any change in the method must be disclosed and the effect quantified.

Market value of assets

The market value of the scheme assets at the date of the most recent actuarial review of the scheme for accounting purposes should be stated.

Level of funding

The level of funding of the scheme on an on-going basis should be quoted in percentage terms. Although the Standard is not completely clear, it is generally accepted that this means:

$$\frac{actuarial\ value\ of\ assets}{value\ of\ past\ service\ liabilities}$$
$$(including\ allowance\ for\ future\ pay\ rises)$$

expressed as a percentage. Appropriate comments should be made if there is any material surplus or deficiency (i.e. the ratio differs materially from 100%).

Accrued benefits deficiency

If there is a deficiency in the scheme in relation to current accrued benefits, the cash amount of this deficiency should be disclosed. In assessing the deficiency, if any, the market value of the assets will usually be compared with the value of accrued benefits based on pensionable service to, and pensionable earnings at, the date of the valuation, including revaluation on the statutory basis or such higher basis as has been promised. If there is a deficiency the action, if any, being taken to deal with it, both now and in the future, should be disclosed.

Changes to pension arrangements

Details of the expected effects on future pension costs of any material changes in the pension arrangements should be given.

Additional payments

Any commitment by the employer to make additional payments over a limited number of years should be disclosed.

PROPOSALS FOR CHANGE

In June 1995, the Accounting Standards Board (ASB) issued a Discussion Paper – "Pension Costs in the Employer's Financial Statements" – which considers possible changes to SSAP 24. An Exposure Draft will follow, with a new Financial Reporting Standard expected sometime in 1996.

The main thrusts of the proposed changes are:

- to reduce the number of options available to companies under SSAP 24, and therefore secure greater consistency;
- to focus the disclosure requirements to ensure that pension costs are properly explained in companies' accounts.

The ASB's preferred approach is to fine-tune the current SSAP 24 in the light of these objectives. However, the Paper also considers a more fundamental change, favoured by a significant minority of the ASB, with the emphasis on current costs, calculated using current market-based assumptions instead of using long-term actuarial assumptions.

Main changes under the preferred approach

- A single actuarial method should be used for calculating normal pension cost – the projected unit method.

- Full allowance should be made for discretionary pension increases.

- Benefit improvements for former employees should be recognised in full immediately.

- Amortisation of surplus or deficiency must be on a straight line method.

- The outstanding cost of retroactive benefit improvements should not be reamortised at each actuarial valuation (unlike experience gains or losses).

- Gains or losses from settlements or curtailments (e.g. bulk transfers, buy-outs, scheme closures or large scale redundancies) should be recognised immediately.

- Disclosures should be significantly increased and should include a reconciliation of scheme assets and liabilities with company balance sheet items, and a table showing movements in the unrecognised surplus or deficiency in the scheme.

Differences under the alternative approach

- Surplus or deficiency would be measured relative to the <u>market</u> values (not the <u>actuarial</u> values) of assets, and would be recognised immediately, rather than gradually, in the employer's balance sheet.

- Surplus or deficiency would be recognised through the profit and loss account if it related to real changes in past service benefits, or through the statement of total recognised gains and losses if it related to changes in assumptions or to experience gains/losses.

- There would be disclosure of the cumulative surplus or deficiency recognised through the statement of total recognised gains or losses, plus a 5 year record of the development of the cumulative surplus or deficiency as a percentage of accrued pension liability.

DISCLOSURE OF DIRECTORS' PENSIONS

COMPANIES ACT 1985

The Companies Act 1985 requires company accounts to make certain disclosures relating to directors' remuneration, including their pension provision. These disclosures include:

- the aggregate amount of directors' emoluments, including pension contributions;

- the aggregate amount of directors' and former directors' pensions, but only if these pensions have <u>not</u> been sufficiently funded by pension contributions.

GREENBURY COMMITTEE REPORT

The Greenbury Committee was established in January 1995 with the following terms of reference:

"To identify good practice in determining Directors' remuneration and prepare a Code of such practice for use by UK PLCs."

The Committee's report was published in July 1995. It recommends a number of areas where the disclosure of directors' remuneration should be tightened, including specific reference to pension provision and costs. A summary of the recommendation relating to pensions is given below:

- To avoid potential conflicts of interest, the company's policy on directors' remuneration, including pension rights, should be determined by a remuneration committee of non-executive directors. The policy should be set out in a report each year to the shareholders, to form part of the company's Annual Reports and Accounts.

- The remuneration committee should consider what elements of remuneration should be pensionable. It is recommended that in general neither annual bonuses nor benefits in kind should be pensionable: if they are pensionable, the report should explain why.

- The report should include full details of all elements in the remuneration package of each individual director by name.

- The report should identify the value of the pension entitlements earned by each individual during the year. It is expected that the value will be based on that part of the cash equivalent transfer value at the year-end that relates to the incremental benefit entitlement generated over the year. It is expected that the Stock Exchange listing rules will be amended to incorporate this disclosure requirement.

PENSIONS ACT 1995

The Pensions Act 1995 received Royal Assent on 19 July 1995. This Act makes the changes in pensions law which have been under discussion since the formation of the Goode Committee in 1992. It also contains a number of provisions aimed at providing equal treatment for men and women in both State and private pension arrangements (*see Section 14*) and makes radical changes to the present system for contracting-out of SERPS (*see Section 12*).

The majority of the changes will not come into effect before 1997, and there is a great deal of procedural detail which has yet to be decided: the Act contains more than 200 references to potential regulations and about 35 statutory instruments are expected to be made over the next year.

A summary of some of the main provisions contained in the Act, together with further indications of the probable eventual regulations based on DSS consultation documents, is set out below.

MEMBER-NOMINATED TRUSTEES

The Act gives the membership of most schemes the right to elect one-third of the trustees, with a minimum of two (where the number of scheme members is less than 100, the minimum is one). Rules for nominating and appointing member-nominated trustees must be drawn up by the existing trustees. The employer may, however, put forward a proposal for the continuation of existing arrangements, or the adoption of new arrangements, for consideration by the membership. If the employer's proposal is not rejected it must be put into effect.

There will be a statutory procedure for obtaining views of scheme members on any of the proposed rules for nomination and/or appointment of trustees and on any alternative proposals put forward by the employer.

SUPERVISION

A new regulatory body – the Occupational Pensions Regulatory Authority (OPRA) – has wide ranging powers to monitor and intervene in the running of occupational pension schemes. OPRA will replace the Occupational Pensions Board and will be funded from a general levy on pension schemes. The scheme actuary and the scheme auditor must report immediately to OPRA if they believe that the employer or the trustees or any of the scheme's advisers are not performing their proper duties, under a procedure known as 'whistle blowing'. OPRA will be able to impose sanctions on trustees, employers and professional advisers who fail in their duties:

- prohibition, suspension or disqualification of trustees;
- disqualification to act as scheme actuary/auditor;
- a maximum fine of £5,000 for individuals and £50,000 for corporate bodies, which may not be paid from trust funds.

In addition, the Act defines a number of criminal offences for which the penalty may be a fine or imprisonment.

MINIMUM FUNDING REQUIREMENT (MFR)

All approved schemes (except pure money purchase schemes and public sector schemes) will be required to maintain sufficient assets to cover guaranteed benefits and to take remedial action if the level of cover falls. The MFR will be phased in over the 5 years from April 1997 to April 2002. Schemes would then have until 2007 before they would be expected to have a 100% MFR funding level.

Actuarial valuation and certificate, and contribution schedule

The trustees must obtain a valuation at least once every three years, to determine the funding level and to provide the basis for them to agree a contribution schedule with the employer. This schedule, showing the rates to be paid by the employer and the members, must be maintained by the trustees and the rates must be certified by the actuary as being adequate to maintain (or restore) a 100% MFR funding level throughout the next 5 years. Additionally, an annual certificate must be obtained, and disclosed to members, giving the actuary's opinion on whether the MFR is likely to be met throughout the 5 year period, based on the contributions payable. If the actuary considers that the contributions will not be adequate to meet the MFR then a new valuation must be made within 6 months, unless the trustees and employer can agree revised contribution rates without it.

Money purchase schemes will be required to maintain a contribution schedule even where other MFR provisions do not apply.

Valuation of assets and liabilities

It is expected that scheme liabilities will be assessed on a new cash equivalent basis using equity-related returns for those at least 10 years away from retirement, phasing in to gilt returns at retirement. Very large schemes will be able to value some of their pensioner liabilities by reference to equity rather than gilt yields. Assets will be taken at market value, with a slight degree of smoothing.

Funding level below 90%

Where a valuation shows a funding level below 90%, the employer will normally be required to restore the funding level to 90% within 12 months, as well as agreeing contribution rates sufficient to achieve the full 100% level within 5 years.

WINDING-UP

New priorities will override existing scheme provisions on a partial or total winding-up, for all schemes subject to the MFR. Transitional provisions are expected to apply between 1997 and 2007, so that GMPs retain their current high priority in the short-term. The new order of priorities will be:

- AVC benefits;
- pensions in payment (excluding pension increases);
- accrued pension rights (excluding pension increases);
- future pension increases; *and lastly*
- any balance of liabilities in accordance with scheme rules.

Any shortfall is a debt on the employer. Any surplus must first be used to provide LPI increases on all benefits (*see below*). Refunds to the employer, if allowed under scheme rules, can only be paid after the trustees have considered other possible uses, and have given notice to members that they intend to make the payment to the employer. Where such a payment is not permitted under scheme rules, the trustees must first use any surplus to increase benefits up to prescribed limits – any remaining surplus may then be repaid to the employer.

INVESTMENT

Trustees have complete power to invest scheme assets as if they were their own, subject to their duty of care and any scheme restrictions. Their decision-making powers may be delegated to an external fund manager, who in turn may sub-delegate part of the portfolio to another fund manager. The trustees as a whole remain responsible for any actions taken, but they need not be liable for the fund manager's actions so long as they have taken steps to ensure that he has appropriate knowledge and experience, and is acting competently and in accordance with the written statement of investment principles.

Statement of investment principles

This statement, which must be prepared by the trustees after taking advice from an experienced investment adviser and after having consulted the employer, must cover, amongst other things:

- the trustees' policy on meeting the MFR;
- the kinds of investment to be held and the balance between them;
- risk and expected return;
- realisation of assets.

The fund manager must have regard to the need for diversification and the suitability of any proposed investment.

CONDUCT OF BUSINESS

Appointing advisers

The trustees must appoint an actuary and an auditor, neither of whom may then act as a trustee to the scheme. The auditor may be either an individual or a firm, but the actuary must be an individual. The trustees must appoint a fund manager authorised or exempt under the Financial Services Act 1986 (FSA) if the scheme has investments covered by the FSA. They may also appoint a legal adviser.

Dealing with disputes

Trustees must appoint an individual to rule on disputes relating to the scheme. The trustees may then be asked to reconsider the dispute, at the complainant's request, and decide whether to uphold or overturn the ruling.

The Pensions Ombudsman's jurisdiction is to be widened to cover disputes between:

- actual or potential beneficiaries of occupational or personal pension schemes and those responsible for the scheme's management;
- trustees or managers of an occupational scheme and the employer; *and*
- trustees or managers of different occupational schemes.

BENEFIT CHANGES

Pension increases

All approved pension schemes will be required to provide Limited Price Indexation (LPI) on all pension payments for service after 5 April 1997, other than those derived from additional voluntary contributions (whether in-house or free-standing). The annual LPI increase is 5% or the increase in RPI if less and any increase granted in excess of the minimum required may be offset against the increase due in the following year.

Transfer values

A new system of transfer value quotation and payment is to be introduced, with strict timescales. The aim is to ensure that, where a member of a salary-related scheme does not delay his decision unduly, the transfer value paid is the amount originally quoted. Transfer values from salary related schemes will be guaranteed for three months from the effective date of calculation.

Most members who left their pension schemes before 1 January 1986 will, for the first time, have a <u>right</u> to take a transfer value.

Transfer values are expected to be required to be at least equal to the new cash equivalent under the MFR.

Divorce settlements

Courts throughout the UK will be required to take pension rights into account when making financial provision orders in divorce settlements. The new provisions will only apply to new settlements effected on or after 6 April 1996 and then only to payments due on or after 6 April 1997.

The value of someone's pension rights will be taken as the cash equivalent. A settlement may be made by redistributing other assets so as to keep the pension rights intact. Alternatively, an order may be made requiring the trustees or managers of the scheme to make payments of part of the member's pension or lump sum to the divorced spouse once the member's pension commences. These orders may be transferred to the new scheme or policy if the member makes a transfer.

COMPENSATION SCHEME

A pension scheme which has 'lost' assets as a result of an offence (such as theft or fraud) committed after 6 April 1997 may apply for compensation to a new Pensions Compensation Board if the employer is insolvent.

The amount of any compensation payments will not exceed 90% of the amount 'lost' (including interest at a prescribed rate) and will also be limited to the amount required to restore the assets to 90% of the liabilities.

The Compensation Scheme will be funded by a levy on occupational pension schemes.

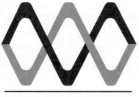

NEW DEVELOPMENTS IN LAST YEAR

2 November 1994:   **New tax charge** of 40% of the value of the fund levied on small self-administered schemes which lose their tax approval.

23 February 1995:   The Inland Revenue's requirements for an **overseas scheme to be treated as 'corresponding'** tightened.

31 March 1995:   The Inland Revenue issued a Statement of Practice concerning the **taxation** implications of receipts of **commission** on the sale of insurance products and **personal pension** schemes.

1 April 1995:   Introduction of **annual levy payments** in place of triennial payments (with transitional arrangements).

13 April 1995:   **Incapacity Benefit** replaces Sickness and Invalidity Benefit.

20 April 1995:   Publication of PIA guidance for **identifying, assessing and dealing with cases of mis-sold personal pensions** for opt-outs and non-joiners.

31 May 1995:   The Equal Access Regulations amended to **prohibit 'indirect' discrimination** in access to pension schemes.

22 June 1995:   Accounting Standards Board (ASB) issued a Discussion Paper on a **successor to SSAP 24.**

29 June 1995:   The House of Lords upheld the decision to vary the pension scheme in the case of **Brooks v Brooks**.

30 June 1995:   Personal pension policyholders able to **defer annuity purchase** on retirement, under provisions of Finance Act 1995.

19 July 1995:   Minimum contributions must be allocated to member's account within three months of being paid to the scheme to **qualify as an appropriate personal pension.**

19 July 1995:   **Pensions Act 1995** given Royal Assent, most provisions to come into effect in 1997 *(see Section 20)*.

SIGNIFICANT PENSION DATES

AVCs

08.04.87	(i) New AVCs cannot be commuted for cash.
	(ii) AVCs can be varied more readily.
26.10.87	FSAVCs available.
06.04.88	Schemes must offer AVC facilities giving reasonable value for money.
27.07.89	FSAVC 'headroom checks' no longer required where contributions do not exceed £2,400p.a.
March 1991	Refunds of surplus AVCs permitted (subject to tax charge).
27.12.93	Regulations on refunds of surplus AVCs effective.
Feb. 1994	FSAVC benefits separated from payment of main scheme benefits.

DISCLOSURE AND ACCOUNTING

May 1986	SORP 1 effective.
01.11.86	Disclosure requirements introduced.
01.07.88	SSAP24 effective for accounting periods from 01.07.88.
15.12.88	FAS 87/8 effective for accounting periods from 15.12.88 (15.12.86 for US plans).
28.09.92	Time limits for disclosure introduced.

EQUAL TREATMENT

06.04.78	Equal access to pension schemes for men and women.
07.11.87	Sex Discrimination Act 1986 came into force: compulsory retirement ages must be the same for men and women.
06.04.88	Protected Rights annuities must be on unisex basis.
17.05.90	Barber judgment (as clarified by later cases and Article 119 protocol): occupational pensions are pay, and benefits in respect of service after 17.05.90 must be equal (unless claims lodged before this date). Applicable to survivors' pensions, but not to actuarial factors in funded defined benefit schemes.
23.06.94	Maternity and family leave provisions of Social Security Act 1989 brought into effect. Benefits during periods of paid maternity absence must continue to accrue based on notional full salary.
16.10.94	All employment rights (other than pay) to be maintained during statutory maternity absence.
31.05.95	(i) Requirement that terms for access to pension schemes can not discriminate between men and women either directly or indirectly introduced into UK law (ECJ had ruled on 28.09.94 that claims could be backdated to 08.04.76 subject to time restrictions under national laws).
	(ii) Claims for backdated membership restricted; cost of claims for post 31.05.95 service to be met, in full, by employer.

IR APPROVAL AND LIMITS

06.04.70	New code approval available.
06.04.73	New code compulsory for new schemes and amended existing schemes.
05.04.80	New code for all approved schemes accepting contributions.
17.03.87	Revised limits for new members on or after 17.03.87.
06.04.87	Controls on surplus.
06.04.88	Tax on refunds to members increased from 10% to 20%.
06.04.88	Membership must be voluntary.
01.07.88	Personal pensions available.
14.03.89 (& 01.06.89)	1989 IR limits regime introduced for members joining newly established schemes on or after 14.03.89 and existing schemes on or after 01.06.89.
27.07.89	Concurrent membership of approved and unapproved schemes permissible.
31.08.91	Changes in PSO practices, including 12:1 conversion factor; relaxation of retained benefits tests; other minor changes.
29.11.91	New PN for new schemes.
04.02.94	Deferral of SSAS annuity purchase until pensioner reaches age 75 permitted.
02.11.94	A tax of 40% of value of the fund levied on SSASs which lose their approval.
30.06.95	Deferral of annuity purchase and income withdrawal permitted for personal pensions.

PROTECTING MEMBERS

29.04.88	Financial Services Act 1986 effective.
17.08.90	No refund to employer unless LPI given.
12.11.90	Independent trustee on insolvency.
02.04.91	Pensions Ombudsman in operation.
May 1991	Pension Schemes Registry established.
31.07.91	First levy due.
09.03.92	Self-investment restrictions effective.
29.06.92	Debt on employer on winding-up of pension scheme.

STATE SCHEME AND CONTRACTING-OUT

06.04.75	Benefits under Graduated Scheme cease to accrue.
06.04.78	Start of SERPS and contracting-out.
05.04.83	Trustees liable for ARPs/PRPs.
01.01.85	Anti-franking introduced for leavers on or after 01.01.85.
01.01.86	Transfer Premiums may be paid.
01.11.86	Contracting-out quality test removed.
06.04.87	(i) Contracting-out via Personal Pension could be backdated to 06.04.87.
	(ii) Trustees liable for CEPs/LRPs.

06.04.88	(i) SERPS benefits reduced for persons retiring after 2000. (ii) GMP accrual rates reduced. (iii) GMPs accrued after 06.04.88 must receive 3% increase from scheme. (iv) Fixed rate GMP revaluation for future leavers reduced to 7.5%. (v) Widowers' GMPs introduced. (vi) Money purchase contracting-out introduced. (vii) 2% incentive payments introduced.
17.05.90	Protected rights under COMPs may commence at any age between 60 and 65.
06.04.93	(i) Revised contracting-out terms. (ii) Fixed rate GMP revaluation for future leavers reduced to 7%. (iii) 2% incentive payments ceased; 1% incentive payments introduced for personal pension contributors aged 30 or over.
19.07.95	State pension age for women changed to 65, with transitional provisions.

TRANSFERS, PRESERVATION AND REVALUATION

06.04.75	Leavers on or after 06.04.75 aged at least 26 and with 5 years' qualifying service entitled to preserved benefits.
01.01.86	(i) Statutory right to cash equivalent for leavers on or after 01.01.86. Non-GMP deferred pensions of such leavers accrued from 01.01.85 to be revalued, broadly at lesser of 5% p.a. or price inflation. (ii) Age 26 requirement for preservation dropped.
06.04.88	Minimum period of qualifying service for entitlement to preserved benefits amended to 2 years, for leavers on or after 06.04.88.
01.01.91	Leavers on or after 01.01.91 receive revaluations on whole non-GMP deferred pension.
29.07.94	Protected Rights may be transferred to a contracted-out occupational scheme of which the individual has previously been a member.

UNAPPROVED BENEFITS

27.07.89	Membership of unapproved schemes permitted to provide benefits on top of those from approved schemes.
01.11.91	Taxation of ex gratia lump sum benefits other than on genuine redundancy or as compensation for loss of office.
01.12.93	Taxation of lump-sum benefits from offshore funded unapproved schemes.

ABBREVIATIONS IN COMMON USE

ABI	Association of British Insurers
ACA	Association of Consulting Actuaries
ACT	Advance Corporation Tax
AGM	Annual General Meeting
APB	Auditing Practices Board
APC	Auditing Practices Committee
APL	Association of Pension Lawyers
APPS	Appropriate Personal Pension Scheme
APT	Association of Pensioneer Trustees
ARP	Accrued Rights Premium
ASB	Accounting Standards Board
ASC	Accounting Standards Committee
AVCs	Additional Voluntary Contributions
BIIBA	British Insurance & Investment Brokers Association
CA	Certified Amount
CA	Companies Act
CBI	Confederation of British Industry
CCA	Current Cost Accounting
CCAB	Consultative Committee of Accounting Bodies
CEA	Comité Européen des Assurances
CEP	Contributions Equivalent Premium
CGT	Capital Gains Tax
CII	Chartered Insurance Institute
CIMPS	Contracted-In Money Purchase Scheme
CIR	Commissioners of Inland Revenue
COE	Contracted-Out Employment
COEG	Contracted-Out Employments Group
COMPS	Contracted-Out Money Purchase Scheme
COPRP	Contracted-Out Protected Rights Premium
COSRS	Contracted-Out Salary Related Scheme
CPA	Compulsory Purchase Annuity
CT	Corporation Tax
CTT	Capital Transfer Tax
DSS	Department of Social Security
DTD	Definitive Trust Deed
EC	European Community
ECON	Employer's Contracting-Out Number
ED	Exposure Draft
EF	Earnings Factor
EGM	Extraordinary General Meeting

EOC	Equal Opportunities Commission
EPB	Equivalent Pension Benefit
FA	Finance Act
FIMBRA	Financial Intermediaries Managers and Brokers Regulatory Association
FRS	Financial Reporting Standard
FSA	Financial Services Act
FSAVCs	Free-Standing Additional Voluntary Contributions
GAD	Government Actuary's Department
GDP	Gross Domestic Product
GMP	Guaranteed Minimum Pension
GN	Guidance Notes
GPPP	Group Personal Pension Plan
HMSO	Her Majesty's Stationery Office
ICTA	Income and Corporation Taxes Act
IHT	Inheritance Tax
IMRO	Investment Management Regulatory Organisation
IPA	Individual Pension Arrangement
IR	Inland Revenue
ITD	Interim Trust Deed
JOM	Joint Office Memorandum
LAUTRO	Life Assurance and Unit Trust Regulatory Organisation
LEL	Lower Earnings Limit
LIC	Life Insurance Council of the ABI
LPI	Limited Price Indexation
LRP	Limited Revaluation Premium
MFR	Minimum Funding Requirement
MLI	Market Level Indicator
NAPF	National Association of Pension Funds
NBV	Net Book Value
NPA	Normal Pension Age
NPD	Normal Pension Date
NRA	Normal Retirement Age
NRD	Normal Retirement Date
OPAS	Occupational Pensions Advisory Service
OPB	Occupational Pensions Board
OPRA	Occupational Pensions Regulatory Authority
PAYE	Pay-As-You-Earn
PAYG	Pay-As-You-Go
PDI	Prolonged Disability Insurance
PHI	Permanent Health Insurance
PIA	Personal Investment Authority
PIL	Payment in Lieu
PLA	Purchased Life Annuity

PMI	The Pensions Management Institute
PN	Practice Notes
PPPRP	Personal Pension Protected Rights Premium
PPS	Personal Pension Scheme
PRAG	Pensions Research Accountants Group
PRP	Pensioners Rights Premium
PSA	Pension Schemes Act
PSO	Pension Schemes Office
PTRAS	Pension Tax Relief at Source
PUP	Paid-Up Pension
ROPP	Rebate Only Personal Pension
RPB	Recognised Professional Body
RPI	Retail Prices Index
SCON	Scheme Contracted-Out Number
SDCS	Simplified Defined Contribution Scheme
SERPS	State Earnings Related Pension Scheme
SFA	Securities and Futures Authority
SFO	Superannuation Funds Office of the Inland Revenue
SFSS	Simplified Final Salary Scheme
SI	Statutory Instrument
SIB	Securities and Investments Board
SIPP	Self-Invested Personal Pension
SORP	Statement of Recommended Practice
SPA	State Pensionable Age
SPC	Society of Pension Consultants
SR	Statutory Regulations
SR&O	Statutory Regulations & Orders
SRO	Self-Regulating Organisation
SSA	Social Security Act
SSAP	Statement of Standard Accounting Practice
SSAPS	Small Self-Administered Pension Scheme
SSAS	Small Self-Administered Scheme
SSB	Short Service Benefit
SSP	State Scheme Pension
SSP	Statutory Sick Pay
SSPA	Social Security Pensions Act
TCN	Third Country National
TUC	Trades Union Congress
TPI	Tax and Prices Index
UEL	Upper Earnings Limit
VAT	Value Added Tax
WGMP	Widow's/Widower's Guaranteed Minimum Pension

Source: PMI/PRAG: *Pensions Terminology: a glossary for pension schemes – revised and updated.* Fourth edition 1992, with additions by Bacon & Woodrow.

GLOSSARY OF TERMS

Bold Text:	Cross references that it is felt might improve the understanding of the term concerned.
Italicised Text:	Terms which, whilst not forming part of the basic definition, provide the reader with additional guidance.

The following abbreviations have been used throughout the text:

DSS	Department of Social Security	S	Section (of an Act)
FA	Finance Act	SSA 73	Social Security Act, 1973
FSA 86	Financial Services Act, 1986	SSA 86	Social Security Act, 1986
ICTA 88	Income and Corporation Taxes Act, 1988	SSA 90	Social Security Act, 1990
JOM	Joint Office Memorandum	SSAP 24	Statement of Standard Accounting Practice 24
OPB	Occupational Pensions Board	SSPA 75	Social Security Pensions Act, 1975
PSO	Pension Schemes Office	SORP 1	Statement of Recommended Practice 1

Note: The Pension Schemes Act 1993, consolidating earlier Social Security legislation relating to pension schemes, came into force on 7 February 1994. For the time being, however, references to earlier legislation have been retained in the following definitions.

DEFINITIONS

20% DIRECTOR   A term sometimes used to refer to a **controlling director**.

ACCELERATED ACCRUAL   Provision by a scheme of an accrual rate greater than one sixtieth of pensionable earnings for each year of pensionable service. Also often used as an alternative term for **uplifted 60ths**.

ACCRUAL RATE   The rate at which pension benefit builds up as pensionable service is completed in a **defined benefit scheme**.

ACCRUED BENEFITS   The benefits for service up to a given point in time, whether **vested rights** or not. They may be calculated in relation to current earnings or projected earnings.

Allowance may also be made for revaluation and/or pension increases required by the scheme rules or legislation.

ACCRUED BENEFITS VALUATION METHOD   A **valuation method** in which the **actuarial liability** at the valuation date relates to:

(a) the benefits for current and deferred pensioners and their dependants, allowing where appropriate for future increases, *and*

(b) the **accrued benefits** for members in service on the valuation date.

A recommended contribution rate may allow for earnings and service projected to the end of a specified period (the control period). In that case allowance may be made for replacing members assumed to leave during that period.

ACCRUED RIGHTS A term sometimes used to describe **accrued benefits**.

The term is given specific definitions for the purposes of preservation (SSA 73), contracting-out and the Disclosure Regulations (SSPA 75).

ACCRUED RIGHTS PREMIUM (ARP) A type of **state scheme premium** which may be paid for a member below **state pensionable age** when a scheme which is contracted-out by reference to the provision of a **GMP** ceases to be contracted-out. In return for the ARP, the state scheme will take over the obligation to provide a **GMP**.

ACTIVE MEMBER A member of a pension scheme who is at present accruing benefits under that scheme in respect of current service.

ACTUARIAL ASSUMPTIONS The set of assumptions as to rates of return, inflation, increase in earnings, mortality etc., used by the actuary in an actuarial valuation or other actuarial calculations.

ACTUARIAL BASIS A term commonly used to mean valuation method and/or actuarial assumptions.

ACTUARIAL CERTIFICATE A certificate given by an actuary, and arising out of actuarial work.

Particular examples are:
(a) the certificate in respect of the OPB solvency test which is required for some contracted-out schemes;
(b) the certificate given to the PSO in connection with the rules for dealing with pension scheme surpluses under ICTA 88.

ACTUARIAL DEFICIENCY The excess of the **actuarial liability** over the **actuarial value of assets**, on the basis of the **valuation method** used.

*If an actuarial report refers to a surplus or deficiency, it must be studied to ascertain precisely what assets and liabilities have been taken into account. In a stricter sense, the terms surplus and deficiency might be used in relation to the results of a **discontinuance valuation.***

ACTUARIAL INCREASE An enhancement of benefits to compensate for the deferment of pension beyond the **normal pension date**.

ACTUARIAL LIABILITY The value placed on the liability of a pension fund for outgoings due after the **valuation date**.

*See **prospective benefits valuation method** and **accrued benefits valuation method.***

ACTUARIAL REDUCTION A reduction made to a member's accrued pension benefits in order to offset any additional cost arising from their payment in advance of the **normal pension date**.

ACTUARIAL REPORT A report on an actuarial valuation, or actuarial advice on the financial effects of changes in a pension scheme.

A report on an actuarial valuation must conform to actuarial guidance issued by the Institute and the Faculty of Actuaries.

ACTUARIAL STATEMENT The statement required by the Disclosure Regulations to be included in the **annual report**. It must show in the prescribed form the security of the accrued and prospective rights of members and be signed by an actuary.

ACTUARIAL SURPLUS The excess of the **actuarial value of assets** over the **actuarial liability** on the basis of the valuation method used. *See notes under **actuarial deficiency.***

ACTUARIAL UNDERTAKING A name commonly used for an undertaking given in a prescribed form by an employer to inform the actuary whether any of the specified events, which are likely to invalidate any certificate required by the OPB for contracting-out purposes, have occurred.

ACTUARIAL VALUATION An investigation by an actuary into the ability of a pension scheme to meet its liabilities. This is usually to assess the **funding level** and a recommended contribution rate based on comparing the **actuarial value of assets** and the **actuarial liability**.

ACTUARIAL VALUE OF ASSETS The value placed on the assets by the actuary. This may be market value, **present value** of estimated income and proceeds of sales or redemption, or some other value.

ACTUARIAL VALUE OF FUTURE CONTRIBUTIONS The **present value** of assumed future contributions and income therefrom.

ACTUARY An adviser on financial questions involving probabilities relating to mortality and other contingencies.

For statutory purposes in the UK, the term automatically includes Fellows of the Institute of Actuaries and of the Faculty of Actuaries. Persons with other actuarial qualifications can be approved by the Secretary of State for a specific purpose of the legislation.

ADDED YEARS The provision of extra pension benefit by reference to an additional period of pensionable service in a **defined benefit scheme**, arising from the receipt of a transfer payment, the paying of additional voluntary contributions or by way of **augmentation**.

ADDITIONAL PENSION The earnings-related element of the state pension, over and above the basic pension.

ADDITIONAL VOLUNTARY CONTRIBUTIONS (AVCs) Contributions over and above a member's normal contributions, if any, which the member elects to pay to the scheme in order to secure additional benefits, either **added years** or **money purchase**. *See also **free-standing additional voluntary contributions.***

ADMINISTRATOR   The person or persons regarded by the PSO and, where relevant, the OPB, as responsible for the management of a pension scheme.

The term may also refer to the person who manages the day-to-day administration of the scheme.

ALLOCATION   1. The facility for a member to give up (or allocate) part of his/her pension in exchange for a pension payable to the member's spouse or dependant.

2. The process for the application of payments to the benefits of individuals under an insured scheme using controlled funding.

ANNUITY   A series of payments, which may be subject to increases, made at stated intervals until a particular event occurs. This event is most commonly the end of a specified period or the death of the person receiving the annuity.

ANTI-FRANKING REQUIREMENTS   The requirements which ban the practice of franking at one time followed by some schemes, whereby the statutory increases in **GMP** were offset against other scheme benefits, rather than being added to a member's total benefits.

The requirements are covered in Ss.41A-41E of SSPA 75 and details of the requirements and permitted exceptions are given in JOM 78 para 170 and JOM 77 paras 170-196 and paras 212-213.

APPROPRIATE ADDITIONS   Amounts to be added when calculating the minimum benefit for the purpose of **anti-franking requirements** in respect of any further benefit accruing after contracted-out employment ceases or any enhancement of the benefits in excess of the **GMP** due to postponed payment.

APPROPRIATE PERSONAL PENSION SCHEME (APPS)   A personal pension scheme or free-standing AVC scheme granted an appropriate scheme certificate by the OPB, enabling its members to use it for the purpose of contracting-out.

APPROPRIATE SCHEME CERTIFICATE   The certificate issued by the OPB to a personal pension scheme or to a free-standing AVC scheme confirming that the scheme satisfies the conditions required for contracting-out.

APPROVED SCHEME   A retirement benefits scheme which is approved by the Inland Revenue under Chapter I of Part XIV of ICTA 88, including a free-standing AVC scheme. The term may also be used to describe a personal pension scheme approved under Chapter IV of that Part. *See also **exempt approved scheme.***

ASSET ALLOCATION STRATEGY   The long-term apportionment of pension scheme assets between the various investment classes such as equities, fixed interest and cash.

ATTAINED AGE METHOD A prospective benefit valuation method in which the **actuarial liability** makes allowance for projected earnings. The **standard contribution rate** is that necessary to cover the cost of all benefits which will accrue to existing members after the **valuation date** by reference to total earnings throughout their future working lifetime projected to the dates on which benefits become payable.

AUGMENTATION The provision of additional benefits in respect of particular members, normally where the cost is borne by the pension scheme and/or the employer.

AVERAGE REMAINING SERVICE LIFE As defined by **SSAP 24**, a weighted average of the expected future service of the current members of the scheme up to their normal pension dates or expected dates of earlier withdrawal or death in service.

BAND (OR BANDED) EARNINGS An alternative term for **upper band earnings**.

BASIC PENSION The single person's flat rate state pension paid to all who have met the minimum National Insurance contribution requirements. A widow, widower or in some cases a married woman may also claim a basic state pension on the contribution record of his or her spouse.

BENEFIT STATEMENT A statement or estimate of benefits payable in respect of an individual on the occurrence of specified events.

BRIDGING PENSION An additional pension paid from a scheme between retirement and **state pensionable age**, which is usually replaced by the state pension payable from that age.

BULK TRANSFER The transfer of a group of members, not necessarily with their consent, from one pension scheme to another, usually with an enhanced transfer payment in comparison with an individual's **cash equivalent**.

The PSO must be consulted about any such transfer payments.

BUY-BACK A term used to describe the payment of a type of **state scheme premium** by means of which a member's rights to SERPS are fully reinstated.

BUY-OUT The purchase by pension scheme trustees of an insurance policy or bond in the name of a member or other beneficiary, in lieu of entitlement to benefit from the scheme, following termination of the member's pensionable service.

Sometimes also used to refer to the purchase of an insurance policy in the name of the trustees.

CAREER AVERAGE SCHEME A scheme where the benefit for each year of membership is related to the pensionable earnings for that year.

126

CASH EQUIVALENT The amount which a member of a pension scheme may, under Schedule 1A of SSPA 75, require to be applied as a transfer payment to another permitted pension scheme or to a buy-out policy.

CASH OPTION An alternative term for **commutation**.

CENTRALISED SCHEME A pension scheme operated on behalf of several employers.

CERTIFIED AMOUNT (CA) That part of a **contributions equivalent premium** which may be recovered out of any refund of scheme contributions to the member.

CLASS A (OR B OR C) MEMBERS Terms derived from specimen rules issued by the PSO, applying to members of occupational schemes who joined during specified periods. Differing Inland Revenue limits apply to each class.

Class A	Members of schemes established on or after 14 March 1989 and all new members of earlier schemes joining on or after 1 June 1989.
Class B	Members of schemes established before 14 March 1989 who joined between 17 March 1987 and 31 May 1989.
Class C	Members who joined schemes before 17 March 1987.

A member may be exempt from treatment as a class A or B member under transitional arrangements. Class B members or (where scheme rules permit) class C members may elect to be treated as class A members, but will then be subject to the **earnings cap**.

CLOSED SCHEME A pension scheme which does not admit new members.

Contributions may or may not continue and benefits may or may not be provided for future service.

COMMON INVESTMENT FUND An arrangement whereby the assets of two or more pension schemes, operated by a single employer or group of employers, are pooled for investment.

COMMUTATION The giving up of a part or all of the pension payable from retirement for an immediate cash sum.

COMMUTATION FACTORS Factors used to determine the amount of pension which needs to be forgone in order to provide a given lump sum benefit.

COMPLIANCE AUDIT 1. An audit carried out to ensure compliance with the rules and regulations imposed by the Financial Services Act.

2. An audit at the instigation of the Inland Revenue's PSO to ensure compliance with Revenue rules and practices as described in JOM 102.

COMPULSORY PURCHASE ANNUITY (CPA) An annuity which must be purchased at retirement for a member retiring from service.

CONCENTRATION OF INVESTMENT Placing a significant proportion of the assets of a pension scheme in any single investment.

The amounts requiring compulsory disclosure and reporting are laid down by the OPB and the Disclosure Regulations.

CONTINUED RIGHTS The term used in the **Practice Notes** to refer to the rights of scheme members who continue to be subject to pre-existing Inland Revenue limits, including both **pre-17 March 1987 continued rights** and **pre-1 June 1989 continued rights**.

CONTRACT-OUT To use a statutory arrangement under which members of a pension scheme which meets certain conditions obtain rights under it in place of part of their earnings-related state scheme benefits. Contributions to the state scheme are reduced in respect of such employees or, in the case of a personal pension scheme or free-standing AVC scheme, partly repaid to the scheme.

CONTRACTED-OUT MONEY PURCHASE SCHEME (COMPS)
A **money purchase scheme** which is contracted-out, usually by reference to the provision of **protected rights**.

*A **money purchase scheme** can also be contracted-out by reference to the provision of a **GMP**, but would then be viewed by the OPB as a **COSRS**, not as a **COMPS**.*

CONTRACTED-OUT PROTECTED RIGHTS PREMIUM (COPRP)
A type of **state scheme premium** which may be paid by a money purchase scheme which is contracted-out by reference to the provision of **protected rights**, in order to purchase benefits under the state scheme for a member, if the scheme ceases to be contracted-out.

CONTRACTED-OUT REBATE 1. The amount by which the employers' and employees' National Insurance contributions are reduced in respect of employees who are contracted-out by virtue of their membership of an occupational pension scheme.

2. The equivalent payment made by the DSS as **minimum contributions** to a personal pension scheme.

CONTRACTED-OUT SALARY RELATED SCHEME (COSRS)
An occupational pension scheme which is contracted-out by reference to the provision of a **GMP**.

CONTRACTING-OUT CERTIFICATE The certificate issued by the OPB, in respect of an occupational pension scheme which satisfies the conditions for contracting-out, confirming the employees in the employments named in the certificate are to be treated as being in contracted-out employment.

CONTRIBUTIONS EQUIVALENT PREMIUM (CEP) A type of **state scheme premium** which may be paid when a member leaves with less than two years **qualifying service** (or five years for a leaver before 6 April 1988), in return for which the state scheme will take over the obligation to provide his/her **GMP.**

CONTRIBUTION HOLIDAY A period during which employers' and/or members' contributions are temporarily suspended, normally when the fund is in surplus. The term is sometimes used loosely when contributions continue to be paid but at a reduced rate.

CONTRIBUTORY SCHEME A scheme which requires contributions from active members unless such contributions are temporarily suspended during a **contribution holiday**.

CONTROLLING DIRECTOR (20% DIRECTOR) A director who, together with his associates, owns or controls 20% or more of the ordinary shares of the employing company. Special restrictions apply to controlling directors who are members of approved schemes. The full definition is set out in the **Practice Notes** (IR12 (1991)).

CORPORATE TRUSTEE A company which acts as a trustee.

CURRENT FUNDING LEVEL The **funding level**, at the present time, where the **actuarial liability** in respect of active members is taken as the **present value** of accrued benefits calculated in relation to current earnings, revalued as for preserved pensions on the statutory basis (or such higher basis as has been promised).

CURRENT UNIT METHOD An accrued benefits valuation in which the **actuarial liability** is based on earnings at the valuation date. The standard contribution rate is that necessary to cover the cost of benefits which will accrue in the year following the valuation date by reference to earnings projected to the end of that year.

CUSTODIAN TRUSTEE A trustee responsible for holding the assets of a trust, other trustees being responsible for the management of the trust including the investment decisions. *See also* **trust corporation**.

DEED OF ADHERENCE A legal document admitting a new employer to a scheme and containing an undertaking by the new employer to comply with the provisions of the scheme.

DEED OF APPOINTMENT A legal document by which a new trustee is appointed.

DEFERRED ANNUITY An annuity which commences from a future date.

DEFERRED PENSIONER A person entitled to **preserved benefits**. Sometimes referred to as a deferred member.

DEFINED BENEFIT SCHEME   A pension scheme in which the rules specify the benefits to be paid, and the scheme is financed accordingly.

DEFINED CONTRIBUTION SCHEME   An alternative term for a **money purchase scheme**.

DEFINITIVE TRUST DEED   The detailed trust deed which follows an **interim trust deed**.

DEPENDANT   A person who is financially dependent on a member or pensioner or was so at the time of death or retirement of the member or pensioner.

For PSO purposes, a spouse qualifies automatically as a dependant and a child of the member or pensioner may always be regarded as a dependant until attaining the age of 18 or ceasing to receive full time educational or vocational training, if later.

DEPOSIT ADMINISTRATION   An insurance policy under which contributions, net of expense charges, are accumulated in a pool to which interest and usually bonuses are added. The proceeds are applied to provide pensions and other benefits as they become due.

DISCLOSURE REGULATIONS   Regulations issued under SSPA 75 requiring disclosure of information about pension schemes and benefits to interested parties.

The term is also used to describe the regulations requiring disclosure of information in relation to insurance policies.

DISCONTINUANCE   The cessation of contributions to a pension scheme leading either to **winding-up** or to the scheme becoming a **frozen scheme**.

DISCONTINUANCE VALUATION   An **actuarial valuation** carried out to assess the position if the scheme were to be discontinued and the trustees were to wind it up in accordance with the requirements of the trust instrument. The valuation may take into account the possible exercise of any discretion to augment benefits.

DISCRETIONARY INCREASE   An increase in a pension in payment or in a preserved benefit arising other than from a system of indexation. Such an increase may be of a regular or an ad hoc nature.

DISCRETIONARY SCHEME   A scheme in which the employees to be offered membership are selected by the employer. Often the benefits, or the contributions from which they are to be provided, are also decided individually for each member.

DOCUMENTATION CERTIFICATE   A form of certificate used, in lieu of submitting detailed scheme documentation, either in seeking Inland Revenue approval in certain cases (an IR documentation certificate) or to satisfy contracting-out requirements (an OPB documentation certificate).

DYNAMISATION/DYNAMISM 1. A term sometimes used to describe indexation.

2. Also used to describe index-linking of earnings, either for calculating scheme benefits, or for determining **final remuneration** for the purpose of PSO limitations.

EARLY LEAVER A person who ceases to be an active member of a pension scheme, other than on death, without being granted an immediate retirement benefit.

EARLY RETIREMENT The retirement of a member with immediate retirement benefit, before normal pension date.

The benefit may be reduced because of early payment. See also ***ill-health early retirement.***

EARMARKED POLICY A term used in the **Practice Notes** to denote a policy held by a pension scheme, where each annuity or sum assured is earmarked to provide benefits for or in respect of an individual member.

EARNINGS CAP Limitation introduced by FA 1989 on the amount of remuneration on which benefits and contributions of a **class A member** may be based. This was set at £60,000 for tax year 1989/90, and is increased annually in line with prices (although no such increase was made for 1993/94). The same limitation applies to **net relevant earnings** for all members of personal pension schemes.

EARNINGS FACTOR (EF) A notional amount of earnings used for the purpose of calculating state scheme benefits or **GMPs**.

ENTRY AGE METHOD A prospective benefits valuation method in which the new entrant contribution rate is taken as the standard contribution rate.

EQUAL ACCESS Identical entry conditions for each sex. This is required by SSPA 75.

EQUIVALENT PENSION BENEFIT (EPB) The benefit which must be provided for an employee who was contracted-out of the former **graduated pension scheme.**

EXEMPT APPROVED SCHEME An approved scheme other than a personal pension scheme which is established under irrevocable trusts (or exceptionally, subject to a formal direction under S.592(1)(b) of ICTA 88) thus giving rise to the tax reliefs specified in ICTA 88.

EXEMPT UNIT TRUST A unitised form of investment normally managed by an investment organisation specifically designed for pension funds and charities which enjoys the same tax advantages as a directly invested pension fund's assets.

131

EXPRESSION OF WISH A means by which a member can indicate a preference as to who should receive any lump sum death benefit. The choice is not binding on the trustees, and as a result Inheritance Tax is normally avoided.

FAS 87 The US Financial Accounting Standards Board's statement which deals with accounting for pensions costs in employer's accounts. FAS 88 applies to employers' accounts when a scheme is wound-up or if benefits are settled on termination of employment.

FINAL PENSIONABLE EARNINGS/PAY/SALARY The pensionable earnings, at or near retirement or leaving service, on which the pension is calculated in a **final salary scheme**. The earnings may be based on the average over a number of consecutive years prior to retirement.

FINAL REMUNERATION The term used by the PSO for the maximum amount of earnings which it will permit to be used for the purpose of calculating maximum approvable benefits.

*The permissible alternatives are set out fully in the **Practice Notes**. See also **earnings cap**.*

FINAL SALARY SCHEME A pension scheme where the benefit is calculated by reference to the member's pensionable earnings for a period ending at or before normal pension date or leaving service, usually also based on pensionable service.

FIXED REVALUATION RATE The rate by which a contracted-out scheme may revalue **GMP** between termination of contracted-out employment and state pensionable age as one of the alternatives to applying **Section 148 Orders** (previously Section 21 Orders).

The rate changes periodically. It was 8.5% for members leaving up to 5 April 1988, 7.5% for members leaving between 6 April 1988 and 5 April 1993, and 7% for those leaving thereafter.

FREE COVER The maximum amount of death or disability benefit which an insurance company covering a group of lives is prepared to insure for each individual without production of evidence of health.

FREE-STANDING AVC SCHEME A scheme established by a **pension provider** to accept free-standing additional voluntary contributions.

FREE-STANDING ADDITIONAL VOLUNTARY CONTRIBUTIONS Contributions to a pension contract separate from a company pension scheme effected by an active member of that scheme. Benefits are secured with a **pension provider** by contributions from the member only.

FROZEN BENEFIT A **preserved benefit**, strictly one not subject to **revaluation**.

FROZEN SCHEME A **closed scheme** where no further contributions are payable and members are entitled to **preserved benefits.**

FULLY INSURED SCHEME A scheme where the trustees have effected an insurance contract in respect of each member which guarantees benefits corresponding at all times to those promised under the rules.

*Sometimes incorrectly used to mean **insured scheme**.*

FUNDING LEVEL The relationship at a specified date between the **actuarial value of assets** and the **actuarial liability**.

The funding level may be calculated separately in respect of different categories of liability, e.g. pensions in payment and AVCs.

FUNDING RATE A term sometimes used to describe the recommended contribution rate.

GRADUATED PENSION SCHEME The state earnings related scheme which commenced on 3 April 1961 and terminated on 5 April 1975.

GROUP PERSONAL PENSION SCHEME An arrangement made for the employees of a particular employer to participate in a personal pension scheme on a grouped basis. This is not a separate scheme; merely a collecting arrangement.

GUARANTEED MINIMUM PENSION (GMP) The minimum pension which an occupational pension scheme must provide as one of the conditions of contracting-out (unless it is contracted-out through the provision of **protected rights**).

For an employee contracted-out under any occupational or personal pension scheme an amount equal to the GMP is deducted from his/her benefits under the state scheme.

ILL-HEALTH EARLY RETIREMENT Retirement on medical grounds before normal pension date. The benefit may exceed that payable on early retirement in other circumstances.

IMMEDIATE ANNUITY An annuity which commences immediately or shortly after its purchase.

INDEPENDENT TRUSTEE An individual or corporate body with no direct or indirect involvement with the pension scheme, sponsoring employer, or members, other than performing the duties of the trustee.

Under provisions introduced by SSA 90, an independent trustee is required to be appointed where an employer has become insolvent.

INDIRECT DISCRIMINATION The unequal treatment of one sex in relation to the other by applying conditions which, while not directly discriminatory, are more likely to be met by one sex than the other.

INLAND REVENUE LIMITS RULE A rule, which must be included in the rules of an approved occupational pension scheme, specifying the maximum approvable benefits for members.

INSURED SCHEME A pension scheme where the sole long-term investment medium is an insurance policy (other than a **managed fund** policy).

INTEGRATION The design of pension scheme benefits to take into account all or part of the state scheme benefits which the member is deemed to receive.

One form of integration involves a state pension disregard.

INTERIM TRUST DEED A form of trust deed commonly used to establish a pension scheme on broadly stated terms leaving the detailed provisions and the rules to be provided later by a **definitive trust deed**.

A scheme may be established by other methods, for example by a board resolution, declaration of trust or exchange of letters.

LATE RETIREMENT The retirement of a member, with immediate retirement benefit, after **normal pension date**.

The benefit may be increased because of late payment.

LATER EARNINGS ADDITION An amount to be added when calculating the minimum benefit for the purpose of **anti-franking requirements** where a member continues in pensionable service after contracted-out employment ceases and the level of earnings is higher when he/she retires or leaves than on ceasing to be contracted-out.

LEVY A levy introduced by SSA 90, based on the active membership of occupational and personal pension schemes, to help meet the costs of the Pensions Ombudsman and the Register.

LIMITED PRICE INDEXATION (LPI) The requirement to increase pensions, once in payment, by 5% per annum or RPI if less.

LIMITED REVALUATION PREMIUM (LRP) A type of **state scheme premium** which may be paid when a member of a scheme contracted-out by means of the **GMP** test ceases to be in contracted-out employment. In return for this premium any subsequent revaluation of **GMP** up to state pensionable age above a specified level (currently 5% per annum) would be provided by the state scheme instead of under the occupational scheme.

This is one of the alternatives to applying **Section 148 Orders** (previously Section 21 Orders).

LINKED QUALIFYING SERVICE Actual service in a previous scheme which gives rise to a **transfer credit**, which ranks as **qualifying service**.

LONG SERVICE BENEFIT The term used in the preservation requirements of SSA 73 to describe the benefit payable at **normal pension age**, with which **short service benefit** must be compared.

LOWER EARNINGS LIMIT (LEL) The minimum amount, approximately equivalent to the **basic pension**, which must be earned in any pay period before National Insurance contributions are payable.

LUMP SUM CERTIFICATE A certificate which must be provided by a transferring scheme in certain circumstances, described in the **Practice Notes**, stating the maximum lump sum available from a transfer payment.

MANAGED FUND An investment contract by means of which an insurance company offers participation in one or more pooled funds. Also used to denote an arrangement where the scheme assets are invested on similar lines to unit trusts by an external investment manager.

MARKET LEVEL INDICATOR (MLI) An index giving a weighted comparison of values of equities and fixed interest securities. Market level indicators are used to adjust the amount of some state scheme premiums.

MATCHING 1. The policy of selecting investments of a nature, incidence or currency similar to that of the expected outgoings.

2. An accounting term, meaning that revenue and costs are matched with one another or 'hedged' so far as their relationship can be established or justifiably assumed.

MEMBER A person who has been admitted to membership of a pension scheme and is entitled to benefit under the scheme.

Sometimes narrowly used to refer only to an **active member.**

For some statutory purposes the term 'members' may include employees who are prospective members.

MINIMUM CONTRIBUTIONS 1. Contributions payable to a personal pension scheme or to a free-standing AVC scheme by the DSS in respect of a member who has elected to contract-out. The contributions consist of a partial rebate of National Insurance contributions, together with the incentive payments where applicable.

2. The term could also be used in respect of any minimum amount which a member is required to contribute in order to be a member of an occupational or personal pension scheme, or in order to make additional voluntary contributions.

MINIMUM CONTRIBUTIONS SCHEME A rebate only personal pension scheme or a contracted-out money purchase scheme to which only payments to the same level as the rebate are made. *See **rebate only personal pension scheme**.*

MINIMUM PAYMENTS The minimum amount which an employer must pay into a money purchase scheme which is contracted-out through the provision of **protected rights**. This amount corresponds to the reduction in National Insurance contributions which applies in respect of employees who are contracted-out.

MODEL RULES Specimen rules produced by the OPB and/or the PSO for certain categories of pension schemes to facilitate approval and/or the issue of a contracting-out or appropriate scheme certificate.

MONEY PURCHASE The determination of an individual member's benefits by reference to contributions paid into the scheme in respect of that member, usually increased by an amount based on the investment return on those contributions.

MONEY PURCHASE CONTRACTED-OUT SCHEME The term used in SSPA 75 (as amended by SSA 86) to describe a **money purchase scheme** which is contracted-out through the provision of **protected rights**.

MONEY PURCHASE SCHEME A scheme where the benefits are determined on a **money purchase** basis.

MONEY PURCHASE UNDERPIN A minimum benefit provided in a defined benefit scheme, calculated on a **money purchase** basis.

NET RELEVANT EARNINGS Earnings from self-employment or non-pensionable employment after deducting losses and certain business charges on income, used in determining the maximum contributions to a retirement annuity or **personal pension scheme** which qualify for tax relief.

With effect from tax year 1989/90 net relevant earnings have been restricted by the **earnings cap**. The maximum contribution below the cap is currently 17.5% of net relevant earnings with higher percentage limits for persons aged over 35, if contributing to a personal pension scheme, or 50, if contributing to a retirement annuity.

NIL CERTIFICATE A certificate indicating that a transfer value is not to be used to provide retirement benefits in lump sum form, such as on a transfer from a **free-standing AVC scheme**.

NOMINATION The naming by a member of the person to whom he/she wishes any death benefit to be paid. The scheme documentation will indicate whether this is binding on the trustees or merely for their consideration. In the latter case (which is the more common) the term **expression of wish** is to be preferred.

NON-CONTRIBUTORY SCHEME A pension scheme which does not require contributions from its active members.

*Not to be confused with a contributory scheme where contributions are suspended during a **contribution holiday**.*

NORMAL PENSION AGE (NPA) The age by reference to which the **normal pension date** is determined.

SSA 73 defines the term for the purposes of the preservation requirements as the earliest age at which a member is entitled as of right to receive unreduced benefits on retirement.

NORMAL PENSION DATE (NPD) The date at which a member of a pension scheme normally becomes entitled to receive his/her retirement benefits.

NORMAL RETIREMENT AGE (NRA) For employment purposes, the age at which employees holding a particular position normally retire from service. This is usually (but not always) the same as **normal pension age**.

NORMAL RETIREMENT DATE (NRD) Commonly used with the same meaning as **normal pension date**.

OCCUPATIONAL PENSION SCHEME An arrangement subject to the SSA 73, organised by an employer or on behalf of a group of employers to provide pensions and/or other benefits for or in respect of one or more employees on leaving service or on death or retirement.

A more detailed definition is to be found in S.51(3)(a) SSA 73.

OCCUPATIONAL PENSIONS ADVISORY SERVICE (OPAS) A grant aided body providing free help and advice to members of the public who have problems concerning their rights under either occupational or personal pension schemes. Its independent service is provided by a network of local volunteer advisers.

OCCUPATIONAL PENSIONS BOARD (OPB) A statutory body set up under SSA 73, with functions derived from that Act and SSPA 75. The Board is responsible for issuing **contracting-out** or **appropriate scheme certificates** for pension schemes which meet the statutory requirements, for supervising those schemes to ensure that **GMPs** and **protected rights** are secure and for ensuring that **equal access** and **preservation** requirements are satisfied. The Board is required to report to the Secretary of State when he/she seeks their advice and to comment on draft regulations affecting occupational pension schemes.

The Board can make grants to persons or organisations who give advice or assistance in connection with occupational or personal pensions activities, and it has been appointed as the Registrar of Occupational and Personal Pension Schemes. The Board can, on application, authorise or direct occupational or personal pension schemes to be modified or wound-up, e.g. in cases where the power to do so does not exist in the **trust deed**.

OLD CODE The legislation before FA 70 relating to approval of occupational pension schemes, and the corresponding Inland Revenue practice.

OPTING-OUT A decision by an employee to leave or not to join an occupational pension scheme of the employer.

This was made a statutory right from 6 April 1988 under SSA 86.

ORDINARY ANNUAL CONTRIBUTIONS A term used in the **Practice Notes** to denote the contributions payable to an occupational pension scheme by the employer on a regular basis in accordance with the scheme documentation.

OVERRIDING LEGISLATION The application of statutory requirements to pension schemes by means of provisions which directly override scheme rules.

*Examples include **revaluation, anti-franking requirements**, rights to a **cash equivalent** under SSPA 75 and the provisions of ICTA 88 and FA 1989 relating to schemes approved before 23 July 1987 and 27 July 1989 respectively.*

PAID-UP BENEFIT A **preserved benefit** which is irrevocably secured for an individual member under a contract of insurance under which premiums have ceased to be payable in respect of that member.

PARTIALLY APPROVED SCHEME A pension scheme only partially approved by the PSO because it provides some benefits which are not approvable, for example for overseas employees.

Not to be confused with partial loss of tax exemptions which occurs under Schedule 22 of ICTA 88 if a pension scheme which is excessively overfunded fails to take action to reduce the surplus.

PAST SERVICE RESERVE A term generally used to describe the **present value** of all benefits accrued at the **valuation date** by reference to earnings projected to the dates on which benefits become payable.

PAY-AS-YOU-GO (PAYG) An arrangement under which benefits are paid out of revenue and no funding is made for future liabilities.

The state scheme is pay-as-you-go.

PENSION COST Under **SSAP 24** the cost of providing pensions, which is charged to the profit and loss account of the employer over the expected service lives or **average remaining service life** of employees in the scheme. The amount may be more or less than the actual payments made to the pension scheme.

PENSION GUARANTEE An arrangement whereby on the early death of a pensioner, the pension scheme pays a further sum or sums to meet a guaranteed total. This total may be established by relation to, for instance, the late member's accumulated contributions or a multiple of the annual rate of pension.

PENSION INCREASE An increase in a pension in payment.

*Such an increase may arise as a result of indexation, or may be a **discretionary increase**. In practice the term may also embrace **revaluation** of preserved benefits.*

PENSION MORTGAGE A mortgage where the lender anticipates the borrower drawing sufficient cash by way of **commutation** from a pension scheme or retirement annuity to cover repayment of the loan. There can be no formal link between the loan and the anticipated cash sum.

PENSION PROVIDER A body by which a personal pension scheme or a free-standing AVC scheme must be established in order to be approved by the Inland Revenue.

PENSION SCHEME An occupational pension scheme, a personal pension scheme or a free-standing AVC scheme.

PENSION SCHEMES OFFICE (PSO) The office of the Inland Revenue which deals with the approval of pension schemes under the relevant tax legislation.

*Prior to 1 April 1992 known as the **Superannuation Funds Office (SFO)**.*

PENSION TAX RELIEF AT SOURCE (PTRAS) The procedure whereby contributions to an occupational pension scheme are deducted from the member's pay before tax is calculated under PAYE, giving immediate tax relief at the highest applicable rate. Such relief is also available for contributions to personal pension schemes but at basic rate only, relief at higher tax rates having to be separately claimed.

PENSIONABLE AGE The term used in legislation to denote **state pensionable age.**

PENSIONABLE EARNINGS The earnings on which benefits and/or contributions are calculated.

One or more elements of earnings (e.g. overtime) may be excluded, and/or there may be a state pension disregard.

PENSIONABLE SERVICE The period of service which is taken into account in calculating pension benefit.

SSA 73 gives the term a statutory definition for the purposes of preservation, which also applies for the purposes of the revaluation and transfer payment requirements of SSPA 75.

PENSIONEER TRUSTEE An individual or company with pensions experience appointed in accordance with the requirements relating to the approval of **small self-administered schemes** under ICTA 88 to act as a trustee of such a scheme.

PENSIONER'S RIGHTS PREMIUM (PRP) A type of **state scheme premium** which may be paid for a member or pensioner over state pensionable age when a **defined benefit scheme** ceases to be contracted-out, in return for which the state scheme will take over the obligation to provide his/her **GMP**.

PENSIONS OMBUDSMAN A post created under SSA 90 to deal with complaints against, and disputes with, occupational and personal pension schemes. The person appointed is completely independent and acts as an impartial adjudicator.

PERMITTED MAXIMUM   The term used in legislation to describe the **earnings cap**.

PERSONAL PENSION ARRANGEMENT   An individual contract made under a **personal pension scheme.**

PERSONAL PENSION CONTRIBUTIONS CERTIFICATE   A certificate issued by a personal pension scheme provider to the member to enable that member to provide his/her Inspector of Taxes with evidence of membership and contributions.

PERSONAL PENSION PROTECTED RIGHTS PREMIUM (PPPRP)
A type of **state scheme premium** which may be paid by a personal pension scheme for a member if the scheme ceases to be contracted-out.

PERSONAL PENSION SCHEME (PPS)   Usually used to mean a scheme approved under Chapter IV of Part XIV of ICTA 88, under which individuals who are self-employed or in non-pensionable employment, not in an occupational pension scheme, make pension provision usually by means of unit trust or deposit account contracts. *See also **self-invested personal pension.***

SSA 86 uses a slightly different definition which excludes a scheme open only to the self-employed but also includes a free-standing AVC scheme.

PRACTICE NOTES (PN)   Notes on the approval of occupational pension schemes by the PSO, currently issued as IR 12 (1991). Schemes approved before November 1991 continue to be subject to the earlier Practice Notes (IR 12 (1979)), but may choose to adopt certain parts of the later Practice Notes.

PRE-1 JUNE 1989 CONTINUED RIGHTS   The rights of a member of an occupational pension scheme who continues to be subject to the Inland Revenue maximum benefit limits which were generally applicable between 17 March 1987 and 31 May 1989. (*The full definition is set out in the **Practice Notes**.*)

*The rights include exemption from the **earnings cap**, as for **pre-17 March 1987 continued rights**, but there are restrictions on **commutation**, and maximum pension is only available after 20 years' service.*

*See also **class B member**.*

PRE-17 MARCH 1987 CONTINUED RIGHTS   The rights of a member of an occupational pension scheme who continues to be subject to the Inland Revenue maximum benefit limits which were generally applicable before 17 March 1987. (*The full definition is set out in the **Practice Notes**.*)

*The rights include exemption from the **earnings cap** and an Inland Revenue maximum pension based on 10 or more years' service.*

*See also **class C member**.*

PRESENT VALUE   The total of the amounts of a series of future payments or receipts discounted at interest to a current date, usually the **valuation date**, and allowing for the probabilities of payment or receipt.

PRESERVATION   The granting by a scheme of **preserved benefits**, in particular in accordance with minimum requirements specified by SSA 73.

PRESERVED BENEFITS   Benefits arising on an individual ceasing to be an **active member** of a pension scheme, payable at a later date.

PRIORITY LIABILITIES   Benefits and other liabilities which are given precedence in accordance with the **priority rule** when a scheme is wound-up.

*Under S.40(3) of SSPA 75 a contracted-out salary related scheme must contain a rule which gives priority, in the event of the scheme winding-up, to **GMPs** and certain other liabilities.*

PRIORITY RULE   The provisions contained in the scheme documentation setting out the order of precedence to be followed if the scheme is wound-up with insufficient assets to meet all liabilities.

PROCEEDS OF POLICY SCHEME   A money purchase scheme where the benefits promised to the members are those which can be provided from the proceeds of an insurance contract effected in respect of each member.

PROJECTED ACCRUED BENEFIT METHOD   A valuation method which compares the accrued **actuarial liability** with the value placed on the scheme assets for valuation purposes. The **actuarial liability** is based on service up to the **valuation date** and makes allowance for projected earnings. Used only in the context of the Pension Scheme Surpluses (Valuation) Regulations 1987 (SI 1987 No 412).

PROJECTED UNIT METHOD   An **accrued benefits valuation method** in which the **actuarial liability** makes allowance for projected earnings. The **standard contribution rate** is that necessary to cover the cost of all benefits which will accrue in the year following the **valuation date** by reference to earnings projected to the dates on which benefits become payable.

This is known in the US as projected unit credit method.

PROSPECTIVE BENEFITS VALUATION METHOD   A **valuation method** in which the **actuarial liability** is the **present value** of:

(a) the benefits for current and deferred pensioners and their dependants, allowing where appropriate for future pension increases; *and*

(b) the benefits which active members will receive in respect of both past and future service, allowing for projected earnings up to their assumed exit dates and, where appropriate, for pension increases thereafter;

less the **present value** *of future contributions payable in respect of current members at the* **standard contribution rate**.

PROTECTED RIGHTS The benefits under an appropriate personal pension scheme or a money purchase contracted-out scheme, deriving respectively from at least the **minimum contributions** or **minimum payments**, which are provided in a specified form as a necessary condition for contracting-out.

The term may also be used in a general sense to describe rights given to certain members on change of rules or change of pension scheme which are superior to those of a new entrant.

PROTECTED RIGHTS ANNUITY The pension provided from **protected rights** under an appropriate personal pension scheme or a money purchase contracted-out scheme by purchase from an insurance company or friendly society.

PROVISIONAL APPROVAL 1. The allowing of tax relief on a provisional basis in respect of employee contributions where an occupational pension scheme is set up under interim documentation. The **Practice Notes** do not use the term. Strictly, Inland Revenue approval is not granted until definitive scheme documentation has been examined.

2. The granting of provisional approval in respect of a personal pension scheme pursuant to S.655(5) ICTA 88 and the Personal Pension Schemes (Provisional Approval) Regulations 1987 (SI 1987 No 1765).

PUBLIC SECTOR PENSION SCHEME An occupational pension scheme for employees of central or local government, a nationalised industry or other statutory body.

PUBLIC SECTOR TRANSFER ARRANGEMENTS The arrangements of the **transfer club** to which certain schemes mainly in the public sector belong.

PUBLIC SERVICE PENSION SCHEME A **public sector pension scheme** the particulars of which are statutorily defined, for example the schemes for the civil service, local authorities, the police and fire services.

PURCHASED LIFE ANNUITY (PLA) An annuity purchased privately by an individual. In accordance with S.656 of ICTA 88, instalments of the annuity are subject to tax only in part.

QUALIFYING SERVICE The term defined in SSA 73 denoting the service to be taken into account to entitle a member to **short service benefit**. The current condition is for at least two years' qualifying service. If a transfer has been received from a personal pension scheme, the member is treated immediately as being entitled to short service benefits. *See also* **linked qualifying service**.

REBATE ONLY PERSONAL PENSION (ROPP)   An **appropriate personal pension scheme** which is funded solely by rebates of National Insurance contributions payable by the DSS to the **pension provider** in due course as a result of an election to contract-out.

REGISTER   The register of occupational and personal pension schemes maintained by the Occupational Pensions Board pursuant to SSA 90 and the Register of Occupational and Personal Pension Schemes Regulations 1990 (SI 1990 No 2278).

Schemes required to register include free-standing AVC schemes, unfunded schemes and overseas schemes. Paid up or frozen schemes are required to register, but are not required to pay the levy.

REGULAR PENSION COST   An accounting term defined in **SSAP 24** as meaning the consistent ongoing cost recognised under the actuarial method used.

RELEVANT BENEFITS   The term used in ICTA 88 and the **Practice Notes** to describe the types of benefits which are within the tax regime governing occupational pension schemes.

The full definition is set out in S.612(1) ICTA 88, and covers any type of financial benefit given in connection with retirement, death or termination of service. The definition does not include benefits provided only in the event of accidental death or disablement during service.

REQUISITE BENEFITS   The scale of benefits which an occupational pension scheme was originally required to provide as one of the conditions of contracting-out. The requirement to provide requisite benefits was removed in November 1986.

RETAINED BENEFITS   Retirement or death benefits in respect of an employee deriving from an earlier period of employment or self-employment. In some circumstances retained benefits must be taken into account in the maximum approvable benefits.

RETIREMENT BENEFITS SCHEME   An arrangement for the provision of benefits consisting of or including **relevant benefits**.

The full definition is set out in S.611 ICTA 88.

REVALUATION   1. The application, particularly to **preserved benefits**, of indexation, or the awarding of **discretionary increases**. SSPA 75 imposes revaluation in the calculation of **GMP** and of preserved benefits other than **GMP**.   2. An accounting term for the revision of the carrying value of an asset, usually having regard to its market value.

REVALUED EARNINGS   A term used to describe index-linking of earnings for calculating benefits.

REVALUED EARNINGS SCHEME A pension scheme where the benefits are based on earnings for a given period revalued in direct proportion to a specified index of prices or earnings.

A notable example is the earnings-related component of the state pension scheme.

REVENUE UNDERTAKING A written undertaking given by the administrators of an approved scheme agreeing to notify the Inland Revenue of certain information or to refer to them before taking certain specified actions.

REVERSIONARY ANNUITY An annuity which commences to be paid on the death of a specified person, normally to a spouse or a dependant.

SALARY SACRIFICE An agreement (which the Inland Revenue requires to be in writing) between the employer and employee whereby the employee forgoes part of his/her earnings in return for a corresponding contribution by the employer to a pension scheme.

*This is not the same as an **additional voluntary contribution.***

SECTION 148 ORDERS Previously Section 21 Orders. The Orders issued each year in accordance with S.148 of the Social Security Administration Act 1992 (previously S.21 of SSPA 75) specifying the rates of increase to be applied to the earnings factors on which the additional pension and **GMPs** are based. This revaluation is based on the increase in national average earnings.

*In respect of early leavers, see also **fixed revaluation rate** and **limited revaluation premium**.*

SECTION 32 POLICY The term used widely to describe an insurance policy used for **buy-out** purposes where the member chooses the insurance company.

The term came into use as a result of S.32 FA 81, which gave prominence to the possibility of effecting such policies (now contained in S.591 ICTA 88).

SEGREGATED FUND An arrangement whereby the investments of a particular pension scheme are managed by an **external investment manager** independently of other funds under its control. Often used to indicate an individual portfolio of stocks and shares in contrast to a pooled fund.

SELF-ADMINISTERED SCHEME A pension scheme where the assets are invested, other than wholly by payment of insurance premiums, by the trustees, an in-house manager or an external investment manager.

Although on the face of it the term self-administered should refer to the method of administering contributions and benefits, in practice the term has become solely related to the way in which the investments are managed.

SELF-INVESTED PERSONAL PENSION (SIPP) A personal pension under which the member has freedom to control investments.

The requirements governing self-invested personal pensions are set out in JOM 101.

SELF-INVESTMENT A term used to describe the investment of a scheme's assets in employer-related investments.

*A 5% limit is imposed on employer-related investments by SSA 90 (with certain exemptions). The PSO imposes separate restrictions on self-investment by **small self-administered schemes**. Requirements as to disclosure and reporting of self-investment are laid down by the OPB and the **Disclosure Regulations**.*

SELF-REGULATING ORGANISATION (SRO) A body authorised by the Securities and Investments Board to regulate and supervise investment business or financial service activities.

SERVICE A period of employment with one or more connected employers.

SHORT SERVICE BENEFIT (SSB) The benefit which must be provided for an **early leaver** under the preservation requirements of SSA 73.

SIMPLIFIED DEFINED CONTRIBUTION SCHEME (SDCS) A money purchase scheme subject to the simplified approval procedure described in Part 22 of the **Practice Notes**.

SMALL SELF-ADMINISTERED SCHEME (SSAS) A self-administered occupational pension scheme with few members (generally less than 12) which is subject on this account to certain special conditions for approval under ICTA 88.

STANDARD CONTRIBUTION RATE The contribution rate required by a particular valuation method before taking into account any differences between the **actuarial liability** and the **actuarial value of assets**.

STATE EARNINGS RELATED PENSION SCHEME (SERPS) A term widely used to describe the additional pension provisions of the state pension scheme.

STATE PENSIONABLE AGE The date from which pensions are normally payable by the state scheme, currently the 65th birthday for men and the 60th birthday for women.

State pensionable age is to be equalised at 65 for men and women. The change is to be phased in over 10 years, starting in 2010.

STATE SCHEME PREMIUM A payment made to the state scheme in certain circumstances. The categories of state scheme premium are: accrued rights premium, contracted-out protected rights premium, contributions equivalent premium, limited revaluation premium, pensioner's rights premium, personal pension protected rights premium, transfer premium.

STATEMENT OF RECOMMENDED PRACTICE 1 (SORP 1) Usually referred to as SORP 1, Statement of Recommended Practice 1 'Pension scheme accounts' was issued in 1986 by the Accounting Standards Committee and gives guidance to current best accounting practice for pension schemes. Its recommendations were effectively made mandatory by the **Disclosure Regulations**.

STATEMENT OF STANDARD ACCOUNTING PRACTICE 24 (SSAP 24) The accounting standard which deals with the accounting for and the disclosure of pension costs and commitments in the financial statements of employers in respect of arrangements for the provision of retirement benefits for their employees.

STATUTORY DISCHARGE The discharge provided in respect of a member who exercises the statutory right to a **cash equivalent** under SSPA 75.

STATUTORY SCHEME A scheme (usually in the public sector) established by Act of Parliament.

SUPERANNUATION FUNDS OFFICE (SFO) *See Pension Schemes Office (PSO).*

SURRENDER 1. A term used in relation to the cancellation of an insurance policy by the payment of a 'surrender value'.

2. A term sometimes used to describe **allocation** or **commutation**.

TOP UP PENSION SCHEME A pension scheme providing benefits which supplement those provided under another scheme.

The term is used in Inland Revenue guidance notes to refer to an unapproved scheme.

TOTAL EARNINGS SCHEME A type of average earnings scheme where the pension is a specified fraction of the member's aggregate earnings throughout the period of membership.

TRANSFER CLUB A group of employers and occupational pension schemes which has agreed to a common basis of **transfer payments**.

TRANSFER CREDIT Under SSA 73 and SSPA 75 the benefit purchased by a **transfer payment**. The effect on **qualifying service** is to link that part of the previous pensionable service which gave rise to the transfer payment to the service in the receiving scheme.

TRANSFER PAYMENT A payment made from a pension scheme to another pension scheme, or to an insurance company to purchase a **buy-out** policy, in lieu of benefits which have accrued to the member or members concerned, to enable the receiving arrangement to provide alternative benefits.

*The **transfer payment** may be made in accordance with the scheme rules or in exercise of a member's statutory rights under SSPA 75.*

TRANSFER PREMIUM A type of **state scheme premium** which can be paid when accrued benefits in excess of **GMPs** have been transferred to an occupational pension scheme which is not contracted-out.

TRANSFER VALUE The amount of the **transfer payment**, usually based on actuarial advice, which the trustees are prepared to make to another pension scheme or an insurance company.

TRIVIAL PENSION A pension which is so small that it can be commuted in full without prejudicing the approval of the scheme by the PSO.

The maximum amount of pension which may be commuted on account of triviality is also governed by preservation and contracting-out requirements.

TRUST A legal concept whereby property is held by one or more persons (the trustees) for the benefit of others (the beneficiaries) for the purposes specified by the trust instrument. The trustees may also be beneficiaries.

TRUST CORPORATION A company empowered under the Public Trustee Act 1906 to act as **custodian trustee** and which is expected to provide professional expertise in managing trusts.

TRUST DEED A legal document, executed in the form of a deed, which establishes, regulates or amends a trust. *See also **interim trust deed** and **definitive trust deed***.

TRUSTEE An individual or company appointed to carry out the purposes of a trust in accordance with the provisions of the trust instrument and general principles of trust law.

UNAPPROVED SCHEME An occupational pension scheme which is not designed for approval by the Inland Revenue. Following FA 1989 an employer may provide benefits for an employee under an unapproved scheme without those benefits being taken into account in calculating maximum approvable benefits under an **approved scheme**.

Such a scheme may be used to provide benefits on earnings in excess of the **earnings cap**. The Inland Revenue has published guidance notes on the tax treatment of unapproved schemes.

The term is sometimes also used to refer to a scheme which is awaiting approval.

UNFUNDED SCHEME A pension scheme for which the employer does not set aside and accumulate assets in advance of the benefits commencing to be paid. The basis may be **pay-as-you-go** or terminal funding.

UNIFORM ACCRUAL   The treatment of retirement benefits as being earned equally over the period of potential pensionable service to **normal pension date**, especially for the purposes of the preservation requirements of SSA 73.

UPLIFTED 60ths   Benefits in excess of one sixtieth of final remuneration for each year of service to the extent permitted by the PSO in an approved occupational pension scheme (only allowable in respect of members with **pre-17 March 1987 continued rights**).

UPPER BAND EARNINGS   Earnings between the **lower earnings limit** and the **upper earnings limit** on which the **additional pension** is calculated.

Also used in the calculation of a GMP.

UPPER EARNINGS LIMIT (UEL)   The maximum amount of earnings (equal to approximately seven times the **lower earnings limit**) on which National Insurance contributions are payable by employees.

VALUATION BASIS   A term commonly used by actuaries to mean **valuation method** and/or **actuarial assumptions**.

VALUATION DATE   The date by reference to which the **actuarial valuation** is carried out.

VALUATION METHOD   An approach used by the actuary in an **actuarial valuation**. The main categories of approach are described under **accrued benefits valuation method** and **prospective benefits valuation method**. A variety of methods can be used but the method or methods used in a particular case should be adequately described in the actuarial report.

VALUE FOR MONEY   A minimum benefit which is related to the member's contributions. SSA 73 preservation requirements originally included such a minimum, but this was removed by amending regulations from 1 January 1986.

VESTED RIGHTS   (a) For active members, benefits to which they would unconditionally be entitled on leaving service;

(b) for deferred pensioners, their preserved benefits;

(c) for pensioners, pensions to which they are entitled;

including where appropriate the related benefits for spouses or other dependants.

WAITING PERIOD   A period of service specified in the rules which an employee must serve before being entitled to join the pension scheme or to receive a particular benefit.

*In some pension schemes the waiting period before being entitled to join may automatically count as pensionable service. Not to be confused with **qualifying service**.*

WIDOW'S/WIDOWER'S GUARANTEED MINIMUM PENSION (WGMP)
The minimum pension which an occupational pension scheme (other than a **money purchase contracted-out scheme**) must provide for the surviving spouse of a member as one of the conditions of contracting-out.

WINDING-UP The process of terminating a pension scheme, usually by applying the assets to the purchase of immediate and deferred annuities for the beneficiaries, or by transferring the assets and liabilities to another pension scheme, in accordance with the scheme documentation. *See also priority rule*.

The definitions used in this Glossary of Terms are taken from *Pensions Terminology – A Glossary for Pension Schemes, Revised and Updated, Fourth Edition 1992*, published by The Pensions Management Institute, whose kind permission to reproduce here is gratefully acknowledged.

The objectives of the Working Party brought together by The Pensions Management Institute and the Pensions Research Accountants Group to review the terms as published in full in the source document were (i) to provide an explanation of terms commonly used by those professionally concerned with occupational pension schemes, for the assistance of all who have to deal with such schemes whether at work or study; (ii) to encourage those concerned to communicate more effectively by the use of a common vocabulary.

For a wider appreciation of terminology than that allowed by the material extracted here, readers are highly recommended to obtain copies of *Pensions Terminology – A Glossary for Pension Schemes*, available from The Pensions Management Institute, PMI House, 4-10 Artillery Lane, London E1 7LS. Telephone: 0171-247 1452.

COMPOUND INTEREST TABLES

	Accumulation of a single unit payment	Present value of a unit payment	Accumulation of an annual unit payment	Present value of an annuity of one unit		Term	
n	$(1+i)^n$	v^n	$s_{\overline{n}\rvert}$	$a_{\overline{n}\rvert}$	$(a_{\overline{n}\rvert})^{-1}$	n	
1	1.030000	.97087379	1.000000	.970874	1.030000	1	
2	1.060900	.94259591	2.030000	1.913470	.522611	2	
3	1.092727	.91514166	3.090900	2.828611	.353530	3	$d = .029126$
4	1.125509	.88848705	4.183627	3.717098	.269027	4	
5	1.159274	.86260878	5.309136	4.579707	.218355	5	$v = .970874$
6	1.194052	.83748426	6.468410	5.417191	.184598	6	
7	1.229874	.81309151	7.662462	6.230283	.160506	7	$i^{(2)} = .029778$
8	1.266770	.78940923	8.892336	7.019692	.142456	8	
9	1.304773	.76641673	10.159106	7.786109	.128434	9	$i^{(4)} = .029668$
10	1.343916	.74409391	11.463879	8.530203	.117231	10	
11	1.384234	.72242128	12.807796	9.252624	.108077	11	$i^{(12)} = .029595$
12	1.425761	.70137988	14.192030	9.954004	.100462	12	
13	1.468534	.68095134	15.617790	10.634955	.094030	13	$\delta = .029559$
14	1.512590	.66111781	17.086324	11.296073	.088526	14	
15	1.557967	.64186195	18.598914	11.937935	.083767	15	$i/i^{(2)} = 1.00744$
16	1.604706	.62316694	20.156881	12.561102	.079611	16	
17	1.652848	.60501645	21.761588	13.166118	.075953	17	$i/i^{(4)} = 1.01118$
18	1.702433	.58739461	23.414435	13.753513	.072709	18	
19	1.753506	.57028603	25.116868	14.323799	.069814	19	$i/i^{(12)} = 1.01368$
20	1.806111	.55367575	26.870374	14.877475	.067216	20	
21	1.860295	.53754928	28.676486	15.415024	.064872	21	$i/\delta = 1.01493$
22	1.916103	.52189250	30.536780	15.936917	.062747	22	
23	1.973587	.50669175	32.452884	16.443608	.060814	23	
24	2.032794	.49193374	34.426470	16.935542	.059047	24	
25	2.093778	.47760557	36.459264	17.413148	.057428	25	
26	2.156591	.46369473	38.553042	17.876842	.055938	26	
27	2.221288	.45018906	40.709634	18.327031	.054564	27	
28	2.287928	.43707675	42.930923	18.764108	.053293	28	
29	2.356566	.42434636	45.218850	19.188455	.052115	29	
30	2.427262	.41198676	47.575416	19.600441	.051019	30	
31	2.500080	.39998715	50.002678	20.000428	.049999	31	
32	2.575083	.38833703	52.502759	20.388766	.049047	32	
33	2.652335	.37702625	55.077841	20.765792	.048156	33	
34	2.731905	.36604490	57.730177	21.131837	.047322	34	
35	2.813862	.35538340	60.462082	21.487220	.046539	35	
36	2.898278	.34503243	63.275944	21.832252	.045804	36	
37	2.985227	.33498294	66.174223	22.167235	.045112	37	
38	3.074783	.32522615	69.159449	22.492462	.044459	38	
39	3.167027	.31575355	72.234233	22.808215	.043844	39	
40	3.262038	.30655684	75.401260	23.114772	.043262	40	
41	3.359899	.29762800	78.663298	23.412400	.042712	41	
42	3.460696	.28895922	82.023196	23.701359	.042192	42	
43	3.564517	.28054294	85.483892	23.981902	.041698	43	
44	3.671452	.27237178	89.048409	24.254274	.041230	44	
45	3.781596	.26443862	92.719861	24.518713	.040785	45	
46	3.895044	.25673653	96.501457	24.775349	.040363	46	
47	4.011895	.24925876	100.39650	25.024708	.039961	47	
48	4.132252	.24199880	104.40840	25.266707	.039578	48	
49	4.256219	.23495029	108.54065	25.501657	.039213	49	
50	4.383906	.22810708	112.79687	25.729764	.038865	50	

3 PER CENT

	Accumulation of a single unit payment	Present value of a unit payment	Accumulation of an annual unit payment	Present value of an annuity of one unit		Term	
n	$(1+i)^n$	v^n	$s_{\overline{n}\|}$	$a_{\overline{n}\|}$	$(a_{\overline{n}\|})^{-1}$	n	
1	1.040000	.96153846	1.000000	.961538	1.040000	1	
2	1.081600	.92455621	2.040000	1.886095	.530196	2	
3	1.124864	.88899636	3.121600	2.775091	.360349	3	$d = .038462$
4	1.169859	.85480419	4.246464	3.629895	.275490	4	
5	1.216653	.82192711	5.416323	4.451822	.224627	5	$v = .961538$
6	1.265319	.79031453	6.632975	5.242137	.190762	6	$i^{(2)} = .039608$
7	1.315932	.75991781	7.898294	6.002055	.166610	7	
8	1.368569	.73069021	9.214226	6.732745	.148528	8	$i^{(4)} = .039414$
9	1.423312	.70258674	10.582795	7.435332	.134493	9	
10	1.480244	.67556417	12.006107	8.110896	.123291	10	$i^{(12)} = .039285$
11	1.539454	.64958093	13.486351	8.760477	.114149	11	$\delta = .039221$
12	1.601032	.62459705	15.025805	9.385074	.106552	12	
13	1.665074	.60057409	16.626838	9.985648	.100144	13	$i/i^{(2)} = 1.00990$
14	1.731676	.57747508	18.291911	10.563123	.094669	14	
15	1.800944	.55526450	20.023588	11.118387	.089941	15	$i/i^{(4)} = 1.01488$
16	1.872981	.53390088	21.824531	11.652296	.085820	16	$i/i^{(12)} = 1.01820$
17	1.947900	.51337325	23.697512	12.165669	.082199	17	
18	2.025817	.49362812	25.645413	12.659247	.078993	18	$i/\delta = 1.01987$
19	2.106849	.47464242	27.671229	13.133939	.076139	19	
20	2.191123	.45638695	29.778079	13.590326	.073582	20	
21	2.278768	.43883360	31.969202	14.029160	.071280	21	
22	2.369919	.42195539	34.247970	14.451115	.069199	22	
23	2.464716	.40572633	36.617889	14.856842	.067309	23	
24	2.563304	.39012147	39.082604	15.246963	.065587	24	
25	2.665836	.37511680	41.645908	15.622080	.064012	25	
26	2.772470	.36068923	44.311745	15.982769	.062567	26	
27	2.883369	.34681657	47.084214	16.329586	.061239	27	
28	2.998703	.33347747	49.967583	16.663063	.060013	28	
29	3.118651	.32065141	52.966286	16.983715	.058880	29	
30	3.243398	.30831867	56.084938	17.292033	.057830	30	
31	3.373133	.29646026	59.328335	17.588494	.056855	31	
32	3.508059	.28505794	62.701469	17.873551	.055949	32	
33	3.648381	.27409417	66.209527	18.147646	.055104	33	
34	3.794316	.26355209	69.857909	18.411198	.054315	34	
35	3.946089	.25341547	73.652225	18.664613	.053577	35	
36	4.103933	.24366872	77.598314	18.908282	.052887	36	
37	4.268090	.23429685	81.702246	19.142579	.052240	37	
38	4.438813	.22528543	85.970336	19.367864	.051632	38	
39	4.616366	.21662061	90.409150	19.584485	.051061	39	
40	4.801021	.20828904	95.025516	19.792774	.050523	40	
41	4.993061	.20027793	99.826536	19.993052	.050017	41	
42	5.192784	.19257493	104.81960	20.185627	.049540	42	
43	5.400495	.18516820	110.01238	20.370795	.049090	43	
44	5.616515	.17804635	115.41288	20.548841	.048665	44	
45	5.841176	.17119841	121.02939	20.720040	.048262	45	
46	6.074823	.16461386	126.87057	20.884654	.047882	46	
47	6.317816	.15828256	132.94559	21.042936	.047522	47	
48	6.570528	.15219476	139.26321	21.195131	.047181	48	
49	6.833349	.14634112	145.83373	21.341472	.046857	49	
50	7.106683	.14071262	152.66708	21.482185	.046550	50	

4 PER CENT

	Accumulation of a single unit payment	Present value of a unit payment	Accumulation of an annual unit payment	Present value of an annuity of one unit		Term	
n	$(1+i)^n$	v^n	$s_{\overline{n}\mid}$	$a_{\overline{n}\mid}$	$(a_{\overline{n}\mid})^{-1}$	n	
1	1.050000	.95238095	1.000000	.952381	1.050000	1	**5** PER CENT
2	1.102500	.90702948	2.050000	1.859410	.537805	2	
3	1.157625	.86383760	3.152500	2.723248	.367209	3	d = .047619
4	1.215506	.82270247	4.310125	3.545951	.282012	4	
5	1.276282	.78352617	5.525631	4.329477	.230975	5	v = .952381
6	1.340096	.74621540	6.801913	5.075692	.197017	6	
7	1.407100	.71068133	8.142008	5.786373	.172820	7	$i^{(2)}$ = .049390
8	1.477455	.67683936	9.549109	6.463213	.154722	8	
9	1.551328	.64460892	11.026564	7.107822	.140690	9	$i^{(4)}$ = .049089
10	1.628895	.61391325	12.577893	7.721735	.129505	10	
11	1.710339	.58467929	14.206787	8.306414	.120389	11	$i^{(12)}$ = .048889
12	1.795856	.55683742	15.917127	8.863252	.112825	12	
13	1.885649	.53032135	17.712983	9.393573	.106456	13	δ = .048790
14	1.979932	.50506795	19.598632	9.898641	.101024	14	
15	2.078928	.48101710	21.578564	10.379658	.096342	15	$i/i^{(2)}$ = 1.01235
16	2.182875	.45811152	23.657492	10.837770	.092270	16	
17	2.292018	.43629669	25.840366	11.274066	.088699	17	$i/i^{(4)}$ = 1.01856
18	2.406619	.41552065	28.132385	11.689587	.085546	18	
19	2.526950	.39573306	30.539004	12.085321	.082745	19	$i/i^{(12)}$ = 1.02271
20	2.653298	.37688948	33.065954	12.462210	.080243	20	
21	2.785963	.35894236	35.719252	12.821153	.077996	21	i/δ = 1.02480
22	2.925261	.34184987	38.505214	13.163003	.075971	22	
23	3.071524	.32557131	41.430475	13.488574	.074137	23	
24	3.225100	.31006791	44.501999	13.798642	.072471	24	
25	3.386355	.29530277	47.727099	14.093945	.070952	25	
26	3.555673	.28124073	51.113454	14.375185	.069564	26	
27	3.733456	.26784832	54.669126	14.643034	.068292	27	
28	3.920129	.25509364	58.402583	14.898127	.067123	28	
29	4.116136	.24294632	62.322712	15.141074	.066046	29	
30	4.321942	.23137745	66.438847	15.372451	.065051	30	
31	4.538039	.22035947	70.760790	15.592811	.064132	31	
32	4.764941	.20986617	75.298829	15.802677	.063280	32	
33	5.003189	.19987254	80.063771	16.002549	.062490	33	
34	5.253348	.19035480	85.066959	16.192904	.061755	34	
35	5.516015	.18129029	90.320307	16.374194	.061072	35	
36	5.791816	.17265741	95.836323	16.546852	.060434	36	
37	6.081407	.16443563	101.62814	16.711287	.059840	37	
38	6.385477	.15660536	107.70955	16.867893	.059284	38	
39	6.704751	.14914797	114.09502	17.017041	.058765	39	
40	7.039989	.14204568	120.79977	17.159086	.058278	40	
41	7.391988	.13528160	127.83976	17.294368	.057822	41	
42	7.761588	.12883962	135.23175	17.423208	.057395	42	
43	8.149667	.12270440	142.99334	17.545912	.056993	43	
44	8.557150	.11686133	151.14301	17.662773	.056616	44	
45	8.985008	.11129651	159.70016	17.774070	.056262	45	
46	9.434258	.10599668	168.68516	17.880066	.055928	46	
47	9.905971	.10094921	178.11942	17.981016	.055614	47	
48	10.401270	.09614211	188.02539	18.077158	.055318	48	
49	10.921333	.09156391	198.42666	18.168722	.055040	49	
50	11.467400	.08720373	209.34800	18.255925	.054777	50	

Term	Accumulation of a single unit payment	Present value of a unit payment	Accumulation of an annual unit payment	Present value of an annuity of one unit		Term
n	$(1+i)^n$	v^n	$s_{\overline{n}\|}$	$a_{\overline{n}\|}$	$(a_{\overline{n}\|})^{-1}$	n
1	1.060000	.94339623	1.000000	.943396	1.060000	1
2	1.123600	.88999644	2.060000	1.833393	.545437	2
3	1.191016	.83961928	3.183600	2.673012	.374110	3
4	1.262477	.79209366	4.374616	3.465106	.288591	4
5	1.338226	.74725817	5.637093	4.212364	.237396	5
6	1.418519	.70496054	6.975319	4.917324	.203363	6
7	1.503630	.66505711	8.393838	5.582381	.179135	7
8	1.593848	.62741237	9.897468	6.209794	.161036	8
9	1.689479	.59189846	11.491316	6.801692	.147022	9
10	1.790848	.55839478	13.180795	7.360087	.135868	10
11	1.898299	.52678753	14.971643	7.886875	.126793	11
12	2.012196	.49696936	16.869941	8.383844	.119277	12
13	2.132928	.46883902	18.882138	8.852683	.112960	13
14	2.260904	.44230096	21.015066	9.294984	.107585	14
15	2.396558	.41726506	23.275970	9.712249	.102963	15
16	2.540352	.39364628	25.672528	10.105895	.098952	16
17	2.692773	.37136442	28.212880	10.477260	.095445	17
18	2.854339	.35034379	30.905653	10.827603	.092357	18
19	3.025600	.33051301	33.759992	11.158116	.089621	19
20	3.207135	.31180473	36.785591	11.469921	.087185	20
21	3.399564	.29415540	39.992727	11.764077	.085005	21
22	3.603537	.27750510	43.392290	12.041582	.083046	22
23	3.819750	.26179726	46.995828	12.303379	.081278	23
24	4.048935	.24697855	50.815577	12.550358	.079679	24
25	4.291871	.23299863	54.864512	12.783356	.078227	25
26	4.549383	.21981003	59.156383	13.003166	.076904	26
27	4.822346	.20736795	63.705766	13.210534	.075697	27
28	5.111687	.19563014	68.528112	13.406164	.074593	28
29	5.418388	.18455674	73.639798	13.590721	.073580	29
30	5.743491	.17411013	79.058186	13.764831	.072649	30
31	6.088101	.16425484	84.801677	13.929086	.071792	31
32	6.453387	.15495740	90.889778	14.084043	.071002	32
33	6.840590	.14618622	97.343165	14.230230	.070273	33
34	7.251025	.13791153	104.18375	14.368141	.069598	34
35	7.686087	.13010522	111.43478	14.498246	.068974	35
36	8.147252	.12274077	119.12087	14.620987	.068395	36
37	8.636087	.11579318	127.26812	14.736780	.067857	37
38	9.154252	.10923885	135.90421	14.846019	.067358	38
39	9.703507	.10305552	145.05846	14.949075	.066894	39
40	10.285718	.09722219	154.76197	15.046297	.066462	40
41	10.902861	.09171905	165.04768	15.138016	.066059	41
42	11.557033	.08652740	175.95054	15.224543	.065683	42
43	12.250455	.08162962	187.50758	15.306173	.065333	43
44	12.985482	.07700908	199.75803	15.383182	.065006	44
45	13.764611	.07265007	212.74351	15.455832	.064700	45
46	14.590487	.06853781	226.50812	15.524370	.064415	46
47	15.465917	.06465831	241.09861	15.589028	.064148	47
48	16.393872	.06099840	256.56453	15.650027	.063898	48
49	17.377504	.05754566	272.95840	15.707572	.063664	49
50	18.420154	.05428836	290.33590	15.761861	.063444	50

6 PER CENT

d = .056604

v = .943396

$i^{(2)}$ = .059126

$i^{(4)}$ = .058695

$i^{(12)}$ = .058411

δ = .058269

$i/i^{(2)}$ = 1.01478

$i/i^{(4)}$ = 1.02223

$i/i^{(12)}$ = 1.02721

i/δ = 1.02971

153

	Accumulation of a single unit payment	Present value of a unit payment	Accumulation of an annual unit payment	Present value of an annuity of one unit		Term
n	$(1+i)^n$	v^n	$s_{\overline{n}|}$	$a_{\overline{n}|}$	$(a_{\overline{n}|})^{-1}$	n
1	1.070000	.93457944	1.000000	.934579	1.070000	1
2	1.144900	.87343873	2.070000	1.808018	.553092	2
3	1.225043	.81629788	3.214900	2.624316	.381052	3
4	1.310796	.76289521	4.439943	3.387211	.295228	4
5	1.402552	.71298618	5.750739	4.100197	.243891	5
6	1.500730	.66634222	7.153291	4.766540	.209796	6
7	1.605781	.62274974	8.654021	5.389289	.185553	7
8	1.718186	.58200910	10.259803	5.971299	.167468	8
9	1.838459	.54393374	11.977989	6.515232	.153486	9
10	1.967151	.50834929	13.816448	7.023582	.142378	10
11	2.104852	.47509280	15.783599	7.498674	.133357	11
12	2.252192	.44401196	17.888451	7.942686	.125902	12
13	2.409845	.41496445	20.140643	8.357651	.119651	13
14	2.578534	.38781724	22.550488	8.745468	.114345	14
15	2.759032	.36244602	25.129022	9.107914	.109795	15
16	2.952164	.33873460	27.888054	9.446649	.105858	16
17	3.158815	.31657439	30.840217	9.763223	.102425	17
18	3.379932	.29586392	33.999033	10.059087	.099413	18
19	3.616528	.27650833	37.378965	10.335595	.096753	19
20	3.869684	.25841900	40.995492	10.594014	.094393	20
21	4.140562	.24151309	44.865177	10.835527	.092289	21
22	4.430402	.22571317	49.005739	11.061240	.090406	22
23	4.740530	.21094688	53.436141	11.272187	.088714	23
24	5.072367	.19714662	58.176671	11.469334	.087189	24
25	5.427433	.18424918	63.249038	11.653583	.085811	25
26	5.807353	.17219549	68.676470	11.825779	.084561	26
27	6.213868	.16093037	74.483823	11.986709	.083426	27
28	6.648838	.15040221	80.697691	12.137111	.082392	28
29	7.114257	.14056282	87.346529	12.277674	.081449	29
30	7.612255	.13136712	94.460786	12.409041	.080586	30
31	8.145113	.12277301	102.07304	12.531814	.079797	31
32	8.715271	.11474113	110.21815	12.646555	.079073	32
33	9.325340	.10723470	118.93343	12.753790	.078408	33
34	9.978114	.10021934	128.25876	12.854009	.077797	34
35	10.676581	.09366294	138.23688	12.947672	.077234	35
36	11.423942	.08753546	148.91346	13.035208	.076715	36
37	12.223618	.08180884	160.33740	13.117017	.076237	37
38	13.079271	.07645686	172.56102	13.193473	.075795	38
39	13.994820	.07145501	185.64029	13.264928	.075387	39
40	14.974458	.06678038	199.63511	13.331709	.075009	40
41	16.022670	.06241157	214.60957	13.394120	.074660	41
42	17.144257	.05832857	230.63224	13.452449	.074336	42
43	18.344555	.05451268	247.77650	13.506962	.074036	43
44	19.628460	.05094643	266.12085	13.557908	.073758	44
45	21.002452	.04761349	285.74931	13.605522	.073500	45
46	22.472623	.04449859	306.75176	13.650020	.073260	46
47	24.045707	.04158747	329.22439	13.691608	.073037	47
48	25.728907	.03886679	353.27009	13.730474	.072831	48
49	27.529930	.03632410	378.99900	13.766799	.072639	49
50	29.457025	.03394776	406.52893	13.800746	.072460	50

7 PER CENT

$d = .065421$

$v = .934579$

$i^{(2)} = .068816$

$i^{(4)} = .068234$

$i^{(12)} = .067850$

$\delta = .067659$

$i/i^{(2)} = 1.01720$

$i/i^{(4)} = 1.02588$

$i/i^{(12)} = 1.03169$

$i/\delta = 1.03461$

	Accumulation of a single unit payment	Present value of a unit payment	Accumulation of an annual unit payment	Present value of an annuity of one unit		Term	
n	$(1+i)^n$	v^n	$s_{\overline{n}|}$	$a_{\overline{n}|}$	$(a_{\overline{n}|})^{-1}$	n	
1	1.075000	.93023256	1.000000	.930233	1.075000	1	$7\frac{1}{2}$**PER**
2	1.155625	.86533261	2.075000	1.795565	.556928	2	**CENT**
3	1.242297	.80496057	3.230625	2.600526	.384538	3	d = .069767
4	1.335469	.74880053	4.472922	3.349326	.298568	4	
5	1.435629	.69655863	5.808391	4.045885	.247165	5	v = .930233
6	1.543302	.64796152	7.244020	4.693846	.213045	6	
7	1.659049	.60275490	8.787322	5.296601	.188800	7	$i^{(2)}$ = .073644
8	1.783478	.56070223	10.446371	5.857304	.170727	8	$i^{(4)}$ = .072978
9	1.917239	.52158347	12.229849	6.378887	.156767	9	
10	2.061032	.48519393	14.147087	6.864081	.145686	10	$i^{(12)}$ = .072539
11	2.215609	.45134319	16.208119	7.315424	.136697	11	δ = .072321
12	2.381780	.41985413	18.423728	7.735278	.129278	12	
13	2.560413	.39056198	20.805508	8.125840	.123064	13	$i/i^{(2)}$ = 1.01841
14	2.752444	.36331347	23.365921	8.489154	.117797	14	
15	2.958877	.33796602	26.118365	8.827120	.113287	15	$i/i^{(4)}$ = 1.02770
16	3.180793	.31438699	29.077242	9.141507	.109391	16	$i/i^{(12)}$ = 1.03393
17	3.419353	.29245302	32.258035	9.433960	.106000	17	
18	3.675804	.27204932	35.677388	9.706009	.103029	18	i/δ = 1.03705
19	3.951489	.25306913	39.353192	9.959078	.100411	19	
20	4.247851	.23541315	43.304681	10.194491	.098092	20	
21	4.566440	.21898897	47.552532	10.413480	.096029	21	
22	4.908923	.20371067	52.118972	10.617191	.094187	22	
23	5.277092	.18949830	57.027895	10.806689	.092535	23	
24	5.672874	.17627749	62.304987	10.982967	.091050	24	
25	6.098340	.16397906	67.977862	11.146946	.089711	25	
26	6.555715	.15253866	74.076201	11.299485	.088500	26	
27	7.047394	.14189643	80.631916	11.441381	.087402	27	
28	7.575948	.13199668	87.679310	11.573378	.086405	28	
29	8.144144	.12278761	95.255258	11.696165	.085498	29	
30	8.754955	.11422103	103.39940	11.810386	.084671	30	
31	9.411577	.10625212	112.15436	11.916638	.083916	31	
32	10.117445	.09883918	121.56593	12.015478	.083226	32	
33	10.876253	.09194343	131.68338	12.107421	.082594	33	
34	11.691972	.08552877	142.55963	12.192950	.082013	34	
35	12.568870	.07956164	154.25161	12.272511	.081483	35	
36	13.511536	.07401083	166.82048	12.346522	.080994	36	
37	14.524901	.06884729	180.33201	12.415370	.080545	37	
38	15.614268	.06404399	194.85691	12.479414	.080132	38	
39	16.785339	.05957580	210.47118	12.538989	.079751	39	
40	18.044239	.05541935	227.25652	12.594409	.079400	40	
41	19.397557	.05155288	245.30076	12.645962	.079077	41	
42	20.852374	.04795617	264.69832	12.693918	.078778	42	
43	22.416302	.04461039	285.55065	12.738528	.078502	43	
44	24.097524	.04149804	307.96699	12.780026	.078247	44	
45	25.904839	.03860283	332.06452	12.818629	.078011	45	
46	27.847702	.03590961	357.96935	12.854539	.077794	46	
47	29.936279	.03340428	385.81706	12.887943	.077592	47	
48	32.181500	.03107375	415.75333	12.919017	.077405	48	
49	34.595113	.02890582	447.93483	12.947922	.077232	49	
50	37.189746	.02688913	482.52995	12.974812	.077072	50	

	Accumulation of a single unit payment	Present value of a unit payment	Accumulation of an annual unit payment	Present value of an annuity of one unit		Term	
n	$(1+i)^n$	v^n	$s_{\overline{n}\|}$	$a_{\overline{n}\|}$	$(a_{\overline{n}\|})^{-1}$	n	**8** PER CENT
1	1.080000	.92592593	1.000000	.925926	1.080000	1	
2	1.166400	.85733882	2.080000	1.783265	.560769	2	
3	1.259712	.79383224	3.246400	2.577097	.388034	3	d = .074074
4	1.360489	.73502985	4.506112	3.312127	.301921	4	
5	1.469328	.68058320	5.866601	3.992710	.250456	5	v = .925926
6	1.586874	.63016963	7.335929	4.622880	.216315	6	$i^{(2)}$ = .078461
7	1.713824	.58349040	8.922803	5.206370	.192072	7	
8	1.850930	.54026888	10.636628	5.746639	.174015	8	$i^{(4)}$ = .077706
9	1.999005	.50024897	12.487558	6.246888	.160080	9	
10	2.158925	.46319349	14.486562	6.710081	.149029	10	$i^{(12)}$ = .077208
11	2.331639	.42888266	16.645487	7.138964	.140076	11	
12	2.518170	.39711376	18.977126	7.536078	.132695	12	δ = .076961
13	2.719624	.36769792	21.495297	7.903776	.126522	13	$i/i^{(2)}$ = 1.01962
14	2.937194	.34046104	24.214920	8.244237	.121297	14	
15	3.172169	.31524170	27.152114	8.559479	.116830	15	$i/i^{(4)}$ = 1.02952
16	3.425943	.29189047	30.324283	8.851369	.112977	16	
17	3.700018	.27026895	33.750226	9.121638	.109629	17	$i/i^{(12)}$ = 1.03616
18	3.996019	.25024903	37.450244	9.371887	.106702	18	
19	4.315701	.23171206	41.446263	9.603599	.104128	19	i/δ = 1.03949
20	4.660957	.21454821	45.761964	9.818147	.101852	20	
21	5.033834	.19865575	50.422921	10.016803	.099832	21	
22	5.436540	.18394051	55.456755	10.200744	.098032	22	
23	5.871464	.17031528	60.893296	10.371059	.096422	23	
24	6.341181	.15769934	66.764759	10.528758	.094978	24	
25	6.848475	.14601790	73.105940	10.674776	.093679	25	
26	7.396353	.13520176	79.954415	10.809978	.092507	26	
27	7.988061	.12518682	87.350768	10.935165	.091448	27	
28	8.627106	.11591372	95.338830	11.051078	.090489	28	
29	9.317275	.10732752	103.96594	11.158406	.089619	29	
30	10.062657	.09937733	113.28321	11.257783	.088827	30	
31	10.867669	.09201605	123.34587	11.349799	.088107	31	
32	11.737083	.08520005	134.21354	11.434999	.087451	32	
33	12.676050	.07888893	145.95062	11.513888	.086852	33	
34	13.690134	.07304531	158.62667	11.586934	.086304	34	
35	14.785344	.06763454	172.31680	11.654568	.085803	35	
36	15.968172	.06262458	187.10215	11.717193	.085345	36	
37	17.245660	.05798572	203.07032	11.775179	.084924	37	
38	18.625276	.05369048	220.31595	11.828869	.084539	38	
39	20.115298	.04971341	238.94122	11.878582	.084185	39	
40	21.724521	.04603093	259.05652	11.924613	.083860	40	
41	23.462483	.04262123	280.78104	11.967235	.083561	41	
42	25.339482	.03946411	304.24352	12.006699	.083287	42	
43	27.366640	.03654084	329.58301	12.043240	.083034	43	
44	29.555972	.03383411	356.94965	12.077074	.082802	44	
45	31.920449	.03132788	386.50562	12.108402	.082587	45	
46	34.474085	.02900730	418.42607	12.137409	.082390	46	
47	37.232012	.02685861	452.90015	12.164267	.082208	47	
48	40.210573	.02486908	490.13216	12.189136	.082040	48	
49	43.427419	.02302693	530.34274	12.212163	.081886	49	
50	46.901613	.02132123	573.77016	12.233485	.081743	50	

Term	Accumulation of a single unit payment	Present value of a unit payment	Accumulation of an annual unit payment	Present value of an annuity of one unit		Term
n	$(1+i)^n$	v^n	$s_{\overline{n}|}$	$a_{\overline{n}|}$	$(a_{\overline{n}|})^{-1}$	n
1	1.085000	.92165899	1.000000	.921659	1.085000	1
2	1.177225	.84945529	2.085000	1.771114	.564616	2
3	1.277289	.78290810	3.262225	2.554022	.391539	3
4	1.385859	.72157428	4.539514	3.275597	.305288	4
5	1.503657	.66504542	5.925373	3.940642	.253766	5
6	1.631468	.61294509	7.429030	4.553587	.219607	6
7	1.770142	.56492635	9.060497	5.118514	.195369	7
8	1.920604	.52066945	10.830639	5.639183	.177331	8
9	2.083856	.47987968	12.751244	6.119063	.163424	9
10	2.260983	.44228542	14.835099	6.561348	.152408	10
11	2.453167	.40763633	17.096083	6.968984	.143493	11
12	2.661686	.37570168	19.549250	7.344686	.136153	12
13	2.887930	.34626883	22.210936	7.690955	.130023	13
14	3.133404	.31914178	25.098866	8.010097	.124842	14
15	3.399743	.29413989	28.232269	8.304237	.120420	15
16	3.688721	.27109667	31.632012	8.575333	.116614	16
17	4.002262	.24985869	35.320733	8.825192	.113312	17
18	4.342455	.23028450	39.322995	9.055476	.110430	18
19	4.711563	.21224378	43.665450	9.267720	.107901	19
20	5.112046	.19561639	48.377013	9.463337	.105671	20
21	5.546570	.18029160	53.489059	9.643628	.103695	21
22	6.018028	.16616738	59.035629	9.809796	.101939	22
23	6.529561	.15314965	65.053658	9.962945	.100372	23
24	7.084574	.14115176	71.583219	10.104097	.098970	24
25	7.686762	.13009378	78.667792	10.234191	.097712	25
26	8.340137	.11990210	86.354555	10.354093	.096580	26
27	9.049049	.11050885	94.694692	10.464602	.095560	27
28	9.818218	.10185148	103.74374	10.566453	.094639	28
29	10.652766	.09387233	113.56196	10.660326	.093806	29
30	11.558252	.08651828	124.21473	10.746844	.093051	30
31	12.540703	.07974035	135.77298	10.826584	.092365	31
32	13.606663	.07349341	148.31368	10.900078	.091742	32
33	14.763229	.06773586	161.92034	10.967813	.091176	33
34	16.018104	.06242936	176.68357	11.030243	.090660	34
35	17.379642	.05753858	192.70168	11.087781	.090189	35
36	18.856912	.05303095	210.08132	11.140812	.089760	36
37	20.459750	.04887645	228.93823	11.189689	.089368	37
38	22.198828	.04504742	249.39798	11.234736	.089010	38
39	24.085729	.04151836	271.59681	11.276255	.088682	39
40	26.133016	.03826577	295.68254	11.314520	.088382	40
41	28.354322	.03526799	321.81555	11.349788	.088107	41
42	30.764439	.03250506	350.16987	11.382293	.087856	42
43	33.379417	.02995858	380.93431	11.412252	.087625	43
44	36.216667	.02761160	414.31373	11.439864	.087414	44
45	39.295084	.02544848	450.53040	11.465312	.087220	45
46	42.635166	.02345482	489.82548	11.488767	.087042	46
47	46.259155	.02161734	532.46065	11.510384	.086878	47
48	50.191183	.01992382	578.71980	11.530308	.086728	48
49	54.457434	.01836297	628.91098	11.548671	.086590	49
50	59.086316	.01692439	683.36842	11.565595	.086463	50

8 ½ PER CENT

d = .078341

v = .921659

$i^{(2)}$ = .083267

$i^{(4)}$ = .082418

$i^{(12)}$ = .081858

δ = .081580

$i/i^{(2)}$ = 1.02082

$i/i^{(4)}$ = 1.03133

$i/i^{(12)}$ = 1.03838

$i/δ$ = 1.04192

Term	Accumulation of a single unit payment	Present value of a unit payment	Accumulation of an annual unit payment	Present value of an annuity of one unit		Term
n	$(1+i)^n$	v^n	$s_{\overline{n}|}$	$a_{\overline{n}|}$	$(a_{\overline{n}|})^{-1}$	n
1	1.090000	.91743119	1.000000	.917431	1.090000	1
2	1.188100	.84167999	2.090000	1.759111	.568469	2
3	1.295029	.77218348	3.278100	2.531295	.395055	3
4	1.411582	.70842521	4.573129	3.239720	.308669	4
5	1.538624	.64993159	5.984711	3.889651	.257092	5
6	1.677100	.59626733	7.523335	4.485919	.222920	6
7	1.828039	.54703424	9.200435	5.032953	.198691	7
8	1.992563	.50186628	11.028474	5.534819	.180674	8
9	2.171893	.46042778	13.021036	5.995247	.166799	9
10	2.367364	.42241081	15.192930	6.417658	.155820	10
11	2.580426	.38753285	17.560293	6.805191	.146947	11
12	2.812665	.35553473	20.140720	7.160725	.139651	12
13	3.065805	.32617865	22.953385	7.486904	.133567	13
14	3.341727	.29924647	26.019189	7.786150	.128433	14
15	3.642482	.27453804	29.360916	8.060688	.124059	15
16	3.970306	.25186976	33.003399	8.312558	.120300	16
17	4.327633	.23107318	36.973705	8.543631	.117046	17
18	4.717120	.21199374	41.301338	8.755625	.114212	18
19	5.141661	.19448969	46.018458	8.950115	.111730	19
20	5.604411	.17843089	51.160120	9.128546	.109546	20
21	6.108808	.16369806	56.764530	9.292244	.107617	21
22	6.658600	.15018171	62.873338	9.442425	.105905	22
23	7.257874	.13778139	69.531939	9.580207	.104382	23
24	7.911083	.12640494	76.789813	9.706612	.103023	24
25	8.623081	.11596784	84.700896	9.822580	.101806	25
26	9.399158	.10639251	93.323977	9.928972	.100715	26
27	10.245082	.09760781	102.72313	10.026580	.099735	27
28	11.167140	.08954845	112.96822	10.116128	.098852	28
29	12.172182	.08215454	124.13536	10.198283	.098056	29
30	13.267678	.07537114	136.30754	10.273654	.097336	30
31	14.461770	.06914783	149.57522	10.342802	.096686	31
32	15.763329	.06343838	164.03699	10.406240	.096096	32
33	17.182028	.05820035	179.80032	10.464441	.095562	33
34	18.728411	.05339481	196.98234	10.517835	.095077	34
35	20.413968	.04898607	215.71075	10.566821	.094636	35
36	22.251225	.04494135	236.12472	10.611763	.094235	36
37	24.253835	.04123309	258.37595	10.652993	.093870	37
38	26.436680	.03782623	282.62978	10.690820	.093538	38
39	28.815982	.03470296	309.06646	10.725523	.093236	39
40	31.409420	.03183758	337.88245	10.757360	.092960	40
41	34.236268	.02920879	369.29187	10.786569	.092708	41
42	37.317532	.02679706	403.52813	10.813366	.092478	42
43	40.676110	.02458446	440.84566	10.837950	.092268	43
44	44.336960	.02255455	481.52177	10.860505	.092077	44
45	48.327286	.02069224	525.85873	10.881197	.091902	45
46	52.676742	.01898371	574.18602	10.900181	.091742	46
47	57.417649	.01741625	626.86276	10.917597	.091595	47
48	62.585237	.01597821	684.28041	10.933575	.091461	48
49	68.217908	.01465891	746.86565	10.948234	.091339	49
50	74.357520	.01344854	815.08356	10.961683	.091227	50

9 PER CENT

$d = .082569$

$v = .917431$

$i^{(2)} = .088061$

$i^{(4)} = .087113$

$i^{(12)} = .086488$

$\delta = .086178$

$i/i^{(2)} = 1.02202$

$i/i^{(4)} = 1.03314$

$i/i^{(12)} = 1.04061$

$i/\delta = 1.04435$

Term	Accumulation of a single unit payment	Present value of a unit payment	Accumulation of an annual unit payment	Present value of an annuity of one unit		Term
n	$(1+i)^n$	v^n	$s_{\overline{n}}$	$a_{\overline{n}}$	$(a_{\overline{n}})^{-1}$	n
1	1.100000	.90909091	1.000000	.909091	1.100000	1
2	1.210000	.82644628	2.100000	1.735537	.576190	2
3	1.331000	.75131480	3.310000	2.486852	.402115	3
4	1.464100	.68301346	4.641000	3.169865	.315471	4
5	1.610510	.62092132	6.105100	3.790787	.263797	5
6	1.771561	.56447393	7.715610	4.355261	.229607	6
7	1.948717	.51315812	9.487171	4.868419	.205405	7
8	2.143589	.46650738	11.435888	5.334926	.187444	8
9	2.357948	.42409762	13.579477	5.759024	.173641	9
10	2.593742	.38554329	15.937425	6.144567	.162745	10
11	2.853117	.35049390	18.531167	6.495061	.153963	11
12	3.138428	.31863082	21.384284	6.813692	.146763	12
13	3.452271	.28966438	24.522712	7.103356	.140779	13
14	3.797498	.26333125	27.974983	7.366687	.135746	14
15	4.177248	.23939205	31.772482	7.606080	.131474	15
16	4.594973	.21762914	35.949730	7.823709	.127817	16
17	5.054470	.19784467	40.544703	8.021553	.124664	17
18	5.559917	.17985879	45.599173	8.201412	.121930	18
19	6.115909	.16350799	51.159090	8.364920	.119547	19
20	6.727500	.14864363	57.274999	8.513564	.117460	20
21	7.400250	.13513057	64.002499	8.648694	.115624	21
22	8.140275	.12284597	71.402749	8.771540	.114005	22
23	8.954302	.11167816	79.543024	8.883218	.112572	23
24	9.849733	.10152560	88.497327	8.984744	.111300	24
25	10.834706	.09229600	98.347059	9.077040	.110168	25
26	11.918177	.08390545	109.18177	9.160945	.109159	26
27	13.109994	.07627768	121.09994	9.237223	.108258	27
28	14.420994	.06934335	134.20994	9.306567	.107451	28
29	15.863093	.06303941	148.63093	9.369606	.106728	29
30	17.449402	.05730855	164.49402	9.426914	.106079	30
31	19.194342	.05209868	181.94342	9.479013	.105496	31
32	21.113777	.04736244	201.13777	9.526376	.104972	32
33	23.225154	.04305676	222.25154	9.569432	.104499	33
34	25.547670	.03914251	245.47670	9.608575	.104074	34
35	28.102437	.03558410	271.02437	9.644159	.103690	35
36	30.912681	.03234918	299.12681	9.676508	.103343	36
37	34.003949	.02940835	330.03949	9.705917	.103030	37
38	37.404343	.02673486	364.04343	9.732651	.102747	38
39	41.144778	.02430442	401.44778	9.756956	.102491	39
40	45.259256	.02209493	442.59256	9.779051	.102259	40
41	49.785181	.02008630	487.85181	9.799137	.102050	41
42	54.763909	.01826027	537.63699	9.817397	.101860	42
43	60.240069	.01660025	592.40069	9.833998	.101688	43
44	66.264076	.01509113	652.64076	9.849089	.101532	44
45	72.890484	.01371921	718.90484	9.862808	.101391	45
46	80.179532	.01247201	791.79532	9.875280	.101263	46
47	88.197485	.01133819	871.97485	9.886618	.101147	47
48	97.017234	.01030745	960.17234	9.896926	.101041	48
49	106.71896	.00937041	1057.1896	9.906296	.100946	49
50	117.39085	.00851855	1163.9085	9.914814	.100859	50

10 PER CENT

$d = .090909$

$v = .909091$

$i^{(2)} = .097618$

$i^{(4)} = .096455$

$i^{(12)} = .095690$

$\delta = .095310$

$i/i^{(2)} = 1.02440$

$i/i^{(4)} = 1.03676$

$i/i^{(12)} = 1.04504$

$i/\delta = 1.04921$

	Accumulation of a single unit payment	Present value of a unit payment	Accumulation of an annual unit payment	Present value of an annuity of one unit		
n	$(1+i)^n$	v^n	$s_{\overline{n}|}$	$a_{\overline{n}|}$	$(a_{\overline{n}|})^{-1}$	n
1	1.110000	.90090090	1.000000	.900901	1.110000	1
2	1.232100	.81162243	2.110000	1.712523	.583934	2
3	1.367631	.73119138	3.342100	2.443715	.409213	3
4	1.518070	.65873097	4.709731	3.102446	.322326	4
5	1.685058	.59345133	6.227801	3.695897	.270570	5
6	1.870415	.53464084	7.912860	4.230538	.236377	6
7	2.076160	.48165841	9.783274	4.712196	.212215	7
8	2.304538	.43392650	11.859434	5.146123	.194321	8
9	2.558037	.39092477	14.163972	5.537048	.180602	9
10	2.839421	.35218448	16.722009	5.889232	.169801	10
11	3.151757	.31728331	19.561430	6.206515	.161121	11
12	3.498451	.28584082	22.713187	6.492356	.154027	12
13	3.883280	.25751426	26.211638	6.749870	.148151	13
14	4.310441	.23199482	30.094918	6.981865	.143228	14
15	4.784589	.20900435	34.405359	7.190870	.139065	15
16	5.310894	.18829202	39.189948	7.379162	.135517	16
17	5.895093	.16963262	44.500843	7.548794	.132471	17
18	6.543553	.15282218	50.395936	7.701617	.129843	18
19	7.263344	.13767764	56.939488	7.839294	.127563	19
20	8.062312	.12403391	64.202832	7.963328	.125576	20
21	8.949166	.11174226	72.265144	8.075070	.123838	21
22	9.933574	.10066870	81.214309	8.175739	.122313	22
23	11.026267	.09069252	91.147884	8.266432	.120971	23
24	12.239157	.08170498	102.17415	8.348137	.119787	24
25	13.585464	.07360809	114.41331	8.421745	.118740	25
26	15.079865	.06631359	127.99877	8.488058	.117813	26
27	16.738650	.05974197	143.07864	8.547800	.116989	27
28	18.579901	.05382160	159.81729	8.601622	.116257	28
29	20.623691	.04848793	178.39719	8.650110	.115605	29
30	22.892297	.04368282	199.02088	8.693793	.115025	30
31	25.410449	.03935389	221.91317	8.733146	.114506	31
32	28.205599	.03545395	247.32362	8.768600	.114043	32
33	31.308214	.03194050	275.52922	8.800541	.113629	33
34	34.752118	.02877522	306.83744	8.829316	.113259	34
35	38.574851	.02592363	341.58955	8.855240	.112927	35
36	42.818085	.02335462	380.16441	8.878594	.112630	36
37	47.528074	.02104020	422.98249	8.899635	.112364	37
38	52.756162	.01895513	470.51056	8.918590	.112125	38
39	58.559340	.01707670	523.26673	8.935666	.111911	39
40	65.000867	.01538441	581.82607	8.951051	.111719	40
41	72.150963	.01385983	646.82693	8.964911	.111546	41
42	80.087569	.01248633	718.97790	8.977397	.111391	42
43	88.897201	.01124895	799.06547	8.988646	.111251	43
44	98.675893	.01013419	887.96267	8.998780	.111126	44
45	109.53024	.00912990	986.63856	9.007910	.111014	45
46	121.57857	.00822513	1096.1688	9.016135	.110912	46
47	134.95221	.00741003	1217.7474	9.023545	.110821	47
48	149.79695	.00667570	1352.6996	9.030221	.110739	48
49	166.27462	.00601415	1502.4965	9.036235	.110666	49
50	184.56483	.00541815	1668.7712	9.041653	.110599	50

11 PER CENT

$d = .099099$

$v = .900901$

$i^{(2)} = .107131$

$i^{(4)} = .105733$

$i^{(12)} = .104815$

$\delta = .104360$

$i/i^{(2)} = 1.02678$

$i/i^{(4)} = 1.04035$

$i/i^{(12)} = 1.04947$

$i/\delta = 1.05404$

	Accumulation of a single unit payment	Present value of a unit payment	Accumulation of an annual unit payment	Present value of an annuity of one unit		Term
Term						
n	$(1+i)^n$	v^n	$s_{\overline{n}|}$	$a_{\overline{n}|}$	$(a_{\overline{n}|})^{-1}$	n
1	1.120000	.89285714	1.000000	.892857	1.120000	1
2	1.254400	.79719388	2.120000	1.690051	.591698	2
3	1.404928	.71178025	3.374400	2.401831	.416349	3
4	1.573519	.63551808	4.779328	3.037349	.329234	4
5	1.762342	.56742686	6.352847	3.604776	.277410	5
6	1.973823	.50663112	8.115189	4.111407	.243226	6
7	2.210681	.45234922	10.089012	4.563757	.219118	7
8	2.475963	.40388323	12.299693	4.967640	.201303	8
9	2.773079	.36061002	14.775656	5.328250	.187679	9
10	3.105848	.32197324	17.548735	5.650223	.176984	10
11	3.478550	.28747610	20.654583	5.937699	.168415	11
12	3.895976	.25667509	24.133133	6.194374	.161437	12
13	4.363493	.22917419	28.029109	6.423548	.155677	13
14	4.887112	.20461981	32.392602	6.628168	.150871	14
15	5.473566	.18269626	37.279715	6.810864	.146824	15
16	6.130394	.16312166	42.753280	6.973986	.143390	16
17	6.866041	.14564434	48.883674	7.119630	.140457	17
18	7.689966	.13003959	55.749715	7.249670	.137937	18
19	8.612762	.11610678	63.439681	7.365777	.135763	19
20	9.646293	.10366677	72.052442	7.469444	.133879	20
21	10.803848	.09255961	81.698736	7.562003	.132240	21
22	12.100310	.08264251	92.502584	7.644646	.130811	22
23	13.552347	.07378796	104.60289	7.718434	.129560	23
24	15.178629	.06588210	118.15524	7.784316	.128463	24
25	17.000064	.05882331	133.33387	7.843139	.127500	25
26	19.040072	.05252081	150.33393	7.895660	.126652	26
27	21.324881	.04689358	169.37401	7.942554	.125904	27
28	23.883866	.04186927	190.69889	7.984423	.125244	28
29	26.749930	.03738327	214.58275	8.021806	.124660	29
30	29.959922	.03337792	241.33268	8.055184	.124144	30
31	33.555113	.02980172	271.29261	8.084986	.123686	31
32	37.581726	.02660868	304.84772	8.111594	.123280	32
33	42.091533	.02375775	342.42945	8.135352	.122920	33
34	47.142517	.02121227	384.52098	8.156564	.122601	34
35	52.799620	.01893953	431.66350	8.175504	.122317	35
36	59.135574	.01691029	484.46312	8.192414	.122064	36
37	66.231843	.01509848	543.59869	8.207513	.121840	37
38	74.179664	.01348078	609.83053	8.220993	.121640	38
39	83.081224	.01203641	684.01020	8.233030	.121462	39
40	93.050970	.01074680	767.09142	8.243777	.121304	40
41	104.21709	.00959536	860.14239	8.253372	.121163	41
42	116.72314	.00856728	964.35948	8.261939	.121037	42
43	130.72991	.00764936	1081.0826	8.269589	.120925	43
44	146.41750	.00682978	1211.8125	8.276418	.120825	44
45	163.98760	.00609802	1358.2300	8.282516	.120736	45
46	183.66612	.00544466	1522.2176	8.287961	.120657	46
47	205.70605	.00486131	1705.8838	8.292822	.120586	47
48	230.39078	.00434045	1911.5898	8.297163	.120523	48
49	258.03767	.00387540	2141.9806	8.301038	.120467	49
50	289.00219	.00346018	2400.0182	8.304498	.120417	50

12 PER CENT

$d = .107143$

$v = .892857$

$i^{(2)} = .116601$

$i^{(4)} = .114949$

$i^{(12)} = .113866$

$\delta = .113329$

$i/i^{(2)} = 1.02915$

$i/i^{(4)} = 1.04394$

$i/i^{(12)} = 1.05387$

$i/\delta = 1.05887$

ANNUITY FACTORS

MALE LIFE ANNUITIES ON PA(90)

Exact Age:	50	55	60	65	70	75
Interest						
0%	26.062	21.806	18.012	14.593	11.563	8.958
1%	22.504	19.190	16.139	13.299	10.705	8.413
2%	19.652	17.040	14.563	12.186	9.951	7.925
3%	17.340	15.258	13.227	11.222	9.286	7.486
4%	15.446	13.767	12.087	10.383	8.695	7.089
5%	13.877	12.508	11.107	9.649	8.169	6.730
6%	12.565	11.437	10.258	9.002	7.698	6.403
7%	11.457	10.520	9.519	8.430	7.275	6.106
8%	10.515	9.727	8.872	7.922	6.894	5.834
9%	9.706	9.038	8.301	7.468	6.549	5.584
10%	9.006	8.435	7.796	7.061	6.236	5.355
11%	8.397	7.905	7.347	6.694	5.950	5.143
12%	7.862	7.435	6.945	6.363	5.689	4.948
13%	7.391	7.017	6.584	6.062	5.450	4.767
14%	6.973	6.643	6.258	5.789	5.230	4.599
15%	6.599	6.307	5.963	5.539	5.028	4.443

Note: The columns represent the present value of a life annuity of one unit per year payable continuously from the exact age given to a male subject to the mortality experience of the PA(90) table and valued at the rates of interest shown.

Source: Institute of Actuaries.

FEMALE LIFE ANNUITIES ON PA(90)

Exact Age:	50	55	60	65	70	75
Interest						
0%	31.470	26.899	22.524	18.414	14.646	11.299
1%	26.608	23.214	19.830	16.525	13.384	10.502
2%	22.804	20.254	17.609	14.929	12.292	9.796
3%	19.789	17.850	15.762	13.570	11.342	9.168
4%	17.370	15.878	14.213	12.405	10.510	8.608
5%	15.406	14.244	12.903	11.401	9.779	8.105
6%	13.793	12.878	11.788	10.530	9.133	7.654
7%	12.455	11.726	10.832	9.769	8.559	7.246
8%	11.332	10.746	10.005	9.102	8.047	6.877
9%	10.383	9.905	9.287	8.514	7.589	6.542
10%	9.572	9.179	8.658	7.992	7.178	6.236
11%	8.873	8.547	8.105	7.527	6.806	5.956
12%	8.268	7.994	7.616	7.111	6.470	5.700
13%	7.738	7.507	7.180	6.738	6.165	5.465
14%	7.272	7.075	6.791	6.401	5.886	5.248
15%	6.860	6.690	6.442	6.095	5.632	5.048

Note: The columns represent the present value of a life annuity of one unit per year payable continuously from the exact age given to a female subject to the mortality experience of the PA(90) table and valued at the rates of interest shown.

Source: Institute of Actuaries.

USEFUL ADDRESSES

Association of British Insurers
51 Gresham Street
London   EC2V 7HQ
Tel: (0171) 600 3333

Association of Consulting Actuaries
No. 1 Wardrobe Place
London   EC4V 5AH
Tel: (0171) 248 3163

Association of Pension Lawyers
c/o Nabarro Nathanson
50 Stratton Street
London   W1X 6NX
Tel: (0171) 493 9933

Association of Pensioneer Trustees
c/o Wolanski & Co. Trustees Limited
114/118 Southampton Row
London   WC1B 5AA
Tel: (0171) 831 9343

Central Office of Information
Hercules Road
London   SE1 7DU
Tel: (0171) 928 2345

Central Statistical Office
Great George Street
London   SW1P 3AQ
Tel: (0171) 270 3000

Chartered Insurance Institute
20 Aldermanbury
London   EC2V 7HY
Tel: (0171) 606 3835

Data Protection Registrar
Wycliffe House
Water Lane
Wilmslow
Cheshire   SK9 5AF
Tel: (01625) 535777

Department of Social Security:
    COE Group
    Newcastle upon Tyne
    NE98 1YX
    Tel: (06451) 50150

Policy Division
The Adelphi
1-11 John Adam Street
London   WC2N 6HT
Tel: (0171) 210 5983

Department of Trade and Industry
1 Victoria Street
London   SW1H 0ET
Tel: (0171) 215 5000

EC Information Services
8 Storey's Gate
London   SW1P 3AT
Tel: (0171) 973 1992

Equal Opportunities Commission
Overseas House
Quay Street
Manchester   M1 3HN
Tel: (0161) 833 9244

Faculty of Actuaries
40/44 Thistle Street
Edinburgh   EH2 1EN
Tel: (0131) 220 4555

HMSO
PO Box 276
London   SW8 5DT
Tel: (0171) 873 0011

IMRO
Lloyds Chambers
1 Portsoken Street
London   E1 8BT
Tel: (0171) 390 5000

Inland Revenue
    Head Office:
    Somerset House
    London   WC2R 1LB
    Tel: (0171) 438 6622

    Pension Schemes Office:
    Yorke House
    PO Box 62
    Castle Meadow Road
    Nottingham   NG2 1BG
    Tel: (0115) 974 000

Institute of Actuaries
Staple Inn Hall
High Holborn
London   WC1V 7QJ
Tel: (0171) 242 0106

Institute of Chartered Accountants in England & Wales
Chartered Accountants Hall
Moorgate Place
London   EC2P 2BJ
Tel: (0171) 920 8100

Institute of Chartered Accountants of Scotland
27 Queen Street
Edinburgh   EH2 1LA
Tel: (0131) 225 5673

Law Society
The Law Society's Hall
113 Chancery Lane
London   WC2A 1PL
Tel: (0171) 242 1222

National Association of Pension Funds Ltd
12-18 Grosvenor Gardens
London   SW1W 0DH
Tel: (0171) 730 0585

Occupational Pensions Advisory Service
11 Belgrave Road
London   SW1V 1RB
Tel: (0171) 233 8080

Occupational Pensions Board
PO Box 2EE
Newcastle upon Tyne   NE99 2EE
Tel: (0191) 225 6414

Pensions Research Accountants Group
c/o GAAPS Ltd
Grafton House
2-3 Golden Square
London   W1R 3AD
Tel: (0171) 437 8899

Pensions Management Institute
PMI House
4-10 Artillery Lane
London   E1 7LS
Tel: (0171) 247 1452

Pensions Ombudsman
11 Belgrave Road
London   SW1V 1RB
Tel: (0171) 834 9144

Pensions Trustees Forum
1 Queen Anne's Gate
London   SW1H 9BT
Tel: (0171) 233 0206

Personal Investment Authority Limited:
(Headquarters)
1 Canada Square
Canary Wharf
London   E14 5AZ
Tel: (0171) 538 8860

Pensions Unit
Hertsmere House
Hertsmere Road
London   E14 4AB
Tel: (0171) 417 7001

PIA Ombudsman Bureau Limited
3rd Floor
Centrepoint
103 New Oxford Street
London   WC1A 1QH
Tel: (0171) 240 3838

Registrar of Pension Schemes
Occupational Pensions Board
PO Box 1NN
Newcastle upon Tyne   NE99 1NN
Tel: (0191) 225 6394

Securities and Investments Board
Gavrelle House
2-14 Bunhill Row
London   EC1Y 8RA
Tel: (0171) 638 1240

Society of Pension Consultants
Ludgate House
Ludgate Circus
London   EC4A 2AB
Tel: (0171) 353 1688/9

Stock Exchange
Old Broad Street
London   EC2N 1HP
Tel: (0171) 588 2355

Note: For brevity, details of principal offices only are included.